My First Resume

Tip: First, read the entire passage. After that, go back and fill in the blanks. You can skip the blanks you're unsure about and finish them later.

qualifications	potential	improvements	grammatical	freshman
intimidating	leadership	habits	contribute	regular

When you're a high school student, writing a résumé can be _____. The good news is that you probably have more work experience than you realize, even if this is your first résumé. Experiences such as childcare, yard work, and volunteerism all _____ to developing key work skills that companies seek. Simply because you have not held a position similar to the one you are seeking does not indicate you lack the requisite abilities to succeed.

Be sure to include any previous employment, especially if it was for pay. Other than that, you can consist of informal work such as pet sitting, cutting grass, snow shoveling, and any other tasks you've done for money. Although you may not have received a _____ income for your informal employment, your talents and reliability as an employee can still be shown via it.

Given that the majority of teenagers have not held many jobs, it is critical to draw on all elements of your life that prove you possess the attitude, willingness to work hard, competencies, and personality necessary for job success.

Please list any _____ positions you held (for example, a president of an organization or as team captain), as well as any honors or awards you have received. Include a list of your duties and accomplishments under each heading.

Employers are more concerned with your work _____ and attitude than anything else. Nobody expects you to be an expert in your field. When recounting an experience, you might use language to the effect that you have perfect or near-perfect attendance and are on time for school and other commitments.

Employers are looking for employees who have a history of positively impacting the company. Ask yourself whether there are any accomplishments that you can include from your time in school, your clubs, or your employment. Use verbs like "upgraded," "started," and "expanded" to describe what you've done if you want to illustrate what you've accomplished. To demonstrate to _____ employers that you are both bright and ambitious, include any demanding advanced academic assignments on your resume.

Keep it short: Keep it simple (But Include All Necessary Information). A single page is all you need. Contact information and previous work experience are both required in some way on every resume. On the other hand, you can exclude things like a career objective or summary.

Create a narrative. Match your talents and expertise to the job's requirements. For example, in the case of a cashier position, if you've never had a position with that precise title before, emphasize your customer service abilities, aptitude for mathematical calculations, work ethic, and ability to operate as part of a team. Examine the job description and make sure your _____ meet the requirements.

It is also appropriate to add information about your academic achievements, such as participation in organizations and the necessary curriculum you finished while producing a college _____ resume or a resume for a college application. Suppose you're applying for work as a front desk receptionist at a hotel. You could want to include the talents you gained while studying hospitality at a school.

Finally, be sure to double- or even triple-check your resume for typos and _____ errors. You may be tempted to send in your resume as soon as you finish it, but take a few minutes to review it.

As a last resort, ask for a second opinion on your resume from friends, family, or school teachers. Have them go it through to see if there's anything you missed or if you can make any _____.

PRACTICE ONLY

Employee Application

Employers use employment applications like this apart of their hiring process. It tells them about the potential employee.

Applicant

Name: Date:

Referral: Phone No.

Fax No.   Email:

Address:

Are You…

A U.S. Citizen?	☐ Yes	☐ No
Over 18 years old?	☐ Yes	☐ No
Licensed to drive?	☐ Yes	☐ No

Employment

Position: Department:

Type: ☐ Full-Time   ☐ Part-Time   ☐ Other (Seasonal/Temp):

Start Date: Starting Salary:

Current Employment: May we contact?   ☐ Yes   ☐ No

Education History

Education	School	Location	Years	Graduated?	Degree(s)
High School					
College					
Graduate					
Other Training/Classes:					
Workshops/Certifications:					

Employment History

Employer	Address	Position	Dates	Reason for Leaving

References

Reference	Relationship	Phone	Email	Address

Applicant Signature   Date

The brag sheet, which is not to be confused with a student resume for college applications, is designed specifically for writing letters of recommendation. However, it is similar to a student resume in that it highlights your achievements, key experiences, leadership abilities, and employment throughout your secondary education. Brag sheets allow you to assist your educator(s) in writing letters of recommendation on your behalf. This form provides them with more information about who you are outside of school and your interests. You may not need a brag sheet right now, but it would be a good idea to practice filling out this form and sharing it with your parents, counselor, or teacher to request a letter of recommendation!

NAME:

BRAG SHEET
College Planning

What is your anticipated college major?

What colleges are you going to apply to?

HS Activities: Please list your HS activities, including clubs, teams, etc., and write the grade in which you participated.   **Grade**

Community Service: Please list your volunteer work and/or church activities.

Awards: Please list any awards (academic and non-academic)

List 3 adjectives to describe yourself:

How excited are you about your future?

Rating

BRAG
SHEET
Life Skill

GPA and class rank (if available)

_____

Students generally have little control over their recommendation letters other than who they choose to write them for and the relationships that necessitate them.

The purpose of a brag sheet is to benefit you while making the writing process as easy for your recommender as possible. As the title suggests, it's one of the best opportunities to brag about yourself. While the primary purpose of a brag sheet is to help guide a teacher recommendation letter, it can also be used for a variety of other purposes.

When you go to an interview for a college that you applied to, bring your brag sheet with you and hand it to the interviewer. It will provide them with a quick overview of your hobbies, academic performance, and future goals. Not only will it highlight the best aspects of you, but it may also lead to more in-depth conversations because they won't have to waste time asking about basic information that you were able to cover in your brag sheet.

Additionally, you can use it when applying to schools and writing essays. It can be difficult and overwhelming to come up with a topic for your essays.

Describe an event or activity that has had an impact on your life.

What are you most proud of and why.

List the positive influences in your life (family, friends, sports, teacher. etc.)

Following High School, What Should You Do?

As a high school senior, you've accomplished a great deal.

This is the culmination of 12 years of hard work. So, what do we do next?

One big goal might be to find a career path.

There are multiple ways to get to your destination. It would help if you first determined your goals and then devised a strategy for achieving them.

Most jobs require a high school diploma or its equivalent. Other jobs require some education or training after you finish high school. If you want to work in certain professions, you'll likely need at least an associate's, bachelor's, master's, or higher degree.

There are a variety of post-secondary options available, including:

1. Four-year university or college
2. Community college with a two-year program
3. Certificate and trade programs
4. Gap year

4-year College or University

To earn a bachelor's degree in a specific field of study, students must attend a four-year college or university. Students earn a bachelor's degree to prepare for a career after college, or they may choose to enroll in a graduate program.

Community College

Community College offers an associate degree program. You can use this degree to start a career right away or transfer to a four-year university to finish your bachelor's degree. The cost of attending a community college is typically lower than that of a four-year institution.

Additionally, smaller class sizes, easier access to tutors, and connecting with instructors are all advantages of a community college. Students who struggled academically in high school may particularly benefit from these benefits.

Trade School

A vocational or technical school may also be referred to as a trade school. It teaches students how to perform certain tasks to land a specific job. You are given a diploma or certificate when you finish the course of study.

Dental hygienist, computer programmer, respiratory therapist, electrical engineer, plumber, mechanic, chef, and cosmetologist are examples of professions.

Military

Many high school students believe that joining the military after graduation is a viable option because it allows them to attend college for less money or even for free after completing their service term. The so-called G.I. Bill provides veterans with benefits for tuition, books, and housing, and it can provide students with peace of mind by allowing them to avoid incurring student loan debt while in school.

Many high school graduates who decide to enlist in the military have specific goals in mind, such as intelligence operations, diplomatic interpreting, and legal support for active duty and officer personnel. Many parents are worried that their child will be sent to a front-line area. Still, the military offers a wide range of career options within its branches, so many who enlist never see any combat action themselves.

Job Corps

If you are between the ages of 16 and 24 and have a low income, you may be eligible for the Job Corps program. Students can earn both a high school diploma and college credit. Job Corps centers can be found across the United States. These programs offer free or low-cost housing, food, health care, financial assistance, and guidance in shifting into a new job.

Health care, construction, information technology, and homeland security are just a few of the many career options available. In addition to finding work or an apprenticeship, many Job Corps alums pursue further education or the military.

Gap Year

Before starting college or a career, many young people take a gap year to explore their interests and earn money. This is when they don't go to school for a whole year. The majority of people who take a gap year use the time to either work full-time, volunteer, or travel.

Students who are determined to return to school after a gap year and complete their degree may suffer some academic setbacks. Still, they may also gain "street smarts" that will benefit them academically in the future. Short-term experiences like this can help students develop life skills that will be useful in college.

Taking a gap year doesn't always entail hopping on a plane and traveling the world. After high school, many students decide to take a year off to find a good job and save money for college. There are two advantages to this option: the ability to pay for college without relying on student loans, and the opportunity to gain work experience.

1. **Community College offers an _____ degree program.**
   a. bachelors
   b. associate

2. **Many young people take a ___ year to explore their interests and earn money.**
   a. gap
   b. half

3. **If you are between the ages of 16 and 24 and have a low income, you may be eligible for the _____ program.**
   a. Military Program
   b. Job Corps

4. **A vocational or technical school may also be referred to as a secondary school.**
   a. False - trade school
   b. True - secondary or post-school

5. **Community College offers an associate degree program.**
   a. True
   b. False

6. **To earn a bachelor's degree, students must attend a _____ college or university.**
   a. two-year
   b. four-year

Test Your Mathematics Knowledge

Score: _____

Date: _____

1. To add fractions_____
   a. the denominators must be the same
   b. the denominators can be same or different
   c. the denominators must be different

2. To add decimals, the decimal points must be?
   a. column and carry the first digit(s)
   b. lined up in any order before you add the columns
   c. lined up vertically before you add the columns

3. When adding like terms_____
   a. the like terms must be same and they must be to the different power.
   b. the exponent must be different and they must be to the same power.
   c. the variable(s) must be the same and they must be to the same power.

4. The concept of math regrouping involves_____
   a. regrouping means that 5x + 2 becomes 50 + 12
   b. the numbers you are adding come out to five digit numbers and 0
   c. rearranging, or renaming, groups in place value

5. _____ indicates how many times a number, or algebraic expression, should be multiplied by itself.
   a. Denominators
   b. Division-quotient
   c. Exponent

6. _____is the numerical value of a number without its plus or minus sign.
   a. Absolute value
   b. Average
   c. Supplementary

7. Any number that is less than zero is called_____
   a. Least common multiple
   b. Equation
   c. Negative number

8. 23 = 2 x 2 x 2 = 8, 8 is the
   a. third power of 2
   b. first power of 2
   c. second power of 2

9. -7, 0, 3, and 7.12223 are
   a. all real numbers
   b. all like fractions
   c. all like terms

10. How do you calculate 2 + 3 x 7?
    a. 2 + 3 x 7 = 2 + 21 = 23
    b. 2 + 7 x 7 = 2 + 21 = 35
    c. 2 + 7 x 3 = 2 + 21 = 23

11. How do you calculate (2 + 3) x (7 - 3)?

    a. (2 + 2) x (7 - 3) = 5 x 4 = 32

    b. (2 + 3) x (7 - 3) = 5 x 4 = 20

    c. (2 + 7) x (2 - 3) = 5 x 4 = 14

12. The Commutative Law of Addition says_____

    a. positive - positive = (add) positive

    b. that it doesn't matter what order you add up numbers, you will always get the same answer

    c. parts of a calculation outside brackets always come first

13. The Zero Properties Law of multiplication says_____

    a. that any number multiplied by 0 equals 0

    b. mathematical operation where four or more numbers are combined to make a sum

    c. Negative - Positive = Subtract

14. Multiplication is when you_____

    a. numbers that are added together in multiplication problems

    b. take one number and add it together a number of times

    c. factor that is shared by two or more numbers

15. When multiplying by 0, the answer is always_____

    a. 0

    b. -0

    c. 1

16. When multiplying by 1, the answer is always the _____

    a. same as the number multiplied by 0

    b. same as the number multiplied by -1

    c. same as the number multiplied by 1

17. You can multiply numbers in_____

    a. any order and multiply by 2 and the answer will be the same

    b. any order you want and the answer will be the same

    c. any order from greater to less than and the answer will be the same

18. Division is_____

    a. set of numbers that are multiplied together to get an answer

    b. breaking a number up into an equal number of parts

    c. division is scaling one number by another

19. If you take 20 things and put them into four equal sized groups

    a. there will be 6 things in each group

    b. there will be 5 things in each group

    c. there will be 10 things in each group

20. The dividend is_____

    a. the number you are multiplied by

    b. the number you are dividing up

    c. the number you are grouping together

21. The divisor is _____

    a. are all multiples of 3

    b. the number you are dividing by

    c. common factor of two numbers

22. The quotient is _____

    a. the answer

    b. answer to a multiplication operation

    c. any number in the problem

23. When dividing something by 1_____
    a. the answer is the original number
    b. the answer produces a given number when multiplied by itself
    c. the answer is the quotient

24. Dividing by 0_____
    a. the answer will always be more than 0
    b. You will always get 1
    c. You cannot divide a number by 0

25. If the answer to a division problem is not a whole number, the number(s) leftover_____
    a. are called the Order Property
    b. are called the denominators
    c. are called the remainder

26. You can figure out the 'mean' by_____
    a. multiply by the sum of two or more numbers
    b. adding up all the numbers in the data and then dividing by the number of numbers
    c. changing the grouping of numbers that are added together

27. The 'median' is the_____
    a. last number of the data set
    b. middle number of the data set
    c. first number of the data set

28. The 'mode' is the number_____
    a. that appears equal times
    b. that appears the least
    c. that appears the most

29. Range is the_____
    a. difference between the less than equal to number and the highest number.
    b. difference between the highest number and the highest number.
    c. difference between the lowest number and the highest number

30. Please Excuse My Dear Aunt Sally: What it means in the Order of Operations is____
    a. Parentheses, Exponents, Multiplication and Division, and Addition and Subtraction
    b. Parentheses, Equal, Multiplication and Decimal, and Addition and Subtraction
    c. Parentheses, Ellipse, Multiplication and Data, and Addition and Subtraction

31. A ratio is_____
    a. a way to show a relationship or compare two numbers of the same kind
    b. short way of saying that you want to multiply something by itself
    c. he sum of the relationship a times x, a times y, and a times z

32. Variables are things_____
    a. that can change or have different values
    b. when something has an exponent
    c. the simplest form using fractions

33. Always perform the same operation to_____of the equation.
    a. when the sum is less than the operation
    b. both sides
    c. one side only

34. The slope intercept form uses the following equation:
    a. $y = mx + b$
    b. $y = x + ab$
    c. $x = mx + c$

35. The point-slope form uses the following equation:

    a. $y - y1 = m(y - x2)$

    b. $y - y1 = m(x - x1)$

    c. $x - y2 = m(x - x1)$

36. Numbers in an algebraic expression that are not variables are called_____

    a. Square

    b. Coefficient

    c. Proportional

37. A coordinate system is _____

    a. a type of cubed square

    b. a coordinate reduced to another proportion plane

    c. a two-dimensional number line

38. Horizontal axis is called_____

    a. h-axis

    b. x-axis

    c. y-axis

39. Vertical axis is called_____

    a. v-axis

    b. y-axis

    c. x-axis

40. Equations and inequalities are both mathematical sentences_____

    a. has y and x variables as points on a graph

    b. reduced ratios to their simplest form using fractions

    c. formed by relating two expressions to each other

Geography: Time Zones

Score: _____

Date: _____

First, go over the entire message. Then go back and fill in the blanks. You can skip the blanks you're unsure about and come back to them later.

different	outside	message	shines	classmate
exist	clocks	time	ball	day

Have you ever tried to call or send a _____ to someone who was on the other side of the country or the world? It can be tough to reach a faraway location from you because the time of _____ may be different from your own. The purpose of time zones and why we have them will be discussed in this session.

Kim, Mike's _____ who recently relocated across the country, is texting him. After a short time, Kim sends Mike a text message saying that it is time for her to go to sleep for the night. The sun is beaming brightly _____, and Mike is confused about why Kim would choose this time of day to go to sleep. 'Can you tell me what _____ it is, please?' Mike asked. 'It's 9:00 p.m. now!' Kim replies.

What exactly is going on here? Was Mike able to travel back in time in some way?

What is happening to Mike and Kim is nothing more than a natural occurrence that occurs on our planet daily. Since Kim relocated across the country, she is now in a _____ time zone than she was previously.

A time zone is a geographical location on the planet with a fixed time that all citizens can observe by setting their _____ to that time. As you go from east to west (or west to east) on the globe's surface, you will encounter different time zones. The greater the distance traveled, the greater the number of time zones crossed.

Time zones are not something that arises in nature by chance. Humans created the concept of time zones and determined which regions of the world are located in which time zones.

Because of time zones, everyone experiences the same pattern of dawn in the early morning and sunset in the late afternoon. We require time zones because the earth is shaped like a _____ and therefore requires them. As the sun beams down on the planet, not every location receives the same amount of sunshine. The sun _____ on one side of the earth and brightens it during the day, while the other side is dark during the night (nighttime). If time zones didn't _____, many people worldwide would experience quite strange sunshine patterns during the day if there were no time zones.

One key skill that everyone should be able to perform is determining whether a location on earth is in a later or earlier time zone than they are. The general guideline is as follows:

If your friend lives in a location that is west of you, they are in a different time zone than you. If they live in a time zone later than yours, they are located east of you.

West is considered to be earlier, whereas the east is considered later.

The following are the primary time zones in the United States:
Eastern (New York, Georgia, Ohio, and other east coast states)
Central (Alabama, Iowa, Minnesota, and more)
Mountain (Arizona, Montana, Utah, and more)
Pacific (California, Nevada, and other west coast states)

Science: Albert Einstein

First, read the entire passage. After that, go back and fill in the blanks. You can skip the blanks you're unsure about and finish them later.

mathematics	boat	Nobel	overnight	top
experiment	paper	books	Germany	failed
pocket	marriage	missed	socks	door

Albert Einstein was born in _____ on March 14, 1879. Because he was Jewish, he fled to the United States to avoid Hitler and the Second World War.

When his grandmother first saw him, she said he was stupid! Little did she know!

He apparently didn't speak until he was four years old, and even then, he would repeat words and sentences until he was seven.

His father gave him a simple _____ compass when he was about five years old, and it quickly became his favorite toy!

He became obsessed with magnetism, which is basically all about magnets and how they work, from that day forward.

Young Einstein didn't like the way his grammar school taught him. He also wasn't particularly fond of authority. As a result, he was expelled from school quite a few times.

He developed an interest in _____ and science at the age of seven.

When Einstein was about ten years old, a much older friend gave him a large stack of science, mathematics, and philosophy _____.

He'd published his first scientific _____ by the age of sixteen. That is absolutely incredible!

Numerous reports have shown that Einstein _____ math in school, but his family has stated that this is not the case. They claimed he was always at the _____ of his class in math and could solve some challenging problems. He was obsessed with geometry and algebra, and no one taught him anything – he taught himself! He was also constantly attempting to prove various mathematical theories on his own.

Yes, he was brilliant.

Although he was not a top student in every subject in school, he certainly made up for it when he and his family moved to Switzerland when he was older.

He began teaching math and physics in 1900.

Einstein was a little disorganized. So, if you're feeling the same way, don't despair; there is still hope!

As an adult, he frequently _____ appointments, and because his mind was all over the place, his lectures were a little difficult to understand.

He didn't wear _____ and had uncombed hair! Even at posh dinners, he'd arrive unkempt, with crumpled clothes and, of course, no socks!

Despite the fact that he was all over the place, a little shabby, and a little difficult to understand, he rocked the world with his Theory of Relativity in 1915. An _____ in 1919 proved the theory correct. He became famous almost _____, and he suddenly received invitations to travel worldwide, as well as honors from all over the world!

In 1921, he was awarded the _____ Prize for Physics. He'd come a long way from the boy who was told he'd never amount to anything!

Today, his other discoveries enabled us to have things like garage _____ openers, televisions, and DVD players. Time magazine named him "Person of the Century" in 1999.

One of his favorite activities was to take a _____ out on a lake and take his notebook with him to think and write everything down. Perhaps this is what inspired him to create his inventions!

Einstein's first _____ produced two sons. His daughter, Lierserl, is believed to have died when she was young. He married twice, and she died before him.

On April 18, 1955, the great scientist died in America.

Government History: How Laws Are Made

Score: _____

Date:_____

Congress is the federal government's legislative branch, and it is in charge of making laws for the entire country. Congress is divided into two legislative chambers: the United States Senate and the United States House of Representatives. Anyone elected to either body has the authority to propose new legislation. A bill is a new law proposal.

People living in the United States and its territories are subject to federal laws.

Bills are created and passed by Congress. The president may then sign the bills into law. Federal courts may examine the laws to see if they are in accordance with the Constitution. If a court finds a law to be unconstitutional, it has the authority to overturn it.

The United States government has enacted several laws to help maintain order and protect the country's people. Each new law must be approved by both houses of Congress as well as the President. Before it becomes a new law in the nation, each law must go through a specific process.

The majority of laws in the United States begin as bills. An idea is the starting point for a bill. That thought could come from anyone, including you! The idea must then be written down and explained as the next step. A bill is the name given to the first draft of an idea. The bill must then be sponsored by a member of Congress. The sponsor is someone who strongly supports the bill and wishes to see it become law. A Senator or a member of the House of Representatives can be the sponsor.

The bill is then introduced in either the House or the Senate by the bill's sponsor. Once submitted, the bill is given a number and is officially recorded as a bill.

The bill is assigned to a committee after it is introduced. Committees are smaller groups of congress members who are experts in specific areas. For example, if the bill concerns classroom size in public schools, it would be referred to the Committee on Education. The committee goes over the bill's specifics. They bring in experts from outside Congress to testify and debate the bill's pros and cons.

The committee may decide to make changes to the bill before it is passed. If the committee finally agrees to pass the bill, it will be sent to the House or Senate's main chamber for approval.

If the bill was introduced in the House, it would first be considered by the House. The bill will be discussed and debated by the representatives. House members will then vote on the bill. If the bill is passed, it will be sent to the Senate for consideration.

The Senate will then follow the same procedure. It will discuss and debate the bill before voting. If the Senate approves the bill, it will be sent to the President.

The President's signature is the final step in a bill becoming law. When the President signs the bill, it becomes law.

The President has the option of refusing to sign the bill. This is known as a veto. The Senate and House can choose to override the President's veto by voting again. The bill must now be approved by a two-thirds majority in both the Senate and the House to override the veto.

A bill must be signed into law by the President within 10-days. If he does not sign it within 10-days, one of two things may occur:

1) It will become law if Congress is in session.

2) It will be considered vetoed if Congress is not in session (this is called a pocket veto).

1. **If the Senate approves the bill, it will be sent to the _____.**
   a. President
   b. House Representee

2. **The _____ may decide to make changes to the bill before it is passed.**
   a. governor
   b. committee

3. **The bill must then be _____ by a member of Congress.**
   a. signed
   b. sponsored

4. **The President has the option of refusing to sign the bill. This is known as a ___.**
   a. voted
   b. veto

5. **The Senate and House can choose to override the President's veto by _____again.**
   a. creating a new bill
   b. voting

6. **The bill is assigned to a committee after it is _____.**
   a. introduced
   b. vetoed

7. **Bills are created and passed by _____.**
   a. The House
   b. Congress

8. **A bill must be signed into law by the President within ___-days.**
   a. 10
   b. 5

9. **The President's _____ is the final step in a bill becoming law.**
   a. signature
   b. saying yes

10. **If the committee agrees to pass the bill, it will be sent to the House or Senate's main ___ for approval.**
    a. chamber
    b. state

Extra Credit: What are some of the weirdest laws in the world? List at least 5.

_____

_____

_____

_____

_____

_____

_____

_____

_____

_____

_____

_____

_____

_____

_____

_____

_____

History: United States Armed Forces

The President of the United States is the Commander in Chief of the United States Armed Forces.

The United States, like many other countries, maintains a military to safeguard its borders and interests. The military has played an essential role in the formation and history of the United States since the Revolutionary War.

The **United States Department of Defense** (DoD) is in charge of controlling each branch of the military, except the United States Coast Guard, which is under the control of the Department of Homeland Security.

The Department of Defense is the world's largest 'company,' employing over 2 million civilians and military personnel.

The United States military is divided into six branches: the Air Force, Army, Coast Guard, Marine Corps, Navy, and Space Force.

The mission of the **United States Air Force** is to defend the country from outside forces. They also provide air support to other branches of the military, such as the Army and Navy.

The **United States Army** is responsible for defending against aggression that threatens the peace and security of the United States.

There are **Army National Guard** units in all 50 states, which their respective governments govern. The Constitution requires only one branch of the military. Members of the National Guard volunteer some of their time to keep the peace. They are not full-time soldiers, but they respond when called upon, for example, to quell violence when the police need assistance.

The primary concern of **the United States Coast Guard** is to protect domestic waterways (lakes, rivers, ports, etc.). The Coast Guard is managed by the United States Department of Homeland Security.

The **Marines** are a quick-response force. They are prepared to fight on both land and sea. The Marine Corps is a branch of the United States Navy. The Marine Corps conducts operations onboard warfare ships all over the world.

The **United States Navy** conducts its missions at sea to secure and protect the world's oceans. Their mission is to ensure safe sea travel and trade.

The **United States Space Force** is the newest branch of the military, established in December 2019. The world's first and currently only independent space force. It is in charge of operating and defending military satellites and ground stations that provide communications, navigation, and Earth observation, such as missile launch detection.

1. **The United States military is divided into ___ branches.**
   a. six
   b. five

2. **_____ is managed by the United States Department of Homeland Security.**
   a. The National Guard
   b. The Coast Guard

3. **The _____ of the United States is the Commander in Chief of the United States Armed Forces.**
   a. Governor
   b. President

4. **The United States maintains a military to safeguard its _____ and interests.**
   a. borders
   b. cities

5. **DoD is in charge of controlling each _____of the military.**
   a. branch
   b. army

6. **The Marines are prepared to fight on both land and ____.**
   a. battlefield
   b. sea

7. **The United States Space Force is in charge of operating and defending military ____ and ground stations.**
   a. soldiers
   b. satellites

8. **The mission of the _____ is to defend the country from outside forces.**
   a. United States DoD Forces
   b. United States Air Force

9. There are _____ units in all 50 states.
   a. Army National Guard
   b. Armed Nations Guard

10. The United States Navy conducts its missions at sea to secure and protect the world's _____.
    a. oceans
    b. borders

11. The primary concern of the United States Coast Guard is to protect_____.
    a. domestic waterways
    b. domesticated cities

12. The United States military is: the Amy Force, Army, Coast Guard, Mario Corps, Old Navy, and Space Force.
    a. True
    b. False

Extra Credit: Has America ever been invaded?

_____

_____

_____

_____

_____

_____

_____

_____

_____

_____

_____

_____

_____

_____

_____

_____

Grammar: Adjectives Matching

Score: _____

Date: _____

Adjectives are words that describe people, places, and things, or nouns. Adjectives are words that describe sounds, shapes, sizes, times, numbers/quantity, textures/touch, and weather. You can remember this by saying to yourself, "an adjective adds something."

If you need to describe a friend or an adult, you can use words that describe their appearance, size, or age. When possible, try to use positive words that describe a person.

1		disappointed		nothing frightens him/her	A
2		anxious		everything is in order around him	B
3		delighted		very pleased	C
4		terrified		always arrives in time	D
5		ashamed		loves being with people	E
6		envious		very surprised and upset	F
7		proud		very frightened	G
8		shocked		wanting something another person has	H
9		brave		feeling bad because you did sg wrong	I
10		hard-working		uprightness and fairness	J
11		organized		worried	K
12		punctual		has 2 or more jobs	L
13		honest		always supports his friends	M
14		outgoing		feeling pleased and satisfied	N
15		loyal		sad because something is worse than expected	O
16		reliable		one can always count on him	P

History: The Thirteen Colonies

In 1776, thirteen British colonies merged to form the United States. Many of these colonies had existed for well over a century, including Virginia's first colony, founded in 1607.

A colony is a region of land that is politically controlled by another country. As was the case with England and the American colonies, the controlling country is usually physically distant from the colony. Colonies are typically founded and settled by people from the home country, but settlers from other countries may also be present. This was especially true of the American colonies, which people from all over Europe populated.

Here is a list of the thirteen colonies, along with the year they were established () and a description of how they were established.

Virginia: John Smith and the London Company set out for Virginia in 1607.

New York: The Dutch founded New York in 1626. In 1664, it became a British colony.

New Hampshire: John Mason was the first landholder in New Hampshire (1623). Eventually, John Wheelwright.

Massachusetts Bay: Puritans seeking religious freedom in Massachusetts Bay (1630).

Maryland (1633) - George and Cecil Calvert established it as a safe haven for Catholics.

Connecticut (1636) - Thomas Hooker, who had been ordered to leave Massachusetts.

Rhode Island: Roger Williams founded Rhode Island (1636) to provide a place of religious freedom for all.

Delaware: Peter Minuit and the New Sweden Company founded Delaware in 1638. In 1664, the British took over.

North Carolina (1663) - Originally a part of the Carolina Province. Separated from South Carolina in 1712.

South Carolina (1663) - Originally a part of the Carolina Province. In 1712, South Carolina seceded from North Carolina.

New Jersey (1664) - Initially settled by the Dutch, the English took control in 1664.

Pennsylvania (1681) William Penn and the Quakers.

Georgia (1732) - James Oglethorpe as a debtor's settlement.

Queen Elizabeth desired to establish colonies in the Americas to expand the British Empire and compete with the Spanish. The English hoped to find riches, create new jobs, and develop trade ports along the Americas' coasts.

Each colony, on the other hand, has its distinct history of how it was founded. Many of the colonies were established by religious leaders or groups seeking religious liberty. Pennsylvania, Massachusetts, Maryland, Rhode Island, and Connecticut were among these colonies. Other colonies were established solely to create new trade opportunities and profits for investors.

The colonies are frequently divided into New England Colonies, Middle Colonies, and Southern Colonies.

New England Colonies: Connecticut, Massachusetts Bay, New Hampshire, Rhode Island

Middle Colonies: Delaware, New Jersey, New York, Pennsylvania

Southern Colonies: Georgia, Maryland, North Carolina, South Carolina, Virginia

1. **The Dutch founded _____ in 1626.**
   a. New Jersey
   b. New York

2. **13 British colonies merged to form the_____.**
   a. United Kingdom
   b. United States

3. **Roger Williams founded _____.**
   a. Maryland
   b. Rhode Island

4. **A colony is a region of _____ that is politically controlled by another country.**
   a. land
   b. township

5. **Middle Colonies:**
   a. Delaware, New Jersey, New York, Pennsylvania
   b. Georgia, Maryland, North Carolina, South Carolina, Texas

6. **Colonies are typically founded and settled by people from the ____ country.**
   a. home
   b. outside

7. **Southern Colonies:**
   a. Maine, New Jersey, New York, Pennsylvania
   b. Georgia, Maryland, North Carolina, South Carolina, Virginia

8. **Many of the colonies were established by _____ leaders or groups seeking religious liberty.**
   a. political
   b. religious

9. **New England Colonies:**
   a. Connecticut, Massachusetts Bay, New Hampshire, Rhode Island
   b. Ohio, Tennessee, New York, Pennsylvania

10. **George and Cecil Calvert established _____ as a safe haven for Catholics.**
   a. Maine
   b. Maryland

11. **The colonies are frequently divided into_____.**
   a. New England Colonies, Middle Colonies, and Southern Colonies
   b. United England Colonies, Midland Colonies, and Southern Colonies.

Confusing Vocab Words

Score: _____

Date: _____

Because English is filled with words that look or sound alike (or both), but mean very different things, it's easy to become confused and use the incorrect word at the wrong time. However, if you are aware of the various meanings of these words, you will not fall into the same traps.

Fill in the blank with the best answer.

1. He _____ [accepts / accept / excepts] defeat well.

2. Please take all the books off the table _____ [exception / accept / except] for the thick one.

3. Lack of sleep _____ [affects / affect / effect] the quality of your work.

4. The _____ [effects / affect / effect] of the light made the room bright.

5. I have a _____ [alot / lot / lots] of friends.

6. The magician preformed a great _____. [illusion / allusion / trick]

7. Dinner was all _____ [already / good / ready] when the guests arrived.

8. The turkey was _____ [al ready / already / all ready] cooked when the guests arrived.

9. _____, [All together / Altogether / altogether] I thought it was a great idea!

10. We were all _____ [altogether / group / together] at the family reunion.

11. The fence kept the dogs _____. [apart / a part / parted]

12. A _____ [section / part / Apart] of the plan is to wake up at dawn.

13. The plane's _____ [assent / descent / ascent] made my ears pop.

14. You could see his _____ [breath / breathing / breathe] in the cold air.

15. If you don't _____, [breath / breathe / breathing] then you are dead.

16. The _____ [capital / capitol / city] of Hawaii is Honolulu.

17. That is the _____ [capital / capitol / captain] building.

18. I _____ [sighted / sited / cited] 10 quotes from the speech.

19. You can not build on that _____. [cite / sight / site]

20. The _____ [cite / site / sight] of land is refreshing.

21. I _____ [complimented / complemented / discouraged] my wife on her cooking.

22. We all have a _____ [conscience / mind / conscious] of right and wrong.

23. The boxer is still _____. [conscience / conscious / knocked out]

24. I went to the city _____ [municipal / counsel / council] meeting.

25. My accountant _____ [directed / counciled / counseled] me on spending habits.

26. The teacher _____ [brought out / illicit / elicited] the correct response.

27. The criminal was arrested for _____ [elicit / illicit / illegal] activities.

28. The baby will cry as soon as _____ [its' / it's / its] mother leaves.

29. _____ [It's / It is / Its] a beautiful day

30. I have a headache, so I'm going to _____ [lay / lain / lie] down.

31. You should never tell a _____. [lay / lie / lye]

32. If you _____ [lose / find / loose] your phone, I will not buy a new one!

33. My pants feel _____, [loose / tight / lose] I need a belt.

34. I _____ [kindly / kind / a bit] of like spicy food.

35. He is a very _____ [kind of / mean / kind] teacher.

Math: Arithmetic Refresher

Score: _____

Date: _____

Select the best answer for each question.

1. Use division to calculate 6/3. The answer is _____.
   a. 2
   b. 4
   c. 3.5

2. Fill in the blank $2 + \sqrt{5}$ _____ $7 - \sqrt{10}$
   a. >
   b. ≤
   c. ≥

3. Use division to calculate 50/10. The answer is _____.
   a. 5.5
   b. 8
   c. 5

4. Which family of numbers begins with the numbers 0, 1, 2, 3, ...?
   a. Integers
   b. Whole numbers
   c. Rational numbers

5. Use division to calculate 7/4. The answer is _____.
   a. 2 R4
   b. 1.5
   c. 1 R3

6. Which of the answer choices is an INCORRECT statement?
   a. 0 > -1
   b. -2 < -4
   c. 32 < -25x

7. Simplify: 7 * 5 - 2 + 11
   a. 44
   b. 23
   c. 21

8. -18 + (-11) = ?
   a. 28
   b. 32
   c. -29

9. 16 - (-7) = ?
   a. 20
   b. 23
   c. 19

10. -12 - (-9) = ?
   a. -3
   b.

11. Simplify: 37 - [5 + {28 - (19 - 7)}]
   a. 16
   b. 36
   c. 46

12. The numbers 1, 2, 3, 4, 5, 6, 7, 8, ..., i.e. natural numbers, are called_____.
   a. Positive integers
   b. Rational integers
   c. Simplify numbers

13. _____is the number you are dividing by.
   a. divisor
   b. equation
   c. dividend

14. _____ is the leftover amount when dividend doesn't divide equally.
   a. remainder
   b. quotient
   c. dividend

Math: Decimals Place Value

Our basic number system is decimals. The decimal system is built around the number ten. It is sometimes referred to as a base-10 number system. Other systems use different base numbers, such as binary numbers, which use base-2.

The place value is one of the first concepts to grasp when learning about decimals. The position of a digit in a number is represented by its place value. It determines the value of the number.

When the numbers 800, 80, and 8 are compared, the digit "8" has a different value depending on its position within the number.

8 - ones place
80 - tens place
800 - hundreds place

The value of the number is determined by the 8's place value. The value of the number increases by ten times as the location moves to the left.

Select the best answer for each question.

1. Which of the following is a decimal number?
   a. 1,852
   b. 1.123
   c. 15

2. For the number 125.928, what is in the tenths place?
   a. 9
   b. 2
   c. 5

3. For the number 359, which number is in the tens place?
   a. 3
   b. 5
   c. 9

4. Write the number 789.1 as an addition problem.
   a. 70 + 800 + 90 + 1
   b. 700 + 80 + 9 + 1 / 10
   c. 700 + 80 + 9+10

5. When we say 7 is in the hundreds place in the number 700, this is the same as 7x102.n.
   a. True
   b. False

6. For the number 2.14, what digit is in the hundredths place?
   a. 4
   b. 1
   c. 2

7. When you start to do arithmetic with decimals, it will be important to_____ properly.
   a. line up the numbers
   b. line up all like numbers
   c. line up numbers ending in 0

8. Depending upon the position of a digit in a number, it has a value called its_____.
   a. tenth place
   b. decimals place
   c. place value

9. The place value of the digit 6 in the number 1673 is 600 as 6 is in the hundreds place.
   a. True
   b. False

10. What is the place value of the digits 2 and 4 in the number 326.471?
    a. 2 is in the tens place. 4 is in the tenths place.
    b. 2 is in the tenths place. 4 is in the tens place.
    c. 2 is in the ones place. 4 is in the tenths place.

Math: Roman Numerals

Score: _____

Date: _____

The Ancient Romans used Roman numerals as their numbering system. We still use them every now and then. They can be found in the Super Bowl's numbering system, after king's names (King Henry IV), in outlines, and elsewhere. Roman numerals are base 10 or decimal numbers, just like the ones we use today. However, they are not entirely positional, and there is no number zero.

Roman numerals use letters rather than numbers. You must know the following seven letters:

I = 1

V = 5

X = 10

L = 50

C = 100

D = 500

M = 1000

Select the best answer for each question.

1. III = __
   a. 33
   b. 30
   c. 3

2. XVI=___
   a. 60
   b. 61
   c. 16

3. IV = 5 - 1 =____
   a. 40
   b. 4
   c. 14

4. What number does the Roman numeral LXXIV represent?
   a. 79
   b. 74
   c. 70

5. Which of the following is the Roman numeral for the number 5?
   a. IV
   b. VI
   c. V

6. How many of the same letters can you put in a row in Roman numerals?
   a. 4 or more
   b. 3
   c. 2

7. Which of the following is the Roman numeral for the number 10?
   a. X
   b. IX
   c. XXI

8. What is the Roman numeral for 33?
   a. XXXIII
   b. XIII
   c. XVIII

9. Which of the following is the Roman numeral for the number 50?
   a. X
   b. L
   c. I

10. Which of the following is the Roman numeral for the number 100?
    a. C
    b. IVV
    c. LII

Music: Antonio Vivaldi
Italian Composer

Score: _____

Date: _____

classical	pianist	Sebastian	performed	red
orphans	success	death	priest	Venice

Antonio Vivaldi was a 17th and 18th-century composer who became one of Europe's most famous figures in _____ music.

Antonio Vivaldi was ordained as a _____ but chose to pursue his passion for music instead. He was a prolific composer who wrote hundreds of works, but he was best known for his concertos in the Baroque style, and he was a highly influential innovator in form and pattern. He was also well-known for his operas, such as Argippo and Bajazet.

Antonio Lucio Vivaldi was born in _____, Italy, on March 4, 1678. Giovanni Battista Vivaldi, his father, was a professional violinist who taught his young son to play. Vivaldi met and learned from some of the finest musicians and composers in Venice through his father. While his violin practice flourished, he could not master wind instruments due to chronic shortness of breath.

Vivaldi sought both religious and musical instruction. He began his studies to become a priest when he was 15 years old. In 1703 he was ordained. Vivaldi was known as "il Prete Rosso," or "the Red Priest," because of his _____ hair. Vivaldi's career as a priest was brief. Due to health issues, he could not deliver mass and was forced to resign from the priesthood shortly after his ordination.

At the age of 25, Vivaldi was appointed master of the violin at Venice's Ospedale della Pietà (Devout Hospital of Mercy). In this capacity, he wrote the majority of his major works over a three-decade period. The Ospedale was a school for _____, with the boys learning trades and the girls learning music. The most talented musicians were invited to join an orchestra that performed Vivaldi's compositions, including religious choral music. The orchestra rose to international prominence under Vivaldi's direction. He was promoted to music director in 1716.

Vivaldi's early fame as a composer and musician did not translate into long-term financial _____. After being overshadowed by younger composers and more modern styles, Vivaldi left Venice for Vienna, Austria, possibly hoping to find a position in the imperial court there. Following the _____ of Charles VI, he found himself without a prominent patron and died in poverty in Vienna on July 28, 1741. He was laid to rest in a simple grave following a funeral service devoid of music.

In the early twentieth century, musicians and scholars revived Vivaldi's music, and many of the composer's unknown works were recovered from obscurity. In 1939, Alfredo Casella, a composer, and _____ organized the revival of Vivaldi Week. Since World War II, Vivaldi's music has been widely performed. The choral composition Gloria, which was reintroduced to the public during Casella's Vivaldi Week, is particularly well-known and is regularly _____ at Christmas celebrations worldwide.

Vivaldi's work, which included nearly 500 concertos, influenced later composers such as Johann _____ Bach.

Nutrition: Reading Labels

Score: _____

Date: _____

Reading food labels can assist you in making educated food choices. Packaged foods and beverages—those in cans, boxes, bottles, jars, and bags—include extensive nutritional and food safety information on their labels or packaging. Keep an eye out for these items on the food label.

On certain foods you purchase, you may notice one of three types of product dates:

"Sell by" indicates how long the manufacturer recommends a store keep foods such as meat, poultry, eggs, or milk products on the shelf—buy them before this date.

The "use by" date indicates how long the food will remain fresh—if you purchase or consume it after that date, some foods may become stale or less tasty.

"Best if used by" (or "best if used before") indicates how long the food will retain its best flavor or quality—it does not suggest a purchase date.

The Food and Drug Administration (FDA) of the United States requires that most packaged foods and beverages bear a Nutrition Facts label. The total number of servings in the container and the food or beverage serving size are listed at the top of the Nutrition Facts label. The serving size indicated on the label is based on the amount of food that most people consume at one time and is not intended to be a guideline for how much to consume.

With permission, read the labels on the containers and answer the questions for each food item. If you do not have any of those items in your home, feel free to find the item online and use that to reference.

Egg carton

1. What store or farm are they from?

2. Are the eggs free range?

3. Where are the eggs produced or brand?

4. When is the best before date?

5. What is the display date if any?

6. How many calories?

7. Can you recycle the egg carton?

8. How much protein?

9. Should I keep the eggs in the fridge?

10. How many eggs were in the carton?

Water Bottle

1. What store is the water from and brand?

2. Does the water contains sodium? If so, how much?

3. What is the percent daily value?

4. Can I recycle the bottle?

5. What telephone number should I call if I have a problem?

6. What is the serving size?

7. How many days do I have to drink the water?

Milk

1. Which store does the milk come from and the brand name?

2. How many pints are in the milk?

3. The milk is ___ _____. A. **Semi-skimmed milk** B. **Whole Milk** C. **Half milk**

4. How much calcium is there?

5. When is the use-by date?

Juice

1. What store is the juice from?

2. How many **ml** are in one bottle?

3. Can I recycle the bottle?

4. What color is the bottle?

5. Should I keep the juice in the fridge?

Science Multiple Choice Quiz: Food Chain and Food Web

Select the best answer for each question.

1. In ecology, it is the sequence of transfers of matter and energy in the form of food from organism to organism.
   a. Food Chain
   b. Food Transport
   c. Food Sequencing

2. _____ can increase the total food supply by cutting out one step in the food chain.
   a. Birds
   b. People
   c. Animals

3. Plants, which convert solar energy to food by photosynthesis, are the _____.
   a. secondary food source
   b. tertiary food source
   c. primary food source

4. _____ help us understand how changes to ecosystems affect many different species, both directly and indirectly.
   a. Food Chain
   b. Food Web
   c. Food Transport

5. _____ eat decaying matter and are the ones who help put nutrients back into the soil for plants to eat.
   a. Decomposers
   b. Consumers
   c. Producers

6. _____ are producers because they produce energy for the ecosystem.
   a. Plants
   b. Decomposers
   c. Animals

7. Each organism in an ecosystem occupies a specific _____ in the food chain or web.
   a. trophic level
   b. space
   c. place

8. What do you call an organism that eats both plants and animals?
   a. Herbivores
   b. Carnivores
   c. Omnivores

9. Carnivore is from the Latin words that means _____.
   a. "plant eaters"
   b. "eats both plants and animals"
   c. "flesh devourers"

10. A food web is all of the interactions between the species within a community that involve the transfer of energy through _____.
    a. reservation
    b. consumption
    c. adaptation

11. Why are animals considered consumers?
    a. because they don't produce energy, they just use it up
    b. because they produce energy for the ecosystem
    c. because they only produce energy for themselves

12. How do plants turn sunlight energy into chemical energy?
    a. through the process of photosynthesis
    b. through the process of adaptation
    c. through the process of cancelation

Science Multiple Choice Quiz:
Temperate Forest Biome

Score: _____

Date: _____

Select the best answer for each question.

1. _____ are found in Northern Hemisphere regions with moist, warm summers and cold winters, primarily in eastern North America, eastern Asia, and western Europe.
   a. Deciduous forests
   b. Wild forests
   c. Rainforests

2. How many types of forest biomes are there?
   a. 2
   b. 3
   c. 4

3. Temperate forests emerged during the period of global cooling that began at the beginning of the _____.
   a. Medieval Era
   b. Paleozoic Era
   c. Cenozoic Era

4. Major temperate forests are located in the following areas, except for:
   a. Eastern China
   b. Japan
   c. Korea

5. What makes a forest a temperate forest?
   a. Temperature, Two seasons, Tropics, and Clay soil.
   b. Temperature, Climate, Wet season, and Loam soil.
   c. Temperature, Four seasons, Lots of rain, and Fertile soil.

6. The three main types of forest biomes are: the rainforest, the temperate forest, and the _____.
   a. Coniferous
   b. Taiga
   c. Broad-leafed

7. Many trees rely on _____ to get through the winter.
   a. temperature
   b. sap
   c. rain

8. Temperate forests are usually classified into two main groups, and these are: _____ and _____.
   a. Deciduous, Evergreen
   b. Coniferous, Deciduous
   c. Indigenous, Evergreen

9. Deciduous is a Latin word that means _____.
   a. "to rise up"
   b. "to subside"
   c. "to fall off"

10. Certain trees in a temperate forest can grow up to how many feet?
    a. 50 feet tall
    b. 90 feet tall
    c. 100 feet tall

11. _____ forests are made up mostly of conifer trees such as cypress, cedar, redwood, fir, juniper, and pine trees.
    a. Broad-leafed
    b. Mixed coniferous and broad-leafed
    c. Coniferous

12. The animals that live in temperate forests have _____ that allow them to _____ in different kinds of weather.
    a. adaptations, survive
    b. compatibility, survive
    c. conformity, thrive

Social Skill Interests: Things To Do

Score: _____

Date: _____

A **hobby** is something that a person actively pursues relaxation and enjoyment. On the other hand, a person may have an **interest** in something because they are curious or concerned. Hobbies usually do not provide monetary compensation. However, a person's interests can vary and may lead to earning money or making a living from them. Hobbies are typically pursued in one's spare time or when one is not required to work. Interests can be followed in one's spare time or while working, as in the case of using one's passion as a source of income. A hobby can be a recreational activity that is done regularly in one's spare time. It primarily consists of participating in sports, collecting items and objects, engaging in creative and artistic pursuits, etc. The desire to learn or understand something is referred to as interest. If a person has a strong interest in a subject, he or she may pursue it as a hobby. However, an interest is not always a hobby. Hobbies such as stamp and flower collecting may not be a source of income for a person, but the items collected can sometimes be sold. Hobbies frequently lead to discoveries and inventions. Interests could be a source of income or something done for free. If a person is interested in cooking or enjoys creating dishes, he can do so at home or make it a career by becoming a chef.

_____

Put the words in the correct category.

pottery	card making	candle making	reading	weaving	knitting
gym	jewellery	chess	surfing	computer games	collecting
woodwork	Soccer	art	swimming	cooking	skateboarding
embroidery	skiing	gardening	writing	chatting	sewing
netball	stamp collecting	football	music	rugby	basketball

Sport (10)	Handcrafts (10)	Interests (10)

Health: Check Your Symptoms

Healthy habits aid in the development of happy and healthy children as well as the prevention of future health issues such as diabetes, hypertension, high cholesterol, heart disease, and cancer.

Chronic diseases and long-term illnesses can be avoided by leading a healthy lifestyle. Self-esteem and self-image are aided by feeling good about yourself and taking care of your health.

Maintain a consistent exercise schedule.

No, you don't have to push yourself to go to the gym and do tough workouts, but you should be as active as possible. You can maintain moving by doing simple floor exercises, swimming, or walking. You can also remain moving by doing some domestic chores around the house.

What matters is that you continue to exercise. At least three to five times a week, devote at least twenty to thirty minutes to exercise. Establish a regimen and make sure you get adequate physical activity each day.

Be mindful of your eating habits.

You must continue to eat healthily in order to maintain a healthy lifestyle. Eat more fruits and vegetables and have fewer carbs, salt, and harmful fat in your diet. Don't eat junk food or sweets.

Avoid skipping meals since your body will crave more food once you resume eating. Keep in mind that you should burn more calories than you consume.

1. **I've got a pain in my head.**
   a. Stiff neck
   b. headache

2. **I was out in the sun too long.**
   a. Sunburn
   b. Fever

3. **I've got a small itchy lump or bump.**
   a. Rash
   b. Insect bite

4. **I might be having a heart attack.**
   a. Cramps
   b. Chest pain

5. **I've lost my voice.**
   a. Laryngitis
   b. Sore throat

6. **I need to blow my nose a lot.**
   a. Runny nose
   b. Blood Nose

7. **I have an allergy. I have a**
   a. Rash
   b. Insect bite

8. **My shoe rubbed my heel. I have a**
   a. Rash
   b. Blister

9. **The doctor gave me antibiotics. I have a/an**
   a. Infection
   b. Cold

10. **I think I want to vomit. I am**
    a. Nauseous
    b. Bloated

11. **My arm is not broken. It is**
    a. Scratched
    b. Sprained

12. **My arm touched the hot stove. It is**
    a. Burned
    b. Bleeding

13. **I have an upset stomach. I might**
    a. Cough
    b. Vomit

14. **The doctor put plaster on my arm. It is**
    a. Sprained
    b. Broken

15. **If you cut your finger it will**
    a. Burn
    b. Bleed

16. **I hit my hip on a desk. It will**
    a. Burn
    b. Bruise

17. **When you have hay-fever you will**
    a. Sneeze
    b. Wheeze

18. **A sharp knife will**
    a. Scratch
    b. Cut

Art: Roman Portrait Sculptures

Alexander	aristocrats	ancestral	shrine	rewarded
sculpture	pattern	mosaics	marble	artistic

Portrait _____ has been practiced since the beginning of Roman history. It was most likely

influenced by the Roman practice of creating _____ images. When a Roman man died, his family

made a wax sculpture of his face and kept it in a special _____ at home. Because these sculptures were

more like records of a person's life than works of art, the emphasis was on realistic detail rather than

_____ beauty.

As Rome became more prosperous and gained access to Greek sculptors, Roman _____

known as patricians began creating these portraits from stone rather than wax.

Roman sculpture was about more than just honoring the dead; it was also about honoring the living. Important

Romans were _____ for their valor or greatness by having statues of themselves erected and

displayed in public. This is one of the earliest of these types of statues that we've discovered, and the

_____ continued all the way until the Republic's demise.

The mosaic is the only form of Roman art that has yet to be discussed. The Romans adored mosaics and created

them with exquisite skill. The Romans created _____ of unprecedented quality and detail using cubes

of naturally colored _____. The floor mosaic depicting _____ the Great at the Battle of

Issus is probably the most famous Roman mosaic.

Parts of Speech Matching

Score: _____

Date: _____

- **NOUN**. used to identify any of a class of people, places, or things
- **PRONOUN**. a word (such as I, he, she, you, it, we, or they) that is used instead of a noun or noun phrase
- **VERB**. a word used to describe an action, state, or occurrence
- **ADJECTIVE**. modify or describe a noun or a pronoun
- **ADVERB**. word that modifies (describes) a verb (she sings loudly), adverbs often end in -ly
- **PREPOSITION**. word or phrase that connects a noun or pronoun to a verb or adjective in a sentence
- **CONJUNCTION**. word used to join words, phrases, sentences, and clauses
- **INTERJECTION**. word or phrase that expresses something in a sudden or exclamatory way, especially an emotion

1	☐	Identify the noun.	verb	A
2	☐	Identify the verb.	mother, truck, banana	B
3	☐	What is an adjective?	Lion	C
4	☐	Three sets of nouns	conjunctions	D
5	☐	Three sets of adverbs	always, beautifully, often	E
6	☐	above, across, against	a word that describes nouns and pronouns	F
7	☐	but, and, because, although	preposition	G
8	☐	Wow! Ouch! Hurrah!	preposition	H
9	☐	Mary and Joe **are** friends.	barked	I
10	☐	Jane ran **around** the corner yesterday.	Interjection	J

Extra Credit: Write at least 3 examples of each: Interjection, Conjunction, Adverb & Preposition

....

....

....

....

Grammar: Contractions
Multiple Choice

Simply put, you replace the letter(s) that were removed from the original words with an apostrophe when you make the contraction.

1. Here is
    a. Here's
    b. Heres'

2. One is
    a. Ones'
    b. One's

3. I will
    a. Il'l
    b. I'll

4. You will
    a. You'll
    b. Yo'ill

5. She will
    a. She'll
    b. She'ill

6. He will
    a. He'ill
    b. He'll

7. It will
    a. It'ill
    b. It'll

8. We will
    a. We'll
    b. We'ill

9. They will
    a. They'ill
    b. They'll

10. That will
    a. That'l
    b. That'll

11. There will
    a. There'ill
    b. There'll

12. This will
    a. This'll
    b. This'ill

13. What will
    a. What'ill
    b. What'll

14. Who will
    a. Who'll
    b. Whol'l

Grammar:
Subjunctive Mood

Wishes, proposals, ideas, imagined circumstances, and assertions that are not true are all expressed in the subjunctive mood. The subjunctive is frequently used to indicate an action that a person hopes or wishes to be able to undertake now or in the future. In general, a verb in the subjunctive mood denotes a scenario or state that is a possibility, hope, or want. It expresses a conditional, speculative, or hypothetical sense of a verb.

When verbs of advice or suggestion are used, the subjunctive mood is utilized. After verbs of recommendation or advice, the subjunctive appears in a phrase beginning with the word -that.

Here are a few verbs that are commonly used in the subjunctive mood to recommend or advise.

- advise, ask, demand, prefer

1. Writers use the subjunctive mood to express _____ or _____ conditions.
   a. imaginary or hoped-for
   b.

2. Which is NOT a common marker of the subjunctive mood?
   a.
   b. memories

3. Which is NOT an example of a hope-for verb?
   a. demand
   b. need

4. Subjunctive mood is used to show a situation is not _____.
   a. fictional or fabricated
   b. entirely factual or certain

5. Which of the below statements is written in the subjunctive mood?
   a. I wish I were a millionaire.
   b. What would you do with a million dollars?

6. The indicative mood is used to state facts and opinions, as in:
   a. My mom's fried chicken is my favorite food in the world.
   b. Smells, taste, chew

7. The imperative mood is used to give commands, orders, and instructions, as in:
   a. Eat your salad.
   b. I love salad!

8. The interrogative mood is used to ask a question, as in:
   a. Have you eaten all of your pizza yet?
   b. I ordered 2 slices of pizza.

9. The conditional mood uses the conjunction "if" or "when" to express a condition and its result, as in:
   a. Blue is my favorite color, so I paint with it often.
   b. If I eat too much lasagna, I'll have a stomach ache later.

10. The subjunctive mood is used to express wishes, proposals, suggestions, or imagined situations, as in:
    a. Yesterday was Monday, and I ate pizza.
    b. I prefer that my mom make pasta rather than tuna.

Biology Vocabulary Words Crossword

Score: _____

Date: _____

Across

1. organelle in which photosynthesis takes place
4. a substance used to kill microorganisms and cure infections
5. any substance that stimulates an immune response in the body
6. a chamber connected to other chambers or passageways
8. major ecological community with distinct climate and flora
9. substance that initiates or accelerates a chemical reaction
13. an eyelike marking
15. any toxin that affects neural tissues

Down

2. a process in which one substance permeates another
6. any of the forms of a gene that can occupy the same locus
7. a digestive juice secreted by the liver
10. a major division of the vertebrate brain
11. the act of dispersing something
12. the environment as it relates to living organisms
14. that which has mass and occupies space

ATRIUM   BIOME   ANTIGEN
ECOLOGY
CHLOROPLAST   MATTER
ABSORPTION   ANTIBIOTIC
DIFFUSION   ALLELE
EYESPOT   NEUROTOXIN
BILE   CEREBELLUM
CATALYST

Biology: Reading Comprehension Viruses

When we catch a cold or get the flu, we are dealing with the effects of a viral infection. Viruses, despite sharing some characteristics with living organisms, are neither cellular nor alive. The presence of cells, the ability to reproduce, the ability to use energy, and the ability to respond to the environment are all important characteristics of living organisms. A virus cannot perform any of these functions on its own.

A virus, on the other hand, is a collection of genetic material encased in a protective coat, which is typically made of proteins. Viruses are obligate parasites because they must replicate on the host. To replicate itself, a virus must first attach to and penetrate a host cell, after which it will go through the various stages of viral infection. These stages are essentially the virus lifecycle. A virus can enter the host cell via one of several methods by interacting with the surface of the host cell. The virus can then replicate itself by utilizing the host's energy and metabolism.

Bacteriophages, viruses that infect bacteria, either use the lysogenic cycle, in which the host cell's offspring carry the virus, or the lytic cycle, in which the host cell dies immediately after viral replication. Once viral shedding has occurred, the virus can infect additional hosts. Viral infections can be productive in the sense that they cause active infection in the host, or they can be nonproductive in the sense that they remain dormant within the host. These two types of infection can result in chronic infections, in which the host goes through cycles of illness and remission, as well as latent infections, in which the virus remains dormant for a period of time before causing illness in the host.

1. A virus is encased in a protective coat, which is typically made of _____.
   a. proteins
   b. molecules
   c. cells

2. To replicate itself, a virus must first attach to and penetrate a ___ cell.
   a. healthy
   b. living atom
   c. host

3. Viruses are neither cellular nor ___.
   a. alive
   b. moving
   c. a threat

4. The virus can replicate itself by utilizing the host's ___and ___.
   a. cells and DNA
   b. molecules and cell
   c. energy and metabolism

5. A virus can remain _____ for a period of time before causing illness in a host.
   a. metabolized
   b. dormant
   c. infected

History Reading Comprehension: Storming of the Bastille

oppression	fortress	prison	prisoners	fortress
military	1000	weapons	battle	French
assassinated	ruled	commoners	Fearful	craftsmen

On July 14, 1789, the Bastille was stormed in Paris, France. The _____ Revolution began with a violent

attack on the government by the people of France.

During the Hundred Years' War, the Bastille was a _____ built in the late 1300s to protect Paris. By

the late 1700s, King Louis XVI had primarily used the Bastille as a state _____.

The majority of the revolutionaries who stormed the Bastille were Paris-based _____ and store

owners. They belonged to the Third Estate, a French social class. Approximately _____ men carried out the

attack.

The Third Estate had recently made the king's demands, including a more significant say in government for the

_____. They were concerned that he was preparing the French army to launch an attack. To arm

themselves, they first took over the Hotel des Invalides in Paris to obtain muskets. However, they lacked gun

powder. The Bastille was rumored to be full of political _____ and symbolized the king's

_____ to many. It also had gunpowder stores, which the revolutionaries required for their

_____.

The revolutionaries approached the Bastille on the morning of July 14. They demanded that the Bastille's

_____ commander, Governor de Launay, hand over the prison and the gunpowder. He flatly refused. The crowd became agitated as the negotiations dragged on. They were able to gain access to the courtyard in the early afternoon. They began to try to break into the main _____ once they were inside the courtyard. _____ soldiers in the Bastille opened fire on the crowd. The _____ had begun. When some of the soldiers joined the crowd's side, the fight took a turn for the worse. De Launay quickly realized the situation was hopeless. He handed over the fort to the revolutionaries, who took control.

During the fighting, approximately 100 revolutionaries were killed. The crowd _____ Governor de Launay and three of his officers after they surrendered.

The storming of the Bastille triggered a chain of events that culminated in King Louis XVI's deposition and the French Revolution. The revolutionaries' success inspired commoners throughout France to rise up and fight against the nobles who had _____ them for so long.

July 14, the date of the storming of the Bastille, is now celebrated as French National Day. In the same way that the Fourth of July is celebrated in the United States. It is known as "The National Celebration" or "The Fourteenth of July" in France.

Write in your own words, what happened in the storming of the Bastille.

History Reading Comprehension: The Great Depression

During the 1930s, the United States experienced a severe economic downturn known as the Great Depression. It started in the United States, Wall Street to be exact, but quickly spread throughout the rest of the world. Many people were out of work, hungry, and homeless during this period. People in the city would wait for hours at soup kitchens to get a bite to eat. Farmers struggled in the Midwest, where a severe drought turned the soil into dust, resulting in massive dust storms.

America's "Great Depression" began with a dramatic stock market crash on "Black Thursday," October 24, 1929, when panicked investors who had lost faith in the American economy quickly sold 16 million shares of stock. However, historians and economists attribute the Great Depression to a variety of factors, including drought, overproduction of goods, bank failures, stock speculation, and consumer debt.

When the Great Depression began, Herbert Hoover was President of the United States. Many people held Hoover responsible for the Great Depression. The shantytowns where homeless people lived were even dubbed "Hoovervilles" after him. Franklin D. Roosevelt was elected president in 1933. He promised the American people a "New Deal."

The New Deal was a set of laws, programs, and government agencies enacted to aid the country in its recovery from the Great Depression. Regulations were imposed on the stock market, banks, and businesses as a result of these laws. They assisted in putting people to work and attempted to house and feed the poor. Many of these laws, such as the Social Security Act, are still in effect today.

The Great Depression came to an end with the outbreak of World War II. The wartime economy re-employed many people and filled factories to capacity.

The Great Depression left an indelible imprint on the United States. The New Deal laws expanded the government's role in people's daily lives significantly. In addition, public works improved the country's infrastructure by constructing roads, schools, bridges, parks, and airports.

Between 1929 and 1933, the stock market lost nearly 90% of its value.
During the Great Depression, approximately 11,000 banks failed, leaving many people without savings.

1. The Great Depression began with the _____.
    a. World War II
    b. economy drought
    c. stock market crash

2. Who was President when the Great Depression began?
    a. Herbert Hoover
    b. George W Bush
    c. Franklin D. Roosevelt

3. The New Deal was a set of _____.
    a. laws, programs, and government agencies
    b. city and state funding
    c. stock market bailout

4. The Great Depression came to an end with the outbreak of _____.
    a. new laws
    b. investors funding
    c. World War II

History: King Tut Reading Comprehension

Tutankhamun was born around 1341 BC as a prince in Egypt's royal court. Pharaoh Akhenaten was his father. Tut was actually born Tutankhaten, but he changed his name after his father died.

Tut was born to one of his father's lesser wives rather than his father's main wife, the powerful Nefertiti. His presence may have caused some tension in the royal courts, as Nefertiti had only daughters and desperately desired to have her own son to succeed to the throne.

Tut's father died when he was seven years old. Tut married his sister (as was common for Pharaohs in Ancient Egypt) and became Pharaoh a few years later. Because he was so young, he needed help ruling the country. Horemheb, a powerful general, and Ay, Tutankhamun's vizier, were the true rulers.

Tutankhamun died when he was about nineteen years old. Archaeologists have no idea what killed him. Some believe he was assassinated, but the most likely cause of death was a leg wound. Scientists discovered that his mummy's leg was broken and infected before he died. This injury was most likely caused by an accident.

Today, Tut is best known for his tomb in the Valley of the Kings. His tomb was most likely built for someone else and was used to bury the young Pharaoh when he died unexpectedly. This may have aided in keeping his tomb hidden from thieves for thousands of years. As a result, when archeologist Howard Carter discovered the tomb in 1922, it was filled with treasure and artifacts not found in any other Pharaoh's tomb.

Did you know that? Lord Carnarvon, Carter's patron (who was best known as the financial backer of the search for and excavation of Tut), died four months after first entering the tomb. Prompting journalists to popularize a "Curse of the Pharaohs," claiming that hieroglyphs on the tomb walls foretold the death of those who disturbed King Tut.

1. **What was King Tut's real name?**
   a. Tutankhaion
   b. Tutankhaten
   c. Tutankhamun

2. **Tut's father died when he was _____ years old.**
   a. 19 yrs old
   b. Twenty-Two
   c. seven

3. **Tutankhamun died when he was about _____ years old.**
   a. nineteen
   b. 16 years old
   c. 21

4. **Nefertiti was the wife of___.**
   a. Tut
   b. Horemheb
   c. Pharaoh Akhenaten

5. **The tomb of young pharaoh Tut is located in the _____.**
   a. Tuts King Egypt
   b. Maine Valley Sons
   c. Valley of the Kings

Jobs and Careers

Tip: After you've answered the easy ones, go back and work on the harder ones.

skill	climbing	monetary	professional	hourly
variety	salaried	experience	graduate	achieve

You might have heard that the education you receive and the information you learn in school will help you get a job when you _____. Or your abilities and skills will benefit you in your future careers. So, what's the truth? How do people decide whether they want a job or a career?

There are several common misconceptions regarding the distinctions between a job and a career. Some people believe that a job is simply an _____ position, whereas a _____ position is a career. Others believe that a career requires a longer educational path that results in exceptional skills and knowledge. The truth is not what most people believe.

A job is a position or set of duties performed for _____ gain, whereas a career is a focused path or journey that a person takes to achieve their professional goals. A career can include a variety of jobs along a career path.

Parents and teachers frequently ask their children what they want to be when they grow up. A career is the answer to that question. A career is a path or _____ journey that a person follows throughout their working life. A career can necessitate extensive education, such as that of a doctor or a lawyer, or it can require extensive _____ training, such as that of an electrician or plumber.

The words "career" and "path" are frequently used interchangeably. A career path is a path that people take to _____ their professional objectives. Many people work for decades on their career paths, which often include a _____ of jobs along the way. With each job, a person gains _____ and skills that will help them get a better job and achieve their career goals.

Another term associated with careers is the concept of people _____ a "career ladder". When people climb the metaphorical career ladder, they progress step by step from one better job to the next. Careers take years to develop and achieve. Sometimes a lot of education is required at the start of a career before a person can start moving up the ladder, whereas other careers require years of experience in the field to get to the top.

Proofreading Shakespeare: Romeo and Juliet

There are **24** mistakes in this passage. 5 capitals missing. 3 unnecessary capitals. 4 unnecessary apostrophes. 3 punctuation marks missing or incorrect. 2 incorrect homophones. 7 incorrectly spelled words.

In 1597, William Shakespeare published "Romeo and Juliet" which would go on to become one of the world's most famous love stories. The plot of Shakespeare's pley takes place in Verona, where the two main characters romeo and Juliet, meet and fall in love Both are descended from two feuding families, the Capulets, and the Montagues. As a result, thay choose to keep their luve hidden and are married by Friar Laurence. Romeo gets into a fight with Juliet"s cousin Tybalt, whom he Kills in a Brawl despite his best efforts. Romeo is expelled from Verona and escapes to Mantua.

When juliet's parents press her to marry, she Seeks the assistance of Friar Laurence once more, who provides her with a sleeping potion designed to simulate her death. In a letter that never reaches Romeo, he explains his plan. Disgusted by the alleged death of his beloved Juliet, Rumeo returns to Verona and commits suicide at Juliet's open coffin. Juliet awakens from her slumber, sees what has happened, and decides to end her liphe. The two feuding families now recognize their complicity and reconcile at their children's graves.

The medieval old town of Verona is ideal for putting oneself in the shoes of Romeo and juliet. Every year, many loving couples and tourists come to walk in the footsteps of romeo and Juliet. A photograph of Juliet's famous balcony, a visit to Romeo's home, or sum queit time spent at Julia's grave. No matter were you look in the city, you wall find loving couple's who stick declarations of love and initials on small slips of paper to the walls or immortalize themselve's on the walls or stones of house's - often illegally.

Although Shakespeare's drama never corresponded to reality, verona has a unique charm, especially for lovers, who imagine they can feel the true story behind the literary work, almost as if Romeo and Juliet had really existed.

Financial: Money, Stocks and Bonds

Score: _____

Date: _____

Tip: First, read the entire passage. After that, go back and fill in the blanks. You can skip the blanks you're unsure about and finish them later.

prices	obligation	currency	issued	barter
stake	coins	exchange	principal	economy
profits	piece	conditions	valuable	gold
NASDAQ	bankruptcy	golden	services	symbols
goods	shareholders	monetary	value	

Three important _____ must be met in order for something to qualify as a financial asset. It has to be:

Something you can have

Something monetary in nature

A contractual claim provides the basis for that monetary value

That last condition may be difficult to grasp at first, but it will become clear in a few minutes.

As a result, financial assets differ from physical assets such as land or _____. You can touch and feel the actual physical asset with land and gold, but you can only touch and feel something (usually a _____ of paper) that represents the asset of value with financial assets.

Money is a government-defined official medium of _____ that consists of cash and _____. Money, _____, cash, and legal tender all refer to the same thing. They are all _____ of a central bank's commitment to keep money's value as stable as possible. Money is a financial asset because its value is derived from the faith and credit of the government that issued it, not from the paper or metal on which it is printed.

Money is obviously a _____ financial asset. We would all have to _____ with one another without a common medium of exchange, trading whatever _____ and _____ we have for something else we need, or trade what we have for something else we could then trade with someone else who has what we need. Consider how complicated that can become!

Stock is another crucial financial asset in the US _____. Stock, like money, is simply a piece of paper that represents something of value. The something of value' represented by stock is a _____ in a company. Stock is also known as 'equity' because you have a stake in its _____ when you own stock in a company.

Consider little Jane's lemonade stand as the most basic example. Jane only has $4 to begin her business, but she requires $10. Jane's parents give her $3 in exchange for 30% of her business, a friend gives her $1 for 10%, and her brother gives her $2 in exchange for 20%. Jane, her parents, a friend, and her brother are now all _____ in her company.

That example, as simple as it is, accurately describes stock. The complexities arise when we attempt to assign a _____ value to that stock. A variety of factors determines a stock's _____. One share of stock in one company does not equal one share of stock in another. The number of shares issued by each company, as well as the size and profitability of each company, will affect the value of your share. Anything that has an impact on a business, good or bad, will affect the stock price.

These are the most basic and fundamental factors that can influence the value of a share of stock. Individual stock _____ are affected by macroeconomic trends as well. Thousands of books have been written in an attempt to discover the _____ rule that determines the exact value of a share of stock.

The value of a stock can fluctuate from minute to minute and even second to second. The New York Stock Exchange and _____ were the world's two largest stock exchanges in 2014. (both located in the United States).

Bonds are the final financial asset we'll look at. Bonds are, in essence, loans. When an organization, such as a company, a city or state, or even the federal government, requires funds, bonds can be _____. Bonds come in various forms, but they are all debt instruments in which the bondholder is repaid their _____ investment, plus interest, at some future maturity date.

The only way a bondholder's money is lost is if the entity that issued the bond declares _____. Bonds are generally safer investments than stocks because they are a legal _____ to repay debt, whereas stocks represent ownership, which can make or lose money.

How It's Made: Money

It's not very often that people think about how the money in their wallets was made or who made it. The federal agency in charge of money creation in the United States is the Department of Treasury. It looks after two branches that make money. The United States Mint produces coins, whereas the United States Bureau of Engraving and Printing produces dollar notes. Let's look at the entire money-making process, from conception to distribution.

Paper money and coin designs are sketched and modeled by designers employed by the United States Department of Treasury. The Secretary of the Treasury selects one of the designs submitted by the designers for production into currency, albeit the final design may be subject to further revisions at this point.

However, why are fresh designs necessary? Technology has made it easier for anyone to create their own counterfeit money. Counterfeiting, the act of creating phony money, is a crime. The government has redesigned our currency to reduce counterfeiting.

Dollar bills and computer paper don't have the same weight and feel. Since paper money is created from a particular cotton and linen blend, it is more difficult to forge. The Bureau of Engraving and Printing also manufactures the ink. Some recent bills (in values of $10 and higher) contain metallic or color-shifting ink to help prevent counterfeiting, which is used on all paper money.

Coins in the United States are created from a combination of metals and alloys. In addition to reducing coin counterfeiting, this usage of bi-metallic elements significantly lowers the cost of minting coins. Coins that are made of pure metal can be worth more than their face value. As a result, instead of utilizing the coins as money, others may opt to melt them and sell the metals they contain.

The Bureau of Engraving and Printing engraves the design onto a plate once it has been created for paper money. The same plate is then replicated numerous times onto a much larger plate that can print multiple bills simultaneously on numerous printers. Ink is applied to the plate, which is then pushed onto the paper. Each side of a sheet of banknotes must dry for 72 hours.

Following the design of the coins, the designs are replicated on stamps that press the design onto the bi-metallic substance. Coins are made from enormous metal sheets, but that's just the beginning. The metal sheets are fed into a machine that punches out coins. Before being stamped with the design, the blank coins are heated and cleaned.

The bills are examined once they've been printed and dried. They remove and discard any bills that have errors. Money that fits the criteria is cut and packaged for distribution. Additionally, the coins are examined, and any that are found to be flawed are disposed of. However, a few of these coins manage to slip through the cracks. When that occurs, the value of these extremely rare coins might skyrocket!

Following an inspection, banks are given the money they require, if needed. After that, the funds are dispersed among the banks' clients. The currency is now in circulation!

Remember, the federal agency in charge of money creation in the United States is the Department of Treasury. The Bureau of Engraving and Printing produces paper currency, whereas the United States Mint produces coins. Numerous safeguards are used during the design, material selection, and production of money to avoid counterfeiting or the production of counterfeit money.

MONEY

1. The _____ agency is in charge of money creation.
   a. federal
   b. government

2. The United States Mint produces coins and dollar bills.
   a. True - coins and dollar bills
   b. False - only coins

3. Each side of a sheet of banknotes must dry for ___ hours.
   a. 72
   b. 24

4. Dollar bills and computer paper don't have the same _____ and feel.
   a. design
   b. weight

5. The metal sheets are fed into a machine that punches out _____.
   a. coins
   b. silver dollars

6. United States Bureau of _____ produces dollar notes.
   a. Engraving and Printing
   b. Engravers and Commission

7. The Secretary of the _____ selects one of the designs submitted by the designers for production.
   a. Treasury
   b. Bank

8. Coins in the United States are created from a combination of _____.
   a. metals and alloys
   b. silver and nickels

9. Before being stamped with the design, the blank coins are _____.
   a. heated and cleaned
   b. shined and reserved

10. Paper money is created from a particular _____ blend, it is more difficult to forge.
    a. parcel and green dye
    b. cotton and linen

Introvert vs. Extrovert

Introvert is a person who prefers calm environments, limits social engagement, or embraces a greater than average preference for solitude.

SYNONYMS:
brooder
loner
solitary

Extrovert is an outgoing, gregarious person who thrives in dynamic environments and seeks to maximize social engagement.

SYNONYMS:
character
exhibitionist
show-off
showboat

Fill in the blank with the correct word. [introvert, introverts, extrovert, extroverts]

1. Sue is the _____ in the family; opinionated, talkative and passionate about politics.

2. He was described as an _____, a reserved man who spoke little.

3. _____ are often described as the life of the party.

4. An _____ is often thought of as a quiet, reserved, and thoughtful individual.

5. _____ enjoy being around other people and tend to focus on the outside world.

6. Typically _____ tend to enjoy more time to themselves.

7. Jane is an _____ whose only hobby is reading.

8. I am still not as "outgoing" as an _____ is.

9. I had been a very _____ person, living life to the full.

10. I am an _____, I am a loner.

11. Because Pat is an _____ who enjoys chatting with others, she is the ideal talk show host.

12. She is basically an _____, uncomfortable with loud women and confrontations.

Dealing With Acne

Acne is a skin disorder that results in bumps. Whiteheads, blackheads, pimples, and pus-filled bumps are all sorts of blemishes. What's the source of these annoying bumps? Pores and hair follicles make up most of your skin's top layer. Sebum (pronounced "see-bum"), the natural oil that moisturizes hair and skin, is produced in the pores by oil glands.

Generally, the glands produce adequate sebum, and the pores are good. However, oil, dead skin cells, and bacteria can block a pore if they accumulate in it to an unhealthy level. Acne may result as a result of this.

Puberty-induced hormonal changes are to blame for acne in children. If your parent suffered from acne as a teen, you will likely as well because your pores may produce more sebum when under stress; stress may worsen acne. Acne is usually gone by the time a person reaches their twenties.

Here are a few tips for preventing breakouts if you suffer from acne:

- It would help if you washed your face with warm water and a light soap or cleanser in the morning before school and before bed.
- Avoid scrubbing your face. Acne can be exacerbated by irritating the skin, so scrubbing is not recommended.
- Makeup should be washed off at the end of the day if you wear it.
- Ensure to wash your face after a workout if you've been sweating heavily.
- Acne-fighting lotions and creams are readily available over-the-counter. Talk to your parents or doctor about the options available to you.

Make sure you follow the guidelines on any acne medication you use. If you're unsure whether you're allergic to the cream or lotion, use a small amount at first. If you don't notice results the next day, don't give up. Acne medication can take weeks or months to take effect. If you use more than recommended, your skin may become extremely dry and red.

Acne-suffering children can seek treatment from their doctor. Doctors can prescribe stronger medications than what you can get over the counter.

The following are some other factors to consider:

- Avoid touching your face if you can.
- Pimples should not be picked, squeezed, or popped.
- Long hair should be kept away from the face, and it should be washed regularly to reduce oil production.

It is possible to get pimples on the hairline by wearing headgear like baseball caps. Stay away from them if you suspect they're contributing to your acne problems.

Despite their best efforts, many children will get acne at some point in their lives. The situation isn't out of the ordinary.

If you suffer from acne, you now have several options for treating it. Remind yourself of this: You are not alone. Take a look around at your buddies and you'll notice that the majority of children and adolescents are dealing with acne, too!

1. Puberty _____ changes are to blame for acne in children.
   a. harmonic
   b. hormonal

2. Pores and hair _____ make up most of your skin's top layer.
   a. follicles
   b. folate

3. Avoid _____ your face.
   a. using cleanser
   b. scrubbing

4. _____ is the oil that moisturizes hair and skin, is produced in the pores by oil glands.
   a. Acne
   b. Sebum

Smart Ways to Deal With a Bully

First, read over the entire passage(s). Then go back and fill in the blanks. You can skip the blanks you're unsure about and come back to them later.

control	popular	confident	ground	society
threats	negative	skip	Fighting	mocking

One of the most serious issues in our _____ today is bullying. It's not uncommon for young people to experience a range of _____ emotions due to this. Bullies may use physical force (such as punches, kicks, or shoves) or verbal abuse (such as calling someone a name, making fun of them, or scaring them) to harm others.

Some examples of bullying include calling someone names, stealing from them and _____ them, or ostracizing them from a group.

Some bullies want to be the center of attention. As a strategy to be _____ or get what they want, they may believe bullying is acceptable. Bullies are usually motivated by a desire to elevate their own status. As a result of picking on someone else, they can feel more power and authority.

Bullies frequently target someone they believe they can _____. Kids who are easily agitated or have difficulty standing up for themselves are likely targets. Getting a strong reaction from someone can give bullies the illusion that they have the power they desire. There are times when bullies pick on someone who is more intelligent than them or who looks different from them somehow.

Preventing a Bully's Attack
Do not give in to the bully. Avoid the bully as much as possible. Of course, you aren't allowed to disappear or _____ class. However, if you can escape the bully by taking a different path, do so.

Bravely stand your _____. Scared people aren't usually the most courageous people. Bullies can be stopped by just showing courage in the face of them. Just how do you present yourself as a fearless person? To send a message that says, "Don't mess with me," stand tall. It is much easier to be brave when you are confident in yourself.

Don't Pay Attention to What the Bully Says or Does. If you can, do your best not to listen to the bully's _____. Act as though you aren't aware of their presence and immediately go away to a safe place. It's what bullies want: a big reaction to their teasing and being mean. If you don't respond to a bully's actions by pretending you don't notice or care, you may be able to stop them.

Defend your rights. Pretend you're _____ and brave. In a loud voice, tell the bully, "No! Stop it!" Then take a step back or even take off running if necessary. No matter what a bully says, say "no" and walk away if it doesn't feel right. If you do what a bully tells you to do, the bully is more likely to keep bullying you; kids who don't stand up for themselves are more likely to be targeted by bullies.

Don't retaliate by being a bully yourself. Don't fight back against someone who's bullying you or your pals by punching, kicking, or shoving them. _____ back only makes the bully happier, and it's also risky since someone can be injured. You're also going to be in a lot of trouble. It's essential to stick with your friends, keep safe, and seek adult assistance.

Inform a responsible adult of the situation. Telling an adult if you're being bullied is crucial. Find someone you can confide in and tell them what's going on with you. It is up to everyone in the school, from teachers to principals to parents to lunchroom assistants, to stop the bullies. As soon as a teacher discovers the bullying, the bully usually stops because they are worried that their parents will punish them for their behavior. Bullying is terrible, and everyone who is bullied or witnesses bullying should speak up.

The Human Bones

At birth, a baby's body has about 300 bones. These bones will one day grow together and become the 206 bones that adults have. Some of a baby's bones are made entirely of cartilage, a special material that helps them grow. Other bones in a baby are partially cartilage-covered. This cartilage is soft and easy to move. During childhood, the cartilage grows and is slowly replaced by bone, with the help of calcium, as you get bigger and stronger.

At about 25, this process will be done. Once this occurs, there is no more room for bone growth; the bones have reached their maximum size. There are a lot of bones that make up a skeleton that is both strong and light.

Spine: It's easy to look at your spine: When you touch your back, you'll feel bumps on it. The spine lets you twist and bend, and it also keeps your body in place. That's not all: It also helps protect the spinal cord, a long group of nerves that sends information from the brain to the rest of your body. You can't just have one or two bones in your spine. It's made of 33! Vertebrae are the bones that make up the spine, and each one is shaped like a ring.

Ribs: Heart, lung, and liver are all essential, and ribs will keep them safe. This makes your chest look like a cage of bones. A few inches below your heart, you can run your fingers along the sides and front of your body to get a sense of the bottom of this cage. It's easy to feel your ribs when you breathe deeply. Some very thin kids can even see some of their ribs through their skin.

Skull: The brain is the most important thing in your body, so your skull protects it the best. There are places where you can feel your skull when you push on your head, like in the back a few inches above your neck. Different bones make up the skull. They protect your brain, while other bones make up the shape of your face. If you touch below your eyes, you can feel the bone that makes the hole where your eye goes.

Arm: When an arm moves, it connects to a large triangular bone on the upper back corner of each side of the ribcage called a "shoulder blade." You have three bones in your arm: the humerus, which is above your elbow, the radius and ulna, which are below your elbow.

Pelvis: The pelvis, a ring of bones at the base of your spine, is where your legs attach. The pelvis, which is like a bowl, holds the spine in place. Large hip bones are in front of the sacrum and coccyx, which are behind. It is made up of the two large hip bones. The pelvis is a hard ring that protects parts of the digestive, urinary, and reproductive systems.

Joint: A joint is where two bones meet. This is how some joints work, and some don't: Fixed joints don't move at all. Young people have a lot of these joints in their skulls, called sutures. These joints close up the bones of the skull in their head. One of these joints is called the parieto-temporal suture, which is the one that runs along the side of the skull. It's called this because it connects the two sides of the skull together.

You need to keep your bones healthy. Drinking milk or eating oranges is good for you. They are calcium-rich. Calcium aids in the development of strong bones.

Have you ever suffered from bone fractures? Ouch! A doctor places the bone in its proper position. During the healing process, it is covered in a cast.

The bones of your body are located below the surface of your skin. They can only be seen with an X-ray machine. An X-ray is a type of picture. It allows medical professionals to see if a bone has been broken.

1. **A baby's body has about _____ bones.**
   a. 320
   b. 300

2. **The _____, which is like a bowl, holds the spine in place.**
   a. pelvis
   b. spinal cord

3. **A _____ is where two bones meet.**
   a. legs
   b. joint

4. **At what age is there no more room for growth?**
   a. 25
   b. 18

5. **Adults have how many bones?**
   a. 206
   b. 200

6. **The _____ lets you twist and bend.**
   a. hip bones
   b. spine

7. **Your skull protects your what?**
   a. brain
   b. joints

8. **Your ribs protect your what?**
   a. Heart, spine, and arms
   b. heart, lung, and liver

9. **The _____ connects to a large triangular bone on the upper back corner of each side of the ribcage.**
   a. shoulder blade
   b. joints blade

10. **You have _____ bones in your arm.**
    a. two
    b. three

US Government: Running for Office

First, read over the entire passage(s). Then go back and fill in the blanks. You can skip the blanks you're unsure about and come back to them later.

political	strategy	presidential	government	outlining
council	rapport	worries	financial	healthcare
requirements	priority	victory	coordinate	memorable

When running for public office, candidates must persuade voters that they are the best candidate for the position. Running for office is a term for this type of endeavor. Running for office can be a full-time job in some cases, such as the _____ race. When running for office, there are a lot of things to do.

To run for office, the first step is to ensure that you meet all of the _____. For example, one must be at least 18 years of age and a US citizen in order to apply.

Almost everyone joins a political party to run for public office these days. The primary election, in which they run to represent that party, is frequently the first election they must win. The Democratic Party and the Republican Party are the two most influential _____ organizations in the United States today.

Without money, it's challenging to run for office. Candidates frequently use billboards, television commercials, and travel to give speeches to promote their campaigns. All of this comes at a price. The people who want to help a candidate win the election provide them with money. As a result, the budget is established. This is critical, as the person with the most significant _____ resources may be able to sway the greatest number of voters, ultimately leading to their victory.

A candidate's campaign staff should be assembled as well. These are people who will assist the candidate in their bid for the presidency. They _____ volunteers, manage funds, plan events, and generally assist the candidate in winning the election. It is the campaign manager's responsibility to lead the campaign team.

Many candidates attempt to stand out from the crowd by creating a memorable campaign slogan. This is a catchy phrase that will stick in voters' minds as they cast their ballots. Calvin Coolidge and Dwight Eisenhower both had _____ campaign slogans, "I Like Ike" for Eisenhower and "Keep Cool with Coolidge" for Coolidge.

At some point, the candidate will begin a public campaign. A lot of "shaking hands and hugging babies" is involved in the process of running for office. There are a lot of speeches they give _____ what they plan to do when they get into the White House. It's their job to explain why they're better than their rivals.

When a candidate runs for office, they usually take a position on several issues relevant to the position for which they are running. A wide range of topics, such as education, clean water, taxation, war, and _____, are examples.

The debate is yet another aspect of running for office. At a debate, all of the candidates for a particular office sit down together to discuss their positions on a specific issue. Candidates take turns speaking and responding to each other's arguments during the debate. The outcome of a debate between two candidates can mean the difference between

_____ and defeat.

After months of campaigning, the election is finally upon us. They'll cast their ballots and then get right back to work. Attending rallies or shaking hands with strangers on the street may be part of their campaign _____. All the candidates can do is wait until the polls close. Family, friends, and campaign members usually gather to see how things turn out. If they are successful, they are likely to deliver a victory speech and then go to a party to celebrate.

Becoming Your Class President

Start working toward your goal of becoming class or high school president as soon as possible if you want to one day hold that position.

If you want to get involved in student _____ your freshman year, go ahead and join, but don't hold your breath waiting to be elected president. Elections for the freshman class council are frequently a complete disaster. Since freshman elections are held within a month of the start of school, no one has had a chance to get to know one another. The person elected president is usually the one whose name has been mentioned the most by other students. A lot of the time, it's not based on competence or trust.

Building trust and _____ with your classmates is essential from the beginning of the school year. This is the most crucial step in the process of becoming a Class Officer President.

Electing someone they like and trust is a top _____ for today's college students. Be a role model for your students. In order to demonstrate your competence, participate in class discussions and get good grades. Avoid being the class clown or the laziest or most absent-minded member of the group.

Become a part of the students' lives. Attend lunch with a variety of people from various backgrounds. Ask them about their _____ and their hopes for the school's future.

Make an effort to attend student _____ meetings even if you aren't currently a member. If you're interested in joining the student council, you may be able to sit in on their meetings, or you may be able to attend an occasional meeting where non-council members can express their concerns and ideas.

Your Identity and Reputation Online

First, read over the entire passage(s). Then go back and fill in the blanks. You can skip the blanks you're unsure about and come back to them later.

persona	remarks	reputation	networking	repercussions
embarrassing	real-life	inappropriate	take-backs	derogatory

Your online identity grows every time you use a social network, send a text, or make a post on a website, for example. Your online _____ may be very different from your real-world persona – the way your friends, parents, and teachers see you.

One of the best things about having an online life is trying on different personas. If you want to change how you act and show up to people, you can. You can also learn more about things that you like. Steps to help you maintain control on the internet can be taken just like in real life.

Here are some things to think about to protect your online identity and reputation:

Nothing is temporary online. The worldwide web is full of opportunities to connect and share with other people. It's also a place with no "_____" or "temporary" situations. It's easy for other people to copy, save, and forward your information even if you delete it.

Add a "private" option for your profiles. Anyone can copy or screen-grab things that you don't want the world to see using social _____ sites. Use caution when using the site's default settings. Each site has its own rules, so read them to ensure you're doing everything you can to keep your information safe.

Keep your passwords safe and change them often. Someone can ruin your _____ by pretending to be you online. The best thing to do is pick passwords that no one can guess. The only people who should know about them are your parents or someone else who you can trust. Your best friend, boyfriend, or girlfriend should not know your passwords.

Don't put up pictures or comments that are _____ or sexually provocative. In the future, things that are funny or cool to you now might not be so cool to someone else, like a teacher or admissions officer. If you don't want your grandmother, coach, or best friend's parents to see it, don't post it. Even on a private page, it could be hacked or copied and sent to someone else.

Don't give in to unwanted advances. There are a lot of inappropriate messages and requests for money that teenagers get when they're on the web. These things can be scary, weird, or even

_____, but they can also be exciting and fun. Do not keep quiet about being bullied online. Tell an adult you trust right away if a stranger or someone you know is bullying you. It's never a good idea to answer. If you respond, you might say something that makes things even worse.

You can go to www.cybertipline.org to report bad behavior or other problems.

Avoid "flaming" by taking a break now and then. Do you want to send an angry text or comment to someone? Relax for a few minutes and realize that the _____ will be there even if you have cooled off or change your mind about them.

People may feel free to write hurtful, _____, or abusive remarks on the internet if they can remain anonymous. We can be painful to others if we share things or make angry comments when we aren't facing someone. If they find out, it could change how they see us. If you wouldn't say it, show it, or do it in person, don't do it online.

Make sure you don't break copyright laws. Don't upload, share, or distribute copyrighted photographs, sounds, or files. Be aware of copyright restrictions. Sharing them is great, but doing so illegally runs the risk of legal _____ down the road.

It's time for a self-evaluation. Take a look at your "digital footprint," which people can find out about you. When you search for your screen name or email address, see what comes up. That's one way to get a sense of what other people think of you online.

In the same way that your _____ identity is formed, your online identity and reputation are also formed. It's different when you're on the internet because you don't always have the chance to explain how you feel or what you mean. Thinking about what you're going to say and being responsible can help you avoid leaving an online trail that you'll later be sorry about.

Proofreading Interpersonal
Skills: Peer Pressure

In this activity, you'll see lots of grammatical *errors*. Correct all the grammar mistakes you see.

There are **30** mistakes in this passage. 3 capitals missing. 5 unnecessary capitals. 3 unnecessary apostrophes. 6 punctuation marks missing or incorrect. 13 incorrectly spelled words.

Tony is mingling with a large group of what he considers to be the school's cool kids. Suddenly, someone in the group begins mocking Tony's friend Rob, who walks with a limp due to a physical dasability.

They begin to imitate rob's limping and Call him 'lame cripple' and other derogatory terms. Although Tony disapproves of their behavior, he does not want to risk being excluded from the group, and thus joins them in mocking Rob.

Peer pressure is the influence exerted on us by member's of our social group. It can manifest in a variety of ways and can lead to us engaging in behaviors we would not normally consider such as Tony joining in and mocking his friend Rob.

However, peer pressure is not always detrimental. Positive peer pressure can motivate us to make better chioces, such as studying harder, staying in school, or seeking a better job. Whan others influence us to make poor Choices, such as smoking, using illicit drugs, or bullying, we succumb to negative peer pressure. We all desire to belong to a group and fit in, so Developing strategies for resisting peer pressure when necessary can be beneficial.

Tony and his friends are engaging in bullying by moking Rob. Bullying is defined as persistent, unwanted. aggressive behavior directed toward another person. It is moust prevalent in school-aged children but can also aphfect adults. Bullying can take on a variety of forms, including the following:

· Verbil bullying is when someone is called names, threatened, or taunted verbally.
· Bullying is physical in nature - hitting spitting, tripping, or poshing someone.
· Social Bullying is intentionally excluding Someone from activities spreading rumors, or embarrassing sumeone.

· Cyberbullying is the act of verbally or socially bullying someone via the internet, such as through social media sites.

Peer pressure exerts a significant influence on an individual's decision to engage in bullying behavoir. In Tony's case, even though Rob is a friend and tony would never consider mocking his disability, his desire to belong to a group outweighs his willingness to defend his friend

Peer pressure is a strong force that is exerted on us by our social group members. Peer pressure is classified into two types: negative peer pressure, which results in poor decision-making, and positive peer pressure, which influences us to make the correct choices. Adolescents are particularly susceptible to peer pressure because of their desire to fit in

Peer pressure can motivate someone to engage in bullying behaviors such as mocking someone, threatening to harm them, taunting them online, or excluding them from an activity. Each year, bullying affect's an astounding 3.2 million school-aged children. Severil strategies for avoiding peer pressure bullying include the following:

- consider your actions by surrounding yourself with good company.
- Acquiring the ability to say no to someone you trust.

Speak up - bullying is never acceptable and is taken extramely seroiusly in schools and the workplace. If someone is attempting to convince you to bully another person, speaking with a trusted adult such as a teacher, coach, counselor, or coworker can frequently help put thing's into perspective and highlight the issue.

Proofreading Skills:
Volunteering

In this activity, you'll see lots of grammatical *errors*. Correct all the grammar mistakes you see.

> There are **10** mistakes in this passage. 3 capitals missing. 4 unnecessary capitals. 3 incorrect homophones.

Your own life can be changed and the lives of others, through volunteer work. to cope with the news that there has been a disaster, you can volunteer to help those in need. Even if you can't contribute financially, you can donate you're time instead.

Volunteering is such an integral part of the American culture that many high schools require their students to participate in community service to graduate.

When you volunteer, you have the freedom to choose what you'd like to do and who or what you think is most deserving of your time. Start with these ideas if you need a little inspiration. We've got just a few examples here.

Encourage the growth and development of young people. Volunteer as a Camp counselor, a Big Brother or Big Sister, or an after-school sports program. Special Olympics games and events are excellent opportunities to know children with special needs.

Spend the holidays doing good deeds for others. Volunteer at a food bank or distribute toys to children in need on Thanksgiving Day, and you'll be doing your part to help those in need. your church, temple, mosque, or another place of worship may also require your assistance.

You can visit an animal shelter and play with the Animals. Volunteers are critical to the well-being of shelter animals. (You also get a good workout when you walk rescued dogs.)

Become a member of a political campaign. Its a great way to learn more about the inner workings of politics if your curious about it. If you are not able To cast a ballot, you can still help elect your preferred candidate.

Help save the planet. Join a river preservation group and lend a hand. Participate in a park cleanup day in your community. Not everyone is cut out for the great outdoors; if you can't see yourself hauling trees up a hill, consider working in the park's office or education center instead.

Take an active role in promoting health-related causes. Many of us know someone afflicted with a medical condition (like cancer, HIV, or diabetes, for example). a charity that helps people with a disease, such as delivering meals, raising money, or providing other assistance, can make you Feel good about yourself.

Find a way to combine your favorite things if you have more than one. For example, if you're a fan of kids and have a talent for arts and crafts, consider volunteering at a children's hospital.

People must fill out an application like this or similar before lenders and banks will issue them a credit card or loans.

Credit Application		PRACTICE ONLY

Name:	Date Birth:	SSN:

Current Address:		Phone:
City:	State:	ZIP:
Own Rent (Please circle)	Monthly payment or rent:	How long?
Previous Address:		
City:	State:	ZIP:
Owned Rented (Please circle)	Monthly payment or rent:	How long?

Employment Information

Current Employer:	How long?
Employer Address:	Phone:

Position:	Hourly Salary (Please circle)	Annual Income:
Previous Employer:		

Address:		How long?

Phone:	E-mail:	Fax:
Position:	Hourly Salary (Please circle)	Annual Income:

Name and relationship of a relative not living with you:
Address:

City:	State:	ZIP:	Phone:

Co-Applicant Information, if for a joint account

Name:	Date Birth:	SSN:

Current Address:		Phone:
City:	State:	ZIP:
Own Rent (Please circle)	Monthly payment or rent:	How long?
Previous Address:		
City:	State:	ZIP:
Owned Rented (Please circle)	Monthly payment or rent:	How long?

Employment Information

Current Employer:	How long?
Employer Address:	Phone:

Position:	Hourly Salary (circle)	Annual Income:
Previous Employer:		
Address:		

Phone:	E-mail:	Fax:
Position:	Hourly Salary (circle)	Annual Income:

Name and relationship of a relative not living with you:
Address:

City:	State:	ZIP:	Phone:

Credit Cards

Name	Account No.	Current Balance	Monthly Payment

Mortgage Company

Account No.:	Address:

Auto Loans

Auto Loans	Account No.	Balance	Monthly Payment

Other Loans, Debts, or Obligations

Description	Account No.	Amount

Other Assets or Sources of Income

	Monthly Value: $
	Monthly Value: $

I/We authorize _____ to verify information provided on this form regarding credit and employment history.

Signature of Applicant	Date

Signature of Co-Applicant, if for joint account	Date

If someone wants to rent an apartment or house, they usually will fill out a document similar to this one here.

Rental Application	PRACTICE ONLY

Applicant information

Name:		
Date of birth:	Ssn:	Phone:
Current address:		
City:	State:	ZIP Code:
Own Rent (Please circle)	Monthly payment or rent:	How long?
Previous address:		
City:	State:	ZIP Code:
Owned Rented (Please circle)	Monthly payment or rent:	How long?

Employment information

Current employer:

Employer address:		How long?
Phone:	E-mail:	Fax:
City:	State:	ZIP Code:
Position:	Hourly Salary (Please circle)	Annual income:

Previous employer:

Address:		How long?
Phone:	E-mail:	Fax:
City:	State:	ZIP Code:
Position:	Hourly Salary (Please circle)	Annual income:

Emergency Contact:

Address:		Phone:
City:	State:	ZIP Code:
Relationship:		

Credit cards

Name	Account no.	Current balance	Monthly payment

Auto loans

Auto loans	Account no.	Balance	Monthly payment

PRACTICE ONLY

This is how some people track their monthly income and expenses. This helps them to plan for how their money will be spent or saved.

Details of Monthly Expenses								
Materials purchased via cash & check				Other expenses paid via cash & check.				
Day	Payment made to	Check number	Amount		Day	Payment made to	Check number	Amount
Amount Carried Forward		Reference			Amount Carried Forward		Reference	

Monthly Budget

EXPENSE	PLAN	ACTUAL	DIFFERENCE
HOUSING			
Mortgage/Rent			
Maintenance			
UTILITIES			
Electric/gas			
Garbage			
Water			
Cable/satellite			
Internet			
Phone/cell phone			
INSURANCE			
Home			
Automobile			
Health/life			
AUTOMOBILE			
Auto payment			
Fuel			
Maintenance/repairs			
Public transportation			
FOOD			
Groceries			
Meals out			
ENTERTAINMENT			
Movie rentals			
Events			
Travel			
SERVICES			
Medical/dental			
Hair/personal care			
Other:			
MISCELLANEOUS			
Clothing			
Toiletries/cosmetics			
Cleaning/laundry			
Pet care			
Other:			
DEBT REPAYMENT			
Loans			
Credit card:			
Credit card:			
Other:			
CHARITY			
SAVINGS			
Totals:			

		Notes:
Monthly income		
Planned spending		
Actual spending		
Over or under amount		

Annual physical exam requirements may vary depending on where you live and school. This form gives you an idea of what info a doctor might share with the school about a student.

PRIVATE PHYSICIAN'S REPORT OF PHYSICAL EXAMINATION OF A PUPIL OF SCHOOL AGE

DATE _____ 20 _____

NAME OF SCHOOL _____ GRADE _____ HOMEROOM _____

NAME OF CHILD			DATE OF BIRTH	SEX
				☐ ☐
Last	First	Middle		M F

ADDRESS

No. and Street	City or Post Office	Borough or Township	County	State	Zip Code

MEDICAL HISTORY IMMUNIZATIONS AND TESTS

VACCINE	DOSES Enter Month, Day, and Year each immunization was given			BOOSTERS & DATES	
Diphtheria and Tetanus (Circle): DTaP, DTP, DT, TD	1 / /	2 / /	3 / /	4 / /	5 / /
Polio (Circle): OPV, IPV	1 / /	2 / /	3 / /	4 / /	5 / /
Measles, Mumps, Rubella	1 / /	2 / /			
Hepatitis B	1 / /	2 / /	3 / /		
HIB	1 / /	2 / /	3 / /		
Varicella	1 / /	2 / /	Varicella Disease or Lab Evidence Date: _____		
Other: _____					

☐ MEDICAL EXEMPTION   The physical condition of the above named child is such that immunization would endanger life or health
☐ RELIGIOUS EXEMPTION   (Includes a strong moral or ethical conviction similar to a religious belief and requires a written statement from the parent/guardian)

If Applicable:

Tuberculin Tests Date Applied	Arm	Device	Antigen	Manufacturer	Signature

Date Read	Results (mm)	Signature			

Follow-Up of significant tuberculin tests:
Parent/Guardian notified of significant findings on _____.

Result of Diagnostic Studies: _____.
Preventive Anti-Tuberculosis – Chemotherapy ordered.   ☐   ☐   _____
                                                       No   Yes   Date

Significant Medical Conditions (√)
If Yes, Explain

	Yes	No	
Allergies	☐	☐	_____
Asthma	☐	☐	_____
Cardiac	☐	☐	_____
Chemical Dependency	☐	☐	_____
Drugs	☐	☐	_____
Alcohol	☐	☐	_____
Diabetes Mellitus	☐	☐	_____
Gastrointestinal Disorder	☐	☐	_____
Hearing Disorder	☐	☐	_____
Hypertension	☐	☐	_____
Neuromuscular Disorder	☐	☐	_____
Orthopedic Condition	☐	☐	_____
Respiratory Illness	☐	☐	_____
Seizure Disorder	☐	☐	_____
Skin Disorder	☐	☐	_____
Vision Disorder	☐	☐	_____
Other (Specify)	☐	☐	_____

Are there any special medical problems or chronic diseases which require restriction of activity, medication or which might affect his/her education? If so, specify _____

Report of Physical Examination (√)

	Normal	Abnormal	Not Examined	Comments
Height (inches)				
Weight (pounds) BMI				
Pulse ( )				
Blood Pressure				
Hair/Scalp				
Skin				
Eyes/Vision				
Ears/Hearing				
Nose and Throat				
Teeth and Gingiva				
Lymph Glands				
Heart – Murmur, etc				
Lung – Adventitious Finding				
Abdomen				
Genitourinary				
Neuromuscular System				
Extremities				
Spine (Presence of Scoliosis)				

_____
Date of Examination

_____   _____
Signature of Examiner   **PRINT Name of Examiner**

_____   _____
Address   **Telephone Number**

When you are a new patient at a clinic, you will likely have to complete a form similar to this.

Patient Information

Patient Information

Patient Name: _____ DOB: _____ Sex: _____

Driver's License: _____ SSN: _____

Home Phone: _____ Cell: _____

Address: _____

Employer: _____ Position: _____

Employer Address: _____ Phone No. _____

Emergency Contact Information

Dependent? _____ If yes, Guardian's Name: _____

Guardian's Phone: _____ Cell: _____

Marital Status: _____ Spouse's Name: _____

Spouse's Employer: _____ Work Phone No. _____

Emergency Contact: _____ Relationship: _____

Home Phone: _____ Cell: _____

Emergency Contact: _____ Relationship: _____

Home Phone: _____ Cell: _____

Insurance

Insured Party: _____ Relationship to Patient: _____

Insurance Company: _____ Phone No. _____

Address: _____

Policy No. _____ Group No. _____

Dual Coverage? _____ 2nd Insurance Company: _____

Insured Party: _____ Relationship to Patient: _____

Phone No. _____ Address: _____

Policy No. _____ Group No. _____

Payment Method: _____ Card/Check No. _____

I verify that the above information is factual and true to the best of my knowledge. I authorize the doctor to employ X-Rays, photographs, anesthetics, medicines, surgeries, and other equipment or aids as he/she deems necessary in order to provide the proper patient care. I understand that payment, proof of insurance, and/or copay is due at the time of service.

I authorize this office to apply benefits on my behalf for the covered services rendered. I certify that the insurance information I have provided is factual and correct.

_____   _____

Patient   Date

Defensive Driving

Score: _____

Date: _____

Avoiding accidents and reducing your risk of being involved in an accident is possible by driving defensively.

On the roadways, you've probably seen that not everyone drives properly, despite many individuals believing they are competent motorists. Some motorists travel at excessively high speeds. Others are careless and end up in the wrong lane. Drivers may drive too closely behind, make quick changes without signaling, or weave in and out of traffic without regard for safety.

Aggressive drivers cause one-third of all traffic accidents. People "multitasking" by talking on the phone, texting or checking messages, or eating while driving is becoming a more significant concern.

You do not influence what other drivers do. However, the dangers posed by other people's poor driving can be avoided by improving your defensive driving skills.

Put Yourself in the Driver's Seat

Here are a few pointers to help you keep in charge of that two-ton steel and glass frame:

Don't lose focus. Driving is primarily a mental task, and there are a lot of things to think about when you're behind the wheel: road conditions, your speed and position, traffic laws, signs, signals, road markings, directions, and other cars around you, checking your mirrors, and so on. The key to safe driving is to keep your attention solely on the task of driving.

A driver's ability to see and respond to possible difficulties is impaired by distractions, such as talking on the phone or eating. If you've been driving for a while, you're not the only one who can get overconfident and let your driving skills fall apart. All drivers must remind themselves to remain focused.

Be on the lookout at all times. When the driver in the car ahead suddenly slams on the brakes, you'll be able to respond swiftly if you're awake and not asleep or under the influence—drinking and using drugs (both prescription and OTC medications) both slow down reaction times and impair judgment in drivers. Similarly, driving when fatigued is a primary cause of car accidents. So get some sleep in advance of your road trip.

Keep an eye on the other person. Being aware of other drivers and road users around you (and what they may suddenly do) is essential to controlling yourself when driving. You can bet the driver will try to get into your lane in front of you if there isn't much room between the car and a slow-moving truck in the same lane, for example. Predicting what the other driver will do and making the necessary adjustments can help lower your risk.

How to Drive Like a Pro:

In order to be prepared for anything, you must drive defensively. Despite your reluctance, you're ready to take action and not rely on the actions of other motorists. Driver error is at blame for 90% of all collisions, according to the Department of Transportation.

You may lessen your danger behind the wheel by following these suggestions for defensive driving:

Safety comes first. To better handle terrible driving from others, you should strive to drive defensively and avoid aggressive and inattentive behaviors yourself. Keep a safe distance from the vehicle ahead of you. To keep yourself safe in the event of a collision, remember to fasten your seatbelt and lock your doors.

Pay attention to your surroundings and stay alert at all times. Frequently check your mirrors and examine the road conditions ahead of you for 20 to 30 seconds. It's important to keep your eyes moving. You can avoid an aggressive driver by slowing down or stopping if they are approaching you. Make an effort to get out of the way of the dangerous vehicle by turning right or exiting at the earliest opportunity, if it is safe to do so. Pedestrians, cyclists, and pets should be observed closely while driving.

Avoid relying on other drivers. Be kind to other people, but watch out for yourself, too. Don't expect another driver to allow you to merge or move out of the way. Prepare yourself for drivers to run red lights and stop signs. Prepare for the worst-case scenario by planning your actions ahead of time.

Use the 3-second to 4-second rule. Since you have the most significant potential of colliding with another vehicle in front of you, employing the 3- to 4-second rule will ensure that you have enough time to bring your car to a stop if necessary. However, this rule only applies to typical traffic in fair weather conditions. Following distance should be increased by a second for each severe weather condition, such as rain and fog, nighttime driving, and following a heavy vehicle.

Please slow down. Speed limits are based on ideal driving conditions and are therefore subject to change. You are obliged to drive at a speed appropriate for the road and weather. Higher speeds also make it more difficult to control your car if something goes wrong. You must slow down if you want to stay in control of your car.

Ensure you have a way out. In all driving conditions, positioning your car so that you can see and be seen is the greatest way to prevent potential threats. Always allow yourself an out – a place where your car can be moved if your immediate course of movement is suddenly obstructed.

Risks must be separated. When confronted with several threats, the best strategy is to deal with each individual. You mustn't take on too many risks at once.

Reduce the amount of time you spend thinking about other things. Any activity that diverts your attention from the task of driving is a form of a distraction. Keep your attention on the road by concentrating solely on the driving task.

Contact your local AAA or your state's Department of Motor Vehicles if you're interested in taking a defensive driving course to enhance your driving knowledge and abilities. Online defensive driving courses are available from a number of certified providers in a variety of states. Insurance premium savings, "positive" safe driving points, or other advantages may be available. Although these programs are pricey, they are well worth it if you want to become a more knowledgeable and careful driver.

1. **You can reduce the likelihood of being involved in an accident by driving _____.**
   a. distinctly driving
   b. defensively

2. **Drivers may drive too closely behind, _____, or zigzag in and out of traffic without regard for safety.**
   a. make quick changes without signaling
   b. make random rear mirrors adjustment

3. **One-third of all traffic accidents are caused by _____ drivers.**
   a. submissive
   b. aggressive

4. **A driver's ability to see and respond to possible difficulties is _____ by _____, such as talking on the phone or eating.**
   a. imperfect, distance
   b. impaired, distractions

5. Drinking and using drugs (both prescription and _____ medications) both slow down reaction times and _____ judgment in drivers.
   a. OTD, impulse
   b. OTC, impair

6. Predicting what the other driver will do and making the necessary _____ can help lower your _____.
   a. speed, adjust
   b. adjustments, risk

7. Driver error is at blame for _____ of all _____, according to the Department of Transportation.
   a. 90%, collisions
   b. 80%, risks

8. Keep a safe _____ from the vehicle ahead of you.
   a. densify
   b. distance

9. Pay attention to your _____ and stay _____ at all times.
   a. surroundings, alert
   b. friends, risk

10. Do not make the mistake of assuming that another driver will move out of the way or enable you to _____ when you are driving.
    a. stop
    b. merge

11. A _____ is anything that takes your mind off of what you're doing.
    a. distraction
    b. dimensions

12. Having an alternative _____ of travel is also crucial.
    a. speed limit
    b. route

13. To maintain vehicle control, you must manage your _____.
    a. speed
    b. distance

14. When driving in _____ conditions, such as rain, fog, nighttime driving, or behind a huge truck or motorcycle, you should _____ the space between you and the vehicle in front of you by an additional second.
    a. poor, increase
    b. fair, decrease

Teen Drinking and Driving

Just Say NO!

Every year, thousands of drunk driving accidents and fatalities are caused by impaired driving. According to statistics, the nation's fatal crashes involved an intoxicated driver. Drinking and driving is dangerous. Even a few drinks can render you unsafe behind the wheel and endanger your life and the lives of others.

Due to a lack of driving experience, teenagers are less adept at identifying and responding to driving hazards, controlling the vehicle, and altering the rate of speed according to varying road conditions. The driving habits of adolescents are also influenced by peer pressure, emotions, and other stressors.

Teenagers are four times more likely to be killed in a car accident at night than during the day because night driving is more challenging. Also, teens are less likely to wear safety belts, making them more likely to get hurt and their injuries worsen. More than three times as many teens are injured in car crashes if they are not buckled up.

Driving under the influence, driving while intoxicated, drunk driving, or impaired driving are all terms used by different states, but generally, a baseline blood alcohol content (BAC) of .08 grams per deciliter (g/dL) or above is considered alcohol-impaired. Driving with even trace levels of alcohol in your system is illegal under zero-tolerance legislation, which applies to drivers younger than 21. States may also impose harsher punishments for drivers with high BACs, vehicle minors, and repeat offenders.

There will be signs of legal impairment, including:

Slur speech
Memory and motor skills limitations
Reduced visual and verbal awareness
Decreased judgment or control
Impaired vision
Nausea

The legal drinking age in the United States is 21 years. Therefore, a minor detected drinking will have committed a misdemeanor of the first degree. In some areas, a student can be detained for a maximum of six months or receive a fine of up to $1,000. The court may decide to impose both of the maximum punishments on you.

Some states combat the problem of underage drinking behind the wheel by applying the same maximum penalties to those caught providing alcohol to someone less than 21 years old. If a police officer has adequate evidence, the student's driver's license may be suspended immediately and revoked on the spot.

Colleges use a code of student conduct to punish students who engage in off-campus behavior that has a significant negative impact on the health or property of members of the university community. Therefore, if a student is convicted of DUI/OVI, he or she may be suspended or expelled from school.

The acronyms DUI, DWI, OMVI, and OVI all refer to the same thing: Driving under the influence of alcohol or drugs is referred to as driving DUI, driving while intoxicated (DWI), operating a motor vehicle while impaired (OMVI), and operating a vehicle while impaired (OVI).

You can:

- Choose never to drink and drive.

- Refuse to ride with a teen driver who has consumed alcohol.
- Knowing and abiding by the state's laws.
- Adhere to the "rules of the road" outlined in their parent-teen driving agreement.
- Wear a seat belt on every trip, regardless of length.
- Observe posted speed restrictions.
- Never text or use a cell phone while driving.

1. **Even just a few beers can put your life and the lives of others in jeopardy if you get behind the wheel of a vehicle while _____.**
   - a. intoxicated
   - b. incinerated
   - c. indecencies

2. **Teenagers, because of their lack of driving experience, are less skilled at recognizing and reacting to driving _____.**
   - a. legislation
   - b. hazards
   - c. stressors

3. **BAC stands for _____.**
   - a. blood alcohol content
   - b. blood alcohology confinement
   - c. blood alcoholic nonattainment

4. **Under the _____ law, which applies to drivers younger than 21, it is against the law to get behind the wheel with any amount of alcohol in your system, even traces of it.**
   - a. zero-tolerance
   - b. zero-non-impaired
   - c. zero-alcohol and beverages

5. **(BAC) of _____ per deciliter (g/dL) or higher is considered to be alcohol-impaired.**
   - a. .02 grams
   - b. .08 grams
   - c. .3% grams

6. **When a police officer has _____, a student's privilege to drive a vehicle can be instantly withdrawn and suspended.**
   - a. parent's permission
   - b. a court order
   - c. sufficient evidence

7. **If a student is found guilty of driving under the influence of alcohol or another controlled substance, the student faces the possibility of being _____ from school.**
   - a. given a warning
   - b. enrolled
   - c. expelled

8. **Driving under the influence of alcohol or drugs is referred to as driving _____.**
   - a. DIU
   - b. DWI
   - c. DUI

9. **Signs of legal impairment**
   - a. Nausea, Diarrhea, Coughing
   - b. Nausea, Slur speech, Impaired vision
   - c. Slur speech, Workaholic, Laughing a lot

10. **Always fasten your _____, no matter how _____ the drive may be.**
   - a. seat belt, short
   - b. belt buckle, fast
   - c. seat belt, long

UNDERSTANDING RIDESHARE

First, read the entire passage. After that, go back and fill in the blanks. You can skip the blanks you're unsure about and finish them later.

ratings	destination	luxury	alternative	fares
carpooling	declining	flagging	smartphone	legislation

The way in which people travel is undergoing significant change. Ride-sharing and ride-hailing services, such as Uber, provide an _____ to the taxi business. When ridesharing startup Uber first debuted its services, the world of private transportation shifted radically. They offered a _____ black car service as an alternative to the usual taxi ride.

In the past, ridesharing was a lot like _____, where the person riding along often paid for half of the trip. Both the driver and passenger were traveling in the same direction, and the rider would contribute to the trip's cost. Ridesharing today is for-profit, and the driver has no _____ in mind rather than providing transportation services like a taxi. A third-party app or website charges a fee to connect riders and drivers.

It's common to see the term "rideshare" replaced with "ride-hail." However, this can be deceptive, as "hailing" usually refers to the act of _____ down a cab from a distance. Hail requests can't be accepted by drivers for ridesharing services like Lyft, Uber, and TappCar because the companies don't support the feature. The _____ also prohibits drivers from receiving hails. Otherwise, the service would be categorized as a taxi service. Instead, users must use their smartphone to "haul" a driver through their preferred ridesharing app.

Rideshare companies use a _____ app to connect drivers with passengers in the local region. The driver opens the app and changes their status to "online" to show they are ready to take a ride.

Customer pick-up and drop-off requests are sent to the driver, who responds by accepting or _____ the ride.

After accepting the trip and picking up the passenger, the driver proceeds to the passenger's destination.

The passenger will exit the vehicle once the driver reaches the final location.

Because payments for _____ are processed within the app, no money exchange occurs between the driver and the passenger.

Additionally, the app enables passengers and drivers to provide _____ for one another. Both the driver and rider benefit from this grading system, which ensures a high level of service and respect for both parties.

My First Resume

When you're a high school student, writing a résumé can be __intimidating__ . The good news is that you probably have more work experience than you realize, even if this is your first résumé. Experiences such as childcare, yard work, and volunteerism all __contribute__ to developing key work skills that companies seek. Simply because you have not held a position similar to the one you are seeking does not indicate you lack the requisite abilities to succeed.

Be sure to include any previous employment, especially if it was for pay. Other than that, you can consist of informal work such as pet sitting, cutting grass, snow shoveling, and any other tasks you've done for money. Although you may not have received a __regular__ income for your informal employment, your talents and reliability as an employee can still be shown via it.

Given that the majority of teenagers have not held many jobs, it is critical to draw on all elements of your life that prove you possess the attitude, willingness to work hard, competencies, and personality necessary for job success.

Please list any __leadership__ positions you held (for example, a president of an organization or as team captain), as well as any honors or awards you have received. Include a list of your duties and accomplishments under each heading.

Employers are more concerned with your work __habits__ and attitude than anything else. Nobody expects you to be an expert in your field. When recounting an experience, you might use language to the effect that you have perfect or near-perfect attendance and are on time for school and other commitments.

Employers are looking for employees who have a history of positively impacting the company. Ask yourself whether there are any accomplishments that you can include from your time in school, your clubs, or your employment. Use verbs like "upgraded," "started," and "expanded" to describe what you've done if you want to illustrate what you've accomplished. To demonstrate to __potential__ employers that you are both bright and ambitious, include any demanding advanced academic assignments on your resume.

Keep it short: Keep it simple (But Include All Necessary Information). A single page is all you need. Contact information and previous work experience are both required in some way on every resume. On the other hand, you can exclude things like a career objective or summary.

Create a narrative. Match your talents and expertise to the job's requirements. For example, in the case of a cashier position, if you've never had a position with that precise title before, emphasize your customer service abilities, aptitude for mathematical calculations, work ethic, and ability to operate as part of a team. Examine the job description and make sure your __qualifications__ meet the requirements.

It is also appropriate to add information about your academic achievements, such as participation in organizations and the necessary curriculum you finished while producing a college __freshman__ resume or a resume for a college application. Suppose you're applying for work as a front desk receptionist at a hotel. You could want to include the talents you gained while studying hospitality at a school.

Finally, be sure to double- or even triple-check your resume for typos and __grammatical__ errors. You may be tempted to send in your resume as soon as you finish it, but take a few minutes to review it.

As a last resort, ask for a second opinion on your resume from friends, family, or school teachers. Have them go it through to see if there's anything you missed or if you can make any __improvements__ .

Following High School, What Should You Do?

1. **Community College offers an _____ degree program.**
   - a. bachelors
   - b. associate

2. **Many young people take a ___ year to explore their interests and earn money.**
   - a. gap
   - b. half

3. **If you are between the ages of 16 and 24 and have a low income, you may be eligible for the _____ program.**
   - a. Military Program
   - b. Job Corps

4. **A vocational or technical school may also be referred to as a secondary school.**
   - a. False - trade school
   - b. True - secondary or post-school

5. **Community College offers an associate degree program.**
   - a. True
   - b. False

6. **To earn a bachelor's degree, students must attend a _____ college or university.˜**
   - a. two-year
   - b. four-year

Test Your Mathematics
Knowledge

1. To add fractions_____
   a. the denominators must be the same
   b. the denominators can be same or different
   c. the denominators must be different

2. To add decimals, the decimal points must be?
   a. column and carry the first digit(s)
   b. lined up in any order before you add the columns
   c. lined up vertically before you add the columns

3. When adding like terms_____
   a. the like terms must be same and they must be to the different power.
   b. the exponent must be different and they must be to the same power.
   c. the variable(s) must be the same and they must be to the same power.

4. The concept of math regrouping involves_____
   a. regrouping means that 5x + 2 becomes 50 + 12
   b. the numbers you are adding come out to five digit numbers and 0
   c. rearranging, or renaming, groups in place value

5. _____ indicates how many times a number, or algebraic expression, should be multiplied by itself.
   a. Denominators
   b. Division-quotient
   c. Exponent

6. _____is the numerical value of a number without its plus or minus sign.
   a. Absolute value
   b. Average
   c. Supplementary

7. Any number that is less than zero is called_____
   a. Least common multiple
   b. Equation
   c. Negative number

8. 23 = 2 x 2 x 2 = 8, 8 is the
   a. third power of 2
   b. first power of 2
   c. second power of 2

9. -7, 0, 3, and 7.12223 are
   a. all real numbers
   b. all like fractions
   c. all like terms

10. How do you calculate 2 + 3 x 7?
   a. 2 + 3 x 7 = 2 + 21 = 23
   b. 2 + 7 x 7 = 2 + 21 = 35
   c. 2 + 7 x 3 = 2 + 21 = 23

11. How do you calculate (2 + 3) x (7 - 3)?

    a. (2 + 2) x (7 - 3) = 5 x 4 = 32

    b. (2 + 3) x (7 - 3) = 5 x 4 = 20

    c. (2 + 7) x (2 - 3) = 5 x 4 = 14

12. The Commutative Law of Addition says_____

    a. positive - positive = (add) positive

    b. that it doesn't matter what order you add up numbers, you will always get the same answer

    c. parts of a calculation outside brackets always come first

13. The Zero Properties Law of multiplication says_____

    a. that any number multiplied by 0 equals 0

    b. mathematical operation where four or more numbers are combined to make a sum

    c. Negative - Positive = Subtract

14. Multiplication is when you_____

    a. numbers that are added together in multiplication problems

    b. take one number and add it together a number of times

    c. factor that is shared by two or more numbers

15. When multiplying by 0, the answer is always_____

    a. 0

    b. -0

    c. 1

16. When multiplying by 1, the answer is always the _____

    a. same as the number multiplied by 0

    b. same as the number multiplied by -1

    c. same as the number multiplied by 1

17. You can multiply numbers in_____

    a. any order and multiply by 2 and the answer will be the same

    b. any order you want and the answer will be the same

    c. any order from greater to less than and the answer will be the same

18. Division is_____

    a. set of numbers that are multiplied together to get an answer

    b. breaking a number up into an equal number of parts

    c. division is scaling one number by another

19. If you take 20 things and put them into four equal sized groups

    a. there will be 6 things in each group

    b. there will be 5 things in each group

    c. there will be 10 things in each group

20. The dividend is_____

    a. the number you are multiplied by

    b. the number you are dividing up

    c. the number you are grouping together

21. The divisor is _____

    a. are all multiples of 3

    b. the number you are dividing by

    c. common factor of two numbers

22. The quotient is _____

    a. the answer

    b. answer to a multiplication operation

    c. any number in the problem

23. When dividing something by 1_____
   a. the answer is the original number
   b. the answer produces a given number when multiplied by itself
   c. the answer is the quotient

24. Dividing by 0_____
   a. the answer will always be more than 0
   b. You will always get 1
   c. You cannot divide a number by 0

25. If the answer to a division problem is not a whole number, the number(s) leftover_____
   a. are called the Order Property
   b. are called the denominators
   c. are called the remainder

26. You can figure out the 'mean' by_____
   a. multiply by the sum of two or more numbers
   b. adding up all the numbers in the data and then dividing by the number of numbers
   c. changing the grouping of numbers that are added together

27. The 'median' is the_____
   a. last number of the data set
   b. middle number of the data set
   c. first number of the data set

28. The 'mode' is the number_____
   a. that appears equal times
   b. that appears the least
   c. that appears the most

29. Range is the_____
   a. difference between the less than equal to number and the highest number.
   b. difference between the highest number and the highest number.
   c. difference between the lowest number and the highest number

30. Please Excuse My Dear Aunt Sally: What it means in the Order of Operations is_____
   a. Parentheses, Exponents, Multiplication and Division, and Addition and Subtraction
   b. Parentheses, Equal, Multiplication and Decimal, and Addition and Subtraction
   c. Parentheses, Ellipse, Multiplication and Data, and Addition and Subtraction

31. A ratio is_____
   a. a way to show a relationship or compare two numbers of the same kind
   b. short way of saying that you want to multiply something by itself
   c. he sum of the relationship a times x, a times y, and a times z

32. Variables are things_____
   a. that can change or have different values
   b. when something has an exponent
   c. the simplest form using fractions

33. Always perform the same operation to_____of the equation.

    a. when the sum is less than the operation

    b. both sides

    c. one side only

34. The slope intercept form uses the following equation:

    a. $y = mx + b$

    b. $y = x + ab$

    c. $x = mx + c$

35. The point-slope form uses the following equation:

    a. $y - y1 = m(y - x2)$

    b. $y - y1 = m(x - x1)$

    c. $x - y2 = m(x - x1)$

36. Numbers in an algebraic expression that are not variables are called____

    a. Square

    b. Coefficient

    c. Proportional

37. A coordinate system is _____

    a. a type of cubed square

    b. a coordinate reduced to another proportion plane

    c. a two-dimensional number line

38. Horizontal axis is called_____

    a. h-axis

    b. x-axis

    c. y-axis

39. Vertical axis is called____

    a. v-axis

    b. y-axis

    c. x-axis

40. Equations and inequalities are both mathematical sentences____

    a. has y and x variables as points on a graph

    b. reduced ratios to their simplest form using fractions

    c. formed by relating two expressions to each other

Geography: Time Zones

Have you ever tried to call or send a __message__ to someone who was on the other side of the country or the world? It can be tough to reach a faraway location from you because the time of __day__ may be different from your own. The purpose of time zones and why we have them will be discussed in this session.

Kim, Mike's __classmate__ who recently relocated across the country, is texting him. After a short time, Kim sends Mike a text message saying that it is time for her to go to sleep for the night. The sun is beaming brightly __outside__, and Mike is confused about why Kim would choose this time of day to go to sleep. 'Can you tell me what __time__ it is, please?' Mike asked. 'It's 9:00 p.m. now!' Kim replies.

What exactly is going on here? Was Mike able to travel back in time in some way?

What is happening to Mike and Kim is nothing more than a natural occurrence that occurs on our planet daily. Since Kim relocated across the country, she is now in a __different__ time zone than she was previously.

A time zone is a geographical location on the planet with a fixed time that all citizens can observe by setting their __clocks__ to that time. As you go from east to west (or west to east) on the globe's surface, you will encounter different time zones. The greater the distance traveled, the greater the number of time zones crossed.

Time zones are not something that arises in nature by chance. Humans created the concept of time zones and determined which regions of the world are located in which time zones.

Because of time zones, everyone experiences the same pattern of dawn in the early morning and sunset in the late afternoon. We require time zones because the earth is shaped like a __ball__ and therefore requires them. As the sun beams down on the planet, not every location receives the same amount of sunshine. The sun __shines__ on one side of the earth and brightens it during the day, while the other side is dark during the night (nighttime). If time-zones didn't __exist__, many people worldwide would experience quite strange sunshine patterns during the day if there were no time zones.

Science: Albert Einstein

Albert Einstein was born in Germany on March 14, 1879. Because he was Jewish, he fled to the United States to avoid Hitler and the Second World War.

His father gave him a simple pocket compass when he was about five years old, and it quickly became his favorite toy!

He developed an interest in mathematics and science at the age of seven.

When Einstein was about ten years old, a much older friend gave him a large stack of science, mathematics, and philosophy books .

He'd published his first scientific paper by the age of sixteen. That is absolutely incredible!

Numerous reports have shown that Einstein failed math in school, but his family has stated that this is not the case. They claimed he was always at the top of his class in math and could solve some challenging problems.

As an adult, he frequently missed appointments, and because his mind was all over the place, his lectures were a little difficult to understand.

He didn't wear socks and had uncombed hair! Even at posh dinners, he'd arrive unkempt, with crumpled clothes and, of course, no socks!

An experiment in 1919 proved the theory correct. He became famous almost overnight , and he suddenly received invitations to travel worldwide, as well as honors from all over the world!

In 1921, he was awarded the Nobel Prize for Physics. He'd come a long way from the boy who was told he'd never amount to anything!

Today, his other discoveries enabled us to have things like garage door openers, televisions, and DVD players. Time magazine named him "Person of the Century" in 1999.

One of his favorite activities was to take a boat out on a lake and take his notebook with him to think and write everything down. Perhaps this is what inspired him to create his inventions!

Einstein's first marriage produced two sons. His daughter, Lierserl, is believed to have died when she was young. He married twice, and she died before him.

Government History: How Laws Are Made

1. If the Senate approves the bill, it will be sent to the _____.
   a. President
   b. House Representee

2. The _____ may decide to make changes to the bill before it is passed.
   a. governor
   b. committee

3. The bill must then be _____ by a member of Congress.
   a. signed
   b. sponsored

4. The President has the option of refusing to sign the bill. This is known as a ___.
   a. voted
   b. veto

5. The Senate and House can choose to override the President's veto by _____ again.
   a. creating a new bill
   b. voting

6. The bill is assigned to a committee after it is _____.
   a. introduced
   b. vetoed

7. Bills are created and passed by _____.
   a. The House
   b. Congress

8. A bill must be signed into law by the President within ___-days.
   a. 10
   b. 5

9. The President's _____ is the final step in a bill becoming law.
   a. signature
   b. saying yes

10. If the committee agrees to pass the bill, it will be sent to the House or Senate's main ___ for approval.
    a. chamber
    b. state

Extra Credit: What are some of the weirdest laws in the world? List at least 5. (Independent student's answers)

[Student worksheet has a 19 line writing exercise here.]

History: United States Armed Forces

1. The United States military is divided into ___ branches.
   - a. six
   - b. five

2. _____ is managed by the United States Department of Homeland Security.
   - a. The National Guard
   - b. The Coast Guard

3. The _____ of the United States is the Commander in Chief of the United States Armed Forces.
   - a. Governor
   - b. President

4. The United States maintains a military to safeguard its _____ and interests.
   - a. borders
   - b. cities

5. DoD is in charge of controlling each _____ of the military.
   - a. branch
   - b. army

6. The Marines are prepared to fight on both land and ____.
   - a. battlefield
   - b. sea

7. The United States Space Force is in charge of operating and defending military ____ and ground stations.
   - a. soldiers
   - b. satellites

8. The mission of the _____ is to defend the country from outside forces.
   - a. United States DoD Forces
   - b. United States Air Force

9. There are _____ units in all 50 states.
   - a. Army National Guard
   - b. Armed Nations Guard

10. The United States Navy conducts its missions at sea to secure and protect the world's _____.
    - a. oceans
    - b. borders

11. The primary concern of the United States Coast Guard is to protect_____.
    - a. domestic waterways
    - b. domesticated cities

12. The United States military is: the Amy Force, Army, Coast Guard, Mario Corps, Old Navy, and Space Force.
    - a. True
    - b. False

Extra Credit: Has America ever been invaded? (Independent student research answer)

[Student worksheet has a 19 line writing exercise here.]

Grammar: Adjectives Matching

Adjectives are words that describe people, places, and things, or nouns. Adjectives are words that describe sounds, shapes, sizes, times, numbers/quantity, textures/touch, and weather. You can remember this by saying to yourself, "an adjective adds something."

If you need to describe a friend or an adult, you can use words that describe their appearance, size, or age. When possible, try to use positive words that describe a person.

#				
1	O	disappointed	→	sad because something is worse than expected
2	K	anxious	→	worried
3	C	delighted	→	very pleased
4	G	terrified	→	very frightened
5	I	ashamed	→	feeling bad because you did sg wrong
6	H	envious	→	wanting something another person has
7	N	proud	→	feeling pleased and satisfied
8	F	shocked	→	very surprised and upset
9	A	brave	→	nothing frightens him/her
10	L	hard-working	→	has 2 or more jobs
11	B	organized	→	everything is in order around him
12	D	punctual	→	always arrives in time
13	J	honest	→	uprightness and fairness
14	E	outgoing	→	loves being with people
15	M	loyal	→	always supports his friends
16	P	reliable	→	one can always count on him

History: The Thirteen Colonies

1. **The Dutch founded _____ in 1626.**
   a. New Jersey
   b. New York

2. **13 British colonies merged to form the_____.**
   a. United Kingdom
   b. United States

3. **Roger Williams founded _____.**
   a. Maryland
   b. Rhode Island

4. **A colony is a region of _____ that is politically controlled by another country.**
   a. land
   b. township

5. **Middle Colonies:**
   a. Delaware, New Jersey, New York, Pennsylvania
   b. Georgia, Maryland, North Carolina, South Carolina, Texas

6. **Colonies are typically founded and settled by people from the ___ country.**
   a. home
   b. outside

7. **Southern Colonies:**
   a. Maine, New Jersey, New York, Pennsylvania
   b. Georgia, Maryland, North Carolina, South Carolina, Virginia

8. **Many of the colonies were established by _____ leaders or groups seeking religious liberty.**
   a. political
   b. religious

9. **New England Colonies:**
   a. Connecticut, Massachusetts Bay, New Hampshire, Rhode Island
   b. Ohio, Tennessee, New York, Pennsylvania

10. **George and Cecil Calvert established _____ as a safe haven for Catholics.**
    a. Maine
    b. Maryland

11. **The colonies are frequently divided into_____.**
    a. New England Colonies, Middle Colonies, and Southern Colonies
    b. United England Colonies, Midland Colonies, and Southern Colonies.

Confusing Vocab Words

1. He __accepts__ [accepts / accept / excepts] defeat well.

2. Please take all the books off the table __except__ [exception / accept / except] for the thick one.

3. Lack of sleep __affects__ [affects / affect / effect] the quality of your work.

4. The __effect__ [effects / affect / effect] of the light made the room bright.

5. I have a __lot__ [alot / lot / lots] of friends.

6. The magician preformed a great __illusion__ [illusion / allusion / trick] .

7. Dinner was all __ready__ [already / good / ready] when the guests arrived.

8. The turkey was __already__ [al ready / already / all ready] cooked when the guests arrived.

9. __Altogether__ [All together / Altogether / altogether] , I thought it was a great idea!

10. We were all __together__ [altogether / group / together] at the family reunion.

11. The fence kept the dogs __apart__ [apart / a part / parted] .

12. A __part__ [section / part / Apart] of the plan is to wake up at dawn.

13. The plane's __ascent__ [assent / descent / ascent] made my ears pop.

14. You could see his __breath__ [breath / breathing / breathe] in the cold air.

15. If you don't __breathe__ [breath / breathe / breathing] , then you are dead.

16. The __capital__ [capital / capitol / city] of Hawaii is Honolulu.

17. That is the __capitol__ [capital / capitol / captain] building.

18. I __cited__ [sighted / sited / cited] 10 quotes from the speech.

19. You can not build on that __site__ [cite / sight / site] .

20. The __sight__ [cite / site / sight] of land is refreshing.

21. I **complimented** [complimented / complemented / discouraged] my wife on her cooking.

22. We all have a **conscience** [conscience / mind / conscious] of right and wrong.

23. The boxer is still **conscious** [conscience / conscious / knocked out] .

24. I went to the city **council** [municipal / counsel / council] meeting.

25. My accountant **counseled** [directed / counciled / counseled] me on spending habits.

26. The teacher **elicited** [brought out / illicit / elicited] the correct response.

27. The criminal was arrested for **illicit** [elicit / illicit / illegal] activities.

28. The baby will cry as soon as **its** [its' / it's / its] mother leaves.

29. **It's** [It's / It is / Its] a beautiful day

30. I have a headache, so I'm going to **lie** [lay / lain / lie] down.

31. You should never tell a **lie** [lay / lie / lye] .

32. If you **lose** [lose / find / loose] your phone, I will not buy a new one!

33. My pants feel **loose** [loose / tight / lose] , I need a belt.

34. I **kind** [kindly / kind / a bit] of like spicy food.

35. He is a very **kind** [kind of / mean / kind] teacher.

Math: Arithmetic Refresher

Select the best answer for each question.

1. Use division to calculate 6/3. The answer is _____.

   a. [2]
   b. 4
   c. 3.5

2. Fill in the blank $2 + \sqrt{5}$ _____ $7 - \sqrt{10}$

   a. [>]
   b. ≤
   c. ≥

3. Use division to calculate 50/10. The answer is _____.

   a. 5.5
   b. 8
   c. [5]

4. Which family of numbers begins with the numbers 0, 1, 2, 3, ...?

   a. Integers
   b. [Whole numbers]
   c. Rational numbers

5. Use division to calculate 7/4. The answer is _____.

   a. 2 R4
   b. 1.5
   c. [1 R3]

6. Which of the answer choices is an INCORRECT statement?

   a. 0 > -1
   b. [-2 < -4]
   c. 32 < -25x

7. Simplify: 7 * 5 - 2 + 11

   a. [44]
   b. 23
   c. 21

8. -18 + (-11) = ?

   a. 28
   b. 32
   c. [-29]

9. 16 - (-7) = ?

   a. 20
   b. [23]
   c. 19

10. -12 - (-9) = ?

   a. [-3]
   b.

11. Simplify: 37 - [5 + {28 - (19 - 7)}]

   a. [16]
   b. 36
   c. 46

12. The numbers 1, 2, 3, 4, 5, 6, 7, 8, ..., i.e. natural numbers, are called____.

   a. [Positive integers]
   b. Rational integers
   c. Simplify numbers

13. _____is the number you are dividing by.

   a. [divisor]
   b. equation
   c. dividend

14. ____ is the leftover amount when dividend doesn't divide equally.

   a. [remainder]
   b. quotient
   c. dividend

Math: Decimals Place Value

Our basic number system is decimals. The decimal system is built around the number ten. It is sometimes referred to as a base-10 number system. Other systems use different base numbers, such as binary numbers, which use base-2.

The place value is one of the first concepts to grasp when learning about decimals. The position of a digit in a number is represented by its place value. It determines the value of the number.

When the numbers 800, 80, and 8 are compared, the digit "8" has a different value depending on its position within the number.

8 - ones place
80 - tens place
800 - hundreds place

The value of the number is determined by the 8's place value. The value of the number increases by ten times as the location moves to the left.

Select the best answer for each question.

1. Which of the following is a decimal number?
   a. 1,852
   b. 1.123
   c. 15

2. For the number 125.928, what is in the tenths place?
   a. 9
   b. 2
   c. 5

3. For the number 359, which number is in the tens place?
   a. 3
   b. 5
   c. 9

4. Write the number 789.1 as an addition problem.
   a. 70 + 800 + 90 + 1
   b. 700 + 80 + 9 + 1 / 10
   c. 700 + 80 + 9+10

5. When we say 7 is in the hundreds place in the number 700, this is the same as 7x102.n.
   a. True
   b. False

6. For the number 2.14, what digit is in the hundredths place?
   a. 4
   b. 1
   c. 2

7. When you start to do arithmetic with decimals, it will be important to _____ properly.
   a. line up the numbers
   b. line up all like numbers
   c. line up numbers ending in 0

8. Depending upon the position of a digit in a number, it has a value called its_____.
   a. tenth place
   b. decimals place
   c. place value

9. The place value of the digit 6 in the number 1673 is 600 as 6 is in the hundreds place.
   a. True
   b. False

10. What is the place value of the digits 2 and 4 in the number 326.471?
    a. 2 is in the tens place. 4 is in the tenths place.
    b. 2 is in the tenths place. 4 is in the tens place.
    c. 2 is in the ones place. 4 is in the tenths place.

Math: Roman Numerals

The Ancient Romans used Roman numerals as their numbering system. We still use them every now and then. They can be found in the Super Bowl's numbering system, after king's names (King Henry IV), in outlines, and elsewhere. Roman numerals are base 10 or decimal numbers, just like the ones we use today. However, they are not entirely positional, and there is no number zero.

Roman numerals use letters rather than numbers. You must know the following seven letters:

I = 1

V = 5

X = 10

L = 50

C = 100

D = 500

M = 1000

Select the best answer for each question.

1. III = __
   a. 33
   b. 30
   c. 3

2. XVI=___
   a. 60
   b. 61
   c. 16

3. IV = 5 - 1 =____
   a. 40
   b. 4
   c. 14

4. What number does the Roman numeral LXXIV represent?
   a. 79
   b. 74
   c. 70

5. Which of the following is the Roman numeral for the number 5?
   a. IV
   b. VI
   c. V

6. How many of the same letters can you put in a row in Roman numerals?
   a. 4 or more
   b. 3
   c. 2

7. Which of the following is the Roman numeral for the number 10?
   a. X
   b. IX
   c. XXI

8. What is the Roman numeral for 33?
   a. XXXIII
   b. XIII
   c. XVIII

9. Which of the following is the Roman numeral for the number 50?
   a. X
   b. L
   c. I

10. Which of the following is the Roman numeral for the number 100?
    a. C
    b. IVV
    c. LII

Music: Antonio Vivaldi
Italian Composer

Antonio Vivaldi was a 17th and 18th-century composer who became one of Europe's most famous figures in __classical__ music.

Antonio Vivaldi was ordained as a __priest__ but chose to pursue his passion for music instead. He was a prolific composer who wrote hundreds of works, but he was best known for his concertos in the Baroque style, and he was a highly influential innovator in form and pattern. He was also well-known for his operas, such as Argippo and Bajazet.

Antonio Lucio Vivaldi was born in __Venice__, Italy, on March 4, 1678. Giovanni Battista Vivaldi, his father, was a professional violinist who taught his young son to play. Vivaldi met and learned from some of the finest musicians and composers in Venice through his father. While his violin practice flourished, he could not master wind instruments due to chronic shortness of breath.

Vivaldi sought both religious and musical instruction. He began his studies to become a priest when he was 15 years old. In 1703 he was ordained. Vivaldi was known as "il Prete Rosso," or "the Red Priest," because of his __red__ hair. Vivaldi's career as a priest was brief. Due to health issues, he could not deliver mass and was forced to resign from the priesthood shortly after his ordination.

At the age of 25, Vivaldi was appointed master of the violin at Venice's Ospedale della Pietà (Devout Hospital of Mercy). In this capacity, he wrote the majority of his major works over a three-decade period. The Ospedale was a school for __orphans__, with the boys learning trades and the girls learning music. The most talented musicians were invited to join an orchestra that performed Vivaldi's compositions, including religious choral music. The orchestra rose to international prominence under Vivaldi's direction. He was promoted to music director in 1716.

Vivaldi's early fame as a composer and musician did not translate into long-term financial __success__. After being overshadowed by younger composers and more modern styles, Vivaldi left Venice for Vienna, Austria, possibly hoping to find a position in the imperial court there. Following the __death__ of Charles VI, he found himself without a prominent patron and died in poverty in Vienna on July 28, 1741. He was laid to rest in a simple grave following a funeral service devoid of music.

In the early twentieth century, musicians and scholars revived Vivaldi's music, and many of the composer's unknown works were recovered from obscurity. In 1939, Alfredo Casella, a composer, and __pianist__ organized the revival of Vivaldi Week. Since World War II, Vivaldi's music has been widely performed. The choral composition Gloria, which was reintroduced to the public during Casella's Vivaldi Week, is particularly well-known and is regularly __performed__ at Christmas celebrations worldwide.

Vivaldi's work, which included nearly 500 concertos, influenced later composers such as Johann __Sebastian__ Bach.

Science Multiple Choice
Quiz: Food Chain and Food
Web

Select the best answer for each question.

1. In ecology, it is the sequence of transfers of matter and energy in the form of food from organism to organism.

   a. Food Chain

   b. Food Transport

   c. Food Sequencing

2. _____ can increase the total food supply by cutting out one step in the food chain.

   a. Birds

   b. People

   c. Animals

3. Plants, which convert solar energy to food by photosynthesis, are the _____.

   a. secondary food source

   b. tertiary food source

   c. primary food source

4. _____ help us understand how changes to ecosystems affect many different species, both directly and indirectly.

   a. Food Chain

   b. Food Web

   c. Food Transport

5. _____ eat decaying matter and are the ones who help put nutrients back into the soil for plants to eat.

   a. Decomposers

   b. Consumers

   c. Producers

6. _____ are producers because they produce energy for the ecosystem.

   a. Plants

   b. Decomposers

   c. Animals

7. Each organism in an ecosystem occupies a specific _____ in the food chain or web.

   a. trophic level

   b. space

   c. place

8. What do you call an organism that eats both plants and animals?

   a. Herbivores

   b. Carnivores

   c. Omnivores

9. Carnivore is from the Latin words that means _____.

   a. "plant eaters"

   b. "eats both plants and animals"

   c. "flesh devourers"

10. A food web is all of the interactions between the species within a community that involve the transfer of energy through _____.

   a. reservation

   b. consumption

   c. adaptation

11. Why are animals considered consumers?

   a. because they don't produce energy, they just use it up

   b. because they produce energy for the ecosystem

   c. because they only produce energy for themselves

12. How do plants turn sunlight energy into chemical energy?

   a. through the process of photosynthesis

   b. through the process of adaptation

   c. through the process of cancelation

Science Multiple Choice Quiz: Temperate Forest Biome

Select the best answer for each question.

1. _____ are found in Northern Hemisphere regions with moist, warm summers and cold winters, primarily in eastern North America, eastern Asia, and western Europe.
   a. Deciduous forests
   b. Wild forests
   c. Rainforests

2. How many types of forest biomes are there?
   a. 2
   b. 3
   c. 4

3. Temperate forests emerged during the period of global cooling that began at the beginning of the _____.
   a. Medieval Era
   b. Paleozoic Era
   c. Cenozoic Era

4. Major temperate forests are located in the following areas, except for:
   a. Eastern China
   b. Japan
   c. Korea

5. What makes a forest a temperate forest?
   a. Temperature, Two seasons, Tropics, and Clay soil.
   b. Temperature, Climate, Wet season, and Loam soil.
   c. Temperature, Four seasons, Lots of rain, and Fertile soil.

6. The three main types of forest biomes are: the rainforest, the temperate forest, and the _____.
   a. Coniferous
   b. Taiga
   c. Broad-leafed

7. Many trees rely on _____ to get through the winter.
   a. temperature
   b. sap
   c. rain

8. Temperate forests are usually classified into two main groups, and these are: _____ and _____.
   a. Deciduous, Evergreen
   b. Coniferous, Deciduous
   c. Indigenous, Evergreen

9. Deciduous is a Latin word that means _____.
   a. "to rise up"
   b. "to subside"
   c. "to fall off"

10. Certain trees in a temperate forest can grow up to how many feet?
    a. 50 feet tall
    b. 90 feet tall
    c. 100 feet tall

11. _____ forests are made up mostly of conifer trees such as cypress, cedar, redwood, fir, juniper, and pine trees.
    a. Broad-leafed
    b. Mixed coniferous and broad-leafed
    c. Coniferous

12. The animals that live in temperate forests have _____ that allow them to _____ in different kinds of weather.
    a. adaptations, survive
    b. compatibility, survive
    c. conformity, thrive

Social Skill Interests: Things To Do

A **hobby** is something that a person actively pursues relaxation and enjoyment. On the other hand, a person may have an **interest** in something because they are curious or concerned. Hobbies usually do not provide monetary compensation. However, a person's interests can vary and may lead to earning money or making a living from them. Hobbies are typically pursued in one's spare time or when one is not required to work. Interests can be followed in one's spare time or while working, as in the case of using one's passion as a source of income. A hobby can be a recreational activity that is done regularly in one's spare time. It primarily consists of participating in sports, collecting items and objects, engaging in creative and artistic pursuits, etc. The desire to learn or understand something is referred to as interest. If a person has a strong interest in a subject, he or she may pursue it as a hobby. However, an interest is not always a hobby. Hobbies such as stamp and flower collecting may not be a source of income for a person, but the items collected can sometimes be sold. Hobbies frequently lead to discoveries and inventions. Interests could be a source of income or something done for free. If a person is interested in cooking or enjoys creating dishes, he can do so at home or make it a career by becoming a chef.

_____

Put the words in the correct category.

pottery	card making	candle making	reading	weaving	knitting
gym	jewellery	chess	surfing	computer games	collecting
woodwork	Soccer	art	swimming	cooking	skateboarding
embroidery	skiing	gardening	writing	chatting	sewing
netball	stamp collecting	football	music	rugby	basketball

Sport (10)	Handcrafts (10)	Interests (10)
Soccer	knitting	reading
rugby	sewing	cooking
football	card making	music
netball	woodwork	stamp collecting
basketball	weaving	gardening
surfing	jewellery	chess
skateboarding	pottery	computer games
skiing	candle making	writing
swimming	embroidery	collecting
gym	art	chatting

Health: Check Your Symptoms

1. **I've got a pain in my head.**
    a. Stiff neck
    b. headache

2. **I was out in the sun too long.**
    a. Sunburn
    b. Fever

3. **I've got a small itchy lump or bump.**
    a. Rash
    b. Insect bite

4. **I might be having a heart attack.**
    a. Cramps
    b. Chest pain

5. **I've lost my voice.**
    a. Laryngitis
    b. Sore throat

6. **I need to blow my nose a lot.**
    a. Runny nose
    b. Blood Nose

7. **I have an allergy. I have a**
    a. Rash
    b. Insect bite

8. **My shoe rubbed my heel. I have a**
    a. Rash
    b. Blister

9. **The doctor gave me antibiotics. I have a/an**
    a. Infection
    b. Cold

10. **I think I want to vomit. I am**
    a. Nauseous
    b. Bloated

11. **My arm is not broken. It is**
    a. Scratched
    b. Sprained

12. **My arm touched the hot stove. It is**
    a. Burned
    b. Bleeding

13. **I have an upset stomach. I might**
    a. Cough
    b. Vomit

14. **The doctor put plaster on my arm. It is**
    a. Sprained
    b. Broken

15. **If you cut your finger it will**
    a. Burn
    b. Bleed

16. **I hit my hip on a desk. It will**
    a. Burn
    b. Bruise

17. **When you have hay-fever you will**
    a. Sneeze
    b. Wheeze

18. **A sharp knife will**
    a. Scratch
    b. Cut

Art: Roman Portrait Sculptures

Alexander	aristocrats	ancestral	shrine	rewarded
sculpture	pattern	mosaics	marble	artistic

Portrait sculpture has been practiced since the beginning of Roman history. It was most likely influenced by

the Roman practice of creating ancestral images. When a Roman man died, his family made a wax sculpture

of his face and kept it in a special shrine at home. Because these sculptures were more like records of a

person's life than works of art, the emphasis was on realistic detail rather than artistic beauty.

As Rome became more prosperous and gained access to Greek sculptors, Roman aristocrats known as

patricians began creating these portraits from stone rather than wax.

Roman sculpture was about more than just honoring the dead; it was also about honoring the living. Important

Romans were rewarded for their valor or greatness by having statues of themselves erected and displayed in

public. This is one of the earliest of these types of statues that we've discovered, and the pattern continued all

the way until the Republic's demise.

The mosaic is the only form of Roman art that has yet to be discussed. The Romans adored mosaics and created

them with exquisite skill. The Romans created mosaics of unprecedented quality and detail using cubes of

naturally colored marble . The floor mosaic depicting Alexander the Great at the Battle of Issus is probably

the most famous Roman mosaic.

Parts of Speech Matching

- NOUN. used to identify any of a class of people, places, or things
- PRONOUN. a word (such as I, he, she, you, it, we, or they) that is used instead of a noun or noun phrase
- VERB. a word used to describe an action, state, or occurrence
- ADJECTIVE. modify or describe a noun or a pronoun
- ADVERB. word that modifies (describes) a verb (she sings loudly), adverbs often end in -ly
- PREPOSITION. word or phrase that connects a noun or pronoun to a verb or adjective in a sentence
- CONJUNCTION. word used to join words, phrases, sentences, and clauses
- INTERJECTION. word or phrase that expresses something in a sudden or exclamatory way, especially an emotion

1	C	Identify the noun.	→	Lion
2	I	Identify the verb.	→	barked
3	F	What is an adjective?	→	a word that describes nouns and pronouns
4	B	Three sets of nouns	→	mother, truck, banana
5	E	Three sets of adverbs	→	always, beautifully, often
6	G, H	above, across, against	→	preposition
7	D	but, and, because, although	→	conjunctions
8	J	Wow! Ouch! Hurrah!	→	Interjection
9	A	Mary and Joe are friends.	→	verb
10	G, H	Jane ran <u>around</u> the corner yesterday.	→	preposition

[Student worksheet has a 4 line writing exercise here.]

Grammar: Contractions
Multiple Choice

Simply put, you replace the letter(s) that were removed from the original words with an apostrophe when you make the contraction.

1. Here is
    a. Here's
    b. Heres'

2. One is
    a. Ones'
    b. One's

3. I will
    a. Il'l
    b. I'll

4. You will
    a. You'll
    b. Yo'ill

5. She will
    a. She'll
    b. She'ill

6. He will
    a. He'ill
    b. He'll

7. It will
    a. It'ill
    b. It'll

8. We will
    a. We'll
    b. We'ill

9. They will
    a. They'ill
    b. They'll

10. That will
    a. That'l
    b. That'll

11. There will
    a. There'ill
    b. There'll

12. This will
    a. This'll
    b. This'ill

13. What will
    a. What'ill
    b. What'll

14. Who will
    a. Who'll
    b. Whol'l

Grammar:
Subjunctive Mood

Wishes, proposals, ideas, imagined circumstances, and assertions that are not true are all expressed in the subjunctive mood. The subjunctive is frequently used to indicate an action that a person hopes or wishes to be able to undertake now or in the future. In general, a verb in the subjunctive mood denotes a scenario or state that is a possibility, hope, or want. It expresses a conditional, speculative, or hypothetical sense of a verb.

When verbs of advice or suggestion are used, the subjunctive mood is utilized. After verbs of recommendation or advice, the subjunctive appears in a phrase beginning with the word -that.

Here are a few verbs that are commonly used in the subjunctive mood to recommend or advise.

- advise, ask, demand, prefer

1. Writers use the subjunctive mood to express _____ or _____conditions.
    a. imaginary or hoped-for
    b.

2. Which is NOT a common marker of the subjunctive mood?
    a.
    b. memories

3. Which is NOT an example of a hope-for verb?
    a. demand
    b. need

4. Subjunctive mood is used to show a situation is not _____.
    a. fictional or fabricated
    b. entirely factual or certain

5. Which of the below statements is written in the subjunctive mood?
    a. I wish I were a millionaire.
    b. What would you do with a million dollars?

6. The indicative mood is used to state facts and opinions, as in:
    a. My mom's fried chicken is my favorite food in the world.
    b. Smells, taste, chew

7. The imperative mood is used to give commands, orders, and instructions, as in:
    a. Eat your salad.
    b. I love salad!

8. The interrogative mood is used to ask a question, as in:
    a. Have you eaten all of your pizza yet?
    b. I ordered 2 slices of pizza.

9. The conditional mood uses the conjunction "if" or "when" to express a condition and its result, as in:
    a. Blue is my favorite color, so I paint with it often.
    b. If I eat too much lasagna, I'll have a stomach ache later.

10. The subjunctive mood is used to express wishes, proposals, suggestions, or imagined situations, as in:
    a. Yesterday was Monday, and I ate pizza.
    b. I prefer that my mom make pasta rather than tuna.

Biology Vocabulary Words Crossword

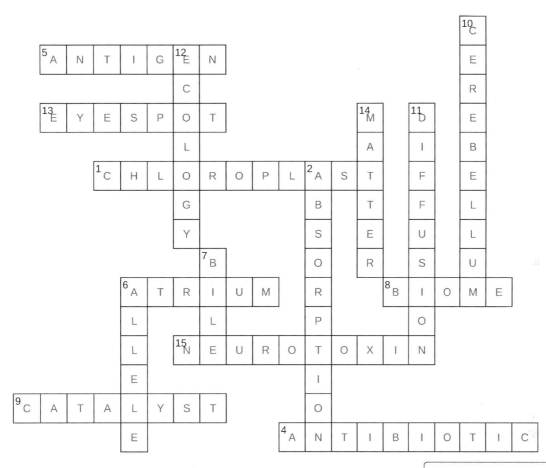

Across

1. organelle in which photosynthesis takes place
4. a substance used to kill microorganisms and cure infections
5. any substance that stimulates an immune response in the body
6. a chamber connected to other chambers or passageways
8. major ecological community with distinct climate and flora
9. substance that initiates or accelerates a chemical reaction
13. an eyelike marking
15. any toxin that affects neural tissues

Down

2. a process in which one substance permeates another
6. any of the forms of a gene that can occupy the same locus
7. a digestive juice secreted by the liver
10. a major division of the vertebrate brain
11. the act of dispersing something
12. the environment as it relates to living organisms
14. that which has mass and occupies space

ATRIUM   BIOME   ANTIGEN
ECOLOGY
CHLOROPLAST   MATTER
ABSORPTION   ANTIBIOTIC
DIFFUSION   ALLELE
EYESPOT   NEUROTOXIN
BILE   CEREBELLUM
CATALYST

Biology: Reading
Comprehension Viruses

When we catch a cold or get the flu, we are dealing with the effects of a viral infection. Viruses, despite sharing some characteristics with living organisms, are neither cellular nor alive. The presence of cells, the ability to reproduce, the ability to use energy, and the ability to respond to the environment are all important characteristics of living organisms. A virus cannot perform any of these functions on its own.

A virus, on the other hand, is a collection of genetic material encased in a protective coat, which is typically made of proteins. Viruses are obligate parasites because they must replicate on the host. To replicate itself, a virus must first attach to and penetrate a host cell, after which it will go through the various stages of viral infection. These stages are essentially the virus lifecycle. A virus can enter the host cell via one of several methods by interacting with the surface of the host cell. The virus can then replicate itself by utilizing the host's energy and metabolism.

Bacteriophages, viruses that infect bacteria, either use the lysogenic cycle, in which the host cell's offspring carry the virus, or the lytic cycle, in which the host cell dies immediately after viral replication. Once viral shedding has occurred, the virus can infect additional hosts. Viral infections can be productive in the sense that they cause active infection in the host, or they can be nonproductive in the sense that they remain dormant within the host. These two types of infection can result in chronic infections, in which the host goes through cycles of illness and remission, as well as latent infections, in which the virus remains dormant for a period of time before causing illness in the host.

1. A virus is encased in a protective coat, which is typically made of _____.
   a. proteins
   b. molecules
   c. cells

2. To replicate itself, a virus must first attach to and penetrate a ___ cell.
   a. healthy
   b. living atom
   c. host

3. Viruses are neither cellular nor __.
   a. alive
   b. moving
   c. a threat

4. The virus can replicate itself by utilizing the host's ___ and ___.
   a. cells and DNA
   b. molecules and cell
   c. energy and metabolism

5. A virus can remain _____ for a period of time before causing illness in a host.
   a. metabolized
   b. dormant
   c. infected

History Reading Comprehension: Storming of the Bastille

1. The French Revolution began with a violent attack on the government by the people of France.
2. During the Hundred Years' War, the Bastille was a fortress built in the late 1300s to protect Paris.
3. By the late 1700s, King Louis XVI had primarily used the Bastille as a state prison .
4. The majority of the revolutionaries who stormed the Bastille were Paris-based craftsmen and store owners.
5. They belonged to the Third Estate, a French social class. Approximately 1000 men carried out the attack.
6. The Third Estate had recently made the king's demands, including a more significant say in government for the commoners .
7. The Bastille was rumored to be full of political prisoners and symbolized the king's oppression to many.
8. It also had gunpowder stores, which the revolutionaries required for their weapons .
9. They demanded that the Bastille's military commander, Governor de Launay, hand over the prison and the gunpowder.
10. They began to try to break into the main fortress once they were inside the courtyard.
11. **Fearful** soldiers in the Bastille opened fire on the crowd.
12. The battle had begun. When some of the soldiers joined the crowd's side, the fight took a turn for the worse.
13. The crowd assassinated Governor de Launay and three of his officers after they surrendered.
14. The revolutionaries' success inspired commoners throughout France to rise up and fight against the nobles who had ruled them for so long.

History Reading Comprehension: The Great Depression

During the 1930s, the United States experienced a severe economic downturn known as the Great Depression. It started in the United States, Wall Street to be exact, but quickly spread throughout the rest of the world. Many people were out of work, hungry, and homeless during this period. People in the city would wait for hours at soup kitchens to get a bite to eat. Farmers struggled in the Midwest, where a severe drought turned the soil into dust, resulting in massive dust storms.

America's "Great Depression" began with a dramatic stock market crash on "Black Thursday," October 24, 1929, when panicked investors who had lost faith in the American economy quickly sold 16 million shares of stock. However, historians and economists attribute the Great Depression to a variety of factors, including drought, overproduction of goods, bank failures, stock speculation, and consumer debt.

When the Great Depression began, Herbert Hoover was President of the United States. Many people held Hoover responsible for the Great Depression. The shantytowns where homeless people lived were even dubbed "Hoovervilles" after him. Franklin D. Roosevelt was elected president in 1933. He promised the American people a "New Deal."

The New Deal was a set of laws, programs, and government agencies enacted to aid the country in its recovery from the Great Depression. Regulations were imposed on the stock market, banks, and businesses as a result of these laws. They assisted in putting people to work and attempted to house and feed the poor. Many of these laws, such as the Social Security Act, are still in effect today.

The Great Depression came to an end with the outbreak of World War II. The wartime economy re-employed many people and filled factories to capacity.

The Great Depression left an indelible imprint on the United States. The New Deal laws expanded the government's role in people's daily lives significantly. In addition, public works improved the country's infrastructure by constructing roads, schools, bridges, parks, and airports.

Between 1929 and 1933, the stock market lost nearly 90% of its value.
During the Great Depression, approximately 11,000 banks failed, leaving many people without savings.

1. The Great Depression began with the _____.
   a. World War II
   b. economy drought
   c. stock market crash

2. Who was President when the Great Depression began?
   a. Herbert Hoover
   b. George W Bush
   c. Franklin D. Roosevelt

3. The New Deal was a set of _____.
   a. laws, programs, and government agencies
   b. city and state funding
   c. stock market bailout

4. The Great Depression came to an end with the outbreak of ____.
   a. new laws
   b. investors funding
   c. World War II

History: King Tut Reading Comprehension

1. What was King Tut's real name?

    a. Tutankhaion

    b. Tutankhaten

    c. Tutankhamun

2. Tut's father died when he was _____ years old.

    a. 19 yrs old

    b. Twenty-Two

    c. seven

3. Tutankhamun died when he was about _____ years old.

    a. nineteen

    b. 16 years old

    c. 21

4. Nefertiti was the wife of____.

    a. Tut

    b. Horemheb

    c. Pharaoh Akhenaten

5. The tomb of young pharaoh Tut is located in the _____.

    a. Tuts King Egypt

    b. Maine Valley Sons

    c. Valley of the Kings

Jobs and Careers

Tip: After you've answered the easy ones, go back and work on the harder ones.

skill	climbing	monetary	professional	hourly
variety	salaried	experience	graduate	achieve

You might have heard that the education you receive and the information you learn in school will help you get a job when you

__graduate__ . Or your abilities and skills will benefit you in your future careers. So, what's the truth? How do people decide whether they

want a job or a career?

There are several common misconceptions regarding the distinctions between a job and a career. Some people believe that a job is

simply an __hourly__ position, whereas a __salaried__ position is a career. Others believe that a career requires a longer educational path

that results in exceptional skills and knowledge. The truth is not what most people believe.

A job is a position or set of duties performed for __monetary__ gain, whereas a career is a focused path or journey that a person takes to

achieve their professional goals. A career can include a variety of jobs along a career path.

Parents and teachers frequently ask their children what they want to be when they grow up. A career is the answer to that question. A

career is a path or __professional__ journey that a person follows throughout their working life. A career can necessitate extensive

education, such as that of a doctor or a lawyer, or it can require extensive __skill__ training, such as that of an electrician or plumber.

The words "career" and "path" are frequently used interchangeably. A career path is a path that people take to __achieve__ their

professional objectives. Many people work for decades on their career paths, which often include a __variety__ of jobs along the way.

With each job, a person gains __experience__ and skills that will help them get a better job and achieve their career goals.

Another term associated with careers is the concept of people __climbing__ a "career ladder". When people climb the metaphorical

career ladder, they progress step by step from one better job to the next. Careers take years to develop and achieve. Sometimes a lot of

education is required at the start of a career before a person can start moving up the ladder, whereas other careers require years of

experience in the field to get to the top.

1 Proofreading Shakespeare:
Romeo and Juliet

There are **24** mistakes in this passage. 5 capitals missing. 3 unnecessary capitals. 4 unnecessary apostrophes. 3 punctuation marks missing or incorrect. 2 incorrect homophones. 7 incorrectly spelled words.

In 1597, William Shakespeare published "Romeo and ~~Juliet"~~ Juliet," which would go on to become one of the world's most famous love stories. The plot of Shakespeare's ~~pley~~ play takes place in Verona, where the two main ~~characters~~ characters, ~~romeo~~ Romeo and Juliet, meet and fall in ~~love~~ love. Both are descended from two feuding families, the Capulets, and the Montagues. As a result, ~~thay~~ they choose to keep their ~~luve~~ love hidden and are married by Friar Laurence. Romeo gets into a fight with ~~Juliet"s~~ Juliet's cousin Tybalt, whom he ~~Kills~~ kills in a ~~Brawl~~ brawl despite his best efforts. Romeo is expelled from Verona and escapes to Mantua.

When ~~juliet's~~ Juliet's parents press her to marry, she ~~Seeks~~ seeks the assistance of Friar Laurence once more, who provides her with a sleeping potion designed to simulate her death. In a letter that never reaches Romeo, he explains his plan. Disgusted by the alleged death of his beloved Juliet, ~~Rumeo~~ Romeo returns to Verona and commits suicide at Juliet's open coffin. Juliet awakens from her slumber, sees what has happened, and decides to end her ~~liphe.~~ life. The two feuding families now recognize their complicity and reconcile at their children's graves.

The medieval old town of Verona is ideal for putting oneself in the shoes of Romeo and ~~juliet.~~ Juliet. Every year, many loving couples and tourists come to walk in the footsteps of ~~romeo~~ Romeo and Juliet. A photograph of Juliet's famous balcony, a visit to Romeo's home, or ~~sum~~ some ~~queit~~ quiet time spent at Julia's grave. No matter ~~were~~ where you look in the city, you ~~wall~~ will find loving ~~couple's~~ couples who stick declarations of love and initials on small slips of paper to the walls or immortalize ~~themselve's~~ themselves on the walls or stones of ~~house's~~ houses - often illegally.

Although Shakespeare's drama never corresponded to reality, ~~verona~~ Verona has a unique charm, especially for lovers, who imagine they can feel the true story behind the literary work, almost as if Romeo and Juliet had really existed.

Financial: Money, Stocks and Bonds

Three important __conditions__ must be met in order for something to qualify as a financial asset.

As a result, financial assets differ from physical assets such as land or __gold__ .

You can touch and feel the actual physical asset with land and gold, but you can only touch and feel something (usually a __piece__ of paper) that represents the asset of value with financial assets.

Money is a government-defined official medium of __exchange__ that consists of cash and __coins__ .

Money, __currency__ , cash, and legal tender all refer to the same thing.

They are all __symbols__ of a central bank's commitment to keep money's value as stable as possible.

Money is obviously a __valuable__ financial asset. We would all have to __barter__ with one another without a common medium of exchange, trading whatever __goods__ and __services__ we have for something else we need, or trade what we have for something else we could then trade with someone else who has what we need.

Stock is another crucial financial asset in the US __economy__ .

Stock, like money, is simply a piece of paper that represents something of value. The something of value' represented by stock is a __stake__ in a company.

Stock is also known as 'equity' because you have a stake in its __profits__ when you own stock in a company.

Jane, her parents, a friend, and her brother are now all __shareholders__ in her company.

The complexities arise when we attempt to assign a __monetary__ value to that stock. A variety of factors determines a stock's __value__ .

These are the most basic and fundamental factors that can influence the value of a share of stock. Individual stock __prices__ are affected by macroeconomic trends as well.

Thousands of books have been written in an attempt to discover the __golden__ rule that determines the exact value of a share of stock.

The New York Stock Exchange and __NASDAQ__ were the world's two largest stock exchanges in 2014. (both located in the United States).

When an organization, such as a company, a city or state, or even the federal government, requires funds, bonds can be __issued__ . Bonds come in various forms, but they are all debt instruments in which the bondholder is repaid their __principal__ investment, plus interest, at some future maturity date.

The only way a bondholder's money is lost is if the entity that issued the bond declares __bankruptcy__ . Bonds are generally safer investments than stocks because they are a legal __obligation__ to repay debt, whereas stocks represent ownership, which can make or lose money.

How It's Made: Money

1. The _____ agency is in charge of money creation.
   - a. federal
   - b. government

2. The United States Mint produces coins and dollar bills.
   - a. True - coins and dollar bills
   - b. False - only coins

3. Each side of a sheet of banknotes must dry for ___ hours.
   - a. 72
   - b. 24

4. Dollar bills and computer paper don't have the same _____ and feel.
   - a. design
   - b. weight

5. The metal sheets are fed into a machine that punches out _____.
   - a. coins
   - b. silver dollars

6. United States Bureau of _____ produces dollar notes.
   - a. Engraving and Printing
   - b. Engravers and Commission

7. The Secretary of the _____ selects one of the designs submitted by the designers for production.
   - a. Treasury
   - b. Bank

8. Coins in the United States are created from a combination of _____.
   - a. metals and alloys
   - b. silver and nickels

9. Before being stamped with the design, the blank coins are _____.
   - a. heated and cleaned
   - b. shined and reserved

10. Paper money is created from a particular _____ blend, it is more difficult to forge.
    - a. parcel and green dye
    - b. cotton and linen

Introvert vs. Extrovert

Introvert is a person who prefers calm environments, limits social engagement, or embraces a greater than average preference for solitude.

SYNONYMS:
brooder
loner
solitary

Extrovert is an outgoing, gregarious person who thrives in dynamic environments and seeks to maximize social engagement.

SYNONYMS:
character
exhibitionist
show-off
showboat

Fill in the blank with the correct word. [introvert, introverts, extrovert, extroverts]

1. Sue is the **extrovert** in the family; opinionated, talkative and passionate about politics.

2. He was described as an **introvert** , a reserved man who spoke little.

3. **Extroverts** are often described as the life of the party.

4. An **introvert** is often thought of as a quiet, reserved, and thoughtful individual.

5. **Extroverts** enjoy being around other people and tend to focus on the outside world.

6. Typically **introverts** tend to enjoy more time to themselves.

7. Jane is an **introvert** whose only hobby is reading.

8. I am still not as "outgoing" as an **extrovert** is.

9. I had been a very **extrovert** person, living life to the full.

10. I am an **introvert** , I am a loner.

11. Because Pat is an **extrovert** who enjoys chatting with others, she is the ideal talk show host.

12. She is basically an **introvert** , uncomfortable with loud women and confrontations.

Dealing With Acne

Acne is a skin disorder that results in bumps. Whiteheads, blackheads, pimples, and pus-filled bumps are all sorts of blemishes. What's the source of these annoying bumps? Pores and hair follicles make up most of your skin's top layer. Sebum (pronounced "see-bum"), the natural oil that moisturizes hair and skin, is produced in the pores by oil glands.

Generally, the glands produce adequate sebum, and the pores are good. However, oil, dead skin cells, and bacteria can block a pore if they accumulate in it to an unhealthy level. Acne may result as a result of this.

Puberty-induced hormonal changes are to blame for acne in children. If your parent suffered from acne as a teen, you will likely as well because your pores may produce more sebum when under stress; stress may worsen acne. Acne is usually gone by the time a person reaches their twenties.

Here are a few tips for preventing breakouts if you suffer from acne:

- It would help if you washed your face with warm water and a light soap or cleanser in the morning before school and before bed.
- Avoid scrubbing your face. Acne can be exacerbated by irritating the skin, so scrubbing is not recommended.
- Makeup should be washed off at the end of the day if you wear it.
- Ensure to wash your face after a workout if you've been sweating heavily.
- Acne-fighting lotions and creams are readily available over-the-counter. Talk to your parents or doctor about the options available to you.

Make sure you follow the guidelines on any acne medication you use. If you're unsure whether you're allergic to the cream or lotion, use a small amount at first. If you don't notice results the next day, don't give up. Acne medication can take weeks or months to take effect. If you use more than recommended, your skin may become extremely dry and red.

Acne-suffering children can seek treatment from their doctor. Doctors can prescribe stronger medications than what you can get over the counter.

The following are some other factors to consider:

- Avoid touching your face if you can.
- Pimples should not be picked, squeezed, or popped.
- Long hair should be kept away from the face, and it should be washed regularly to reduce oil production.

It is possible to get pimples on the hairline by wearing headgear like baseball caps. Stay away from them if you suspect they're contributing to your acne problems.

Despite their best efforts, many children will get acne at some point in their lives. The situation isn't out of the ordinary.

If you suffer from acne, you now have several options for treating it. Remind yourself of this: You are not alone. Take a look around at your buddies and you'll notice that the majority of children and adolescents are dealing with acne, too!

1. Puberty _____ changes are to blame for acne in children.
   a. harmonic
   b. hormonal

2. Pores and hair _____ make up most of your skin's top layer.
   a. follicles
   b. folate

3. Avoid _____ your face.
   a. using cleanser
   b. scrubbing

4. _____ is the oil that moisturizes hair and skin, is produced in the pores by oil glands.
   a. Acne
   b. Sebum

Smart Ways to Deal With a Bully

One of the most serious issues in our society today is bullying. It's not uncommon for young people to experience a range of negative emotions due to this. Bullies may use physical force (such as punches, kicks, or shoves) or verbal abuse (such as calling someone a name, making fun of them, or scaring them) to harm others.

Some examples of bullying include calling someone names, stealing from them and mocking them, or ostracizing them from a group.

Some bullies want to be the center of attention. As a strategy to be popular or get what they want, they may believe bullying is acceptable. Bullies are usually motivated by a desire to elevate their own status. As a result of picking on someone else, they can feel more power and authority.

Bullies frequently target someone they believe they can control . Kids who are easily agitated or have difficulty standing up for themselves are likely targets. Getting a strong reaction from someone can give bullies the illusion that they have the power they desire. There are times when bullies pick on someone who is more intelligent than them or who looks different from them somehow.

Preventing a Bully's Attack
Do not give in to the bully. Avoid the bully as much as possible. Of course, you aren't allowed to disappear or skip class. However, if you can escape the bully by taking a different path, do so.

Bravely stand your ground . Scared people aren't usually the most courageous people. Bullies can be stopped by just showing courage in the face of them. Just how do you present yourself as a fearless person? To send a message that says, "Don't mess with me," stand tall. It is much easier to be brave when you are confident in yourself.

Don't Pay Attention to What the Bully Says or Does. If you can, do your best not to listen to the bully's threats . Act as though you aren't aware of their presence and immediately go away to a safe place. It's what bullies want: a big reaction to their teasing and being mean. If you don't respond to a bully's actions by pretending you don't notice or care, you may be able to stop them.

Defend your rights. Pretend you're confident and brave. In a loud voice, tell the bully, "No! Stop it!" Then take a step back or even take off running if necessary. No matter what a bully says, say "no" and walk away if it doesn't feel right. If you do what a bully tells you to do, the bully is more likely to keep bullying you; kids who don't stand up for themselves are more likely to be targeted by bullies.

Don't retaliate by being a bully yourself. Don't fight back against someone who's bullying you or your pals by punching, kicking, or shoving them. Fighting back only makes the bully happier, and it's also risky since someone can be injured. You're also going to be in a lot of trouble. It's essential to stick with your friends, keep safe, and seek adult assistance.

Inform a responsible adult of the situation. Telling an adult if you're being bullied is crucial. Find someone you can confide in and tell them what's going on with you. It is up to everyone in the school, from teachers to principals to parents to lunchroom assistants, to stop the bullies. As soon as a teacher discovers the bullying, the bully usually stops because they are worried that their parents will punish them for their behavior. Bullying is terrible, and everyone who is bullied or witnesses bullying should speak up.

The Human Bones

1. A baby's body has about _____ bones.

    a. 320

    b. 300

2. The _____, which is like a bowl, holds the spine in place.

    a. pelvis

    b. spinal cord

3. A _____ is where two bones meet.

    a. legs

    b. joint

4. At what age is there no more room for growth?

    a. 25

    b. 18

5. Adults have how many bones?

    a. 206

    b. 200

6. The _____ lets you twist and bend.

    a. hip bones

    b. spine

7. Your skull protects your what?

    a. brain

    b. joints

8. Your ribs protect your what?

    a. Heart, spine, and arms

    b. heart, lung, and liver

9. The _____ connects to a large triangular bone on the upper back corner of each side of the ribcage.

    a. shoulder blade

    b. joints blade

10. You have _____ bones in your arm.

    a. two

    b. three

US Government: Running for Office

When running for public office, candidates must persuade voters that they are the best candidate for the position. Running for office is a term for this type of endeavor. Running for office can be a full-time job in some cases, such as the __presidential__ race. When running for office, there are a lot of things to do.

To run for office, the first step is to ensure that you meet all of the __requirements__. For example, one must be at least 18 years of age and a US citizen in order to apply.

Almost everyone joins a political party to run for public office these days. The primary election, in which they run to represent that party, is frequently the first election they must win. The Democratic Party and the Republican Party are the two most influential __political__ organizations in the United States today.

Without money, it's challenging to run for office. Candidates frequently use billboards, television commercials, and travel to give speeches to promote their campaigns. All of this comes at a price. The people who want to help a candidate win the election provide them with money. As a result, the budget is established. This is critical, as the person with the most significant __financial__ resources may be able to sway the greatest number of voters, ultimately leading to their victory.

A candidate's campaign staff should be assembled as well. These are people who will assist the candidate in their bid for the presidency. They __coordinate__ volunteers, manage funds, plan events, and generally assist the candidate in winning the election. It is the campaign manager's responsibility to lead the campaign team.

Many candidates attempt to stand out from the crowd by creating a memorable campaign slogan. This is a catchy phrase that will stick in voters' minds as they cast their ballots. Calvin Coolidge and Dwight Eisenhower both had __memorable__ campaign slogans, "I Like Ike" for Eisenhower and "Keep Cool with Coolidge" for Coolidge.

At some point, the candidate will begin a public campaign. A lot of "shaking hands and hugging babies" is involved in the process of running for office. There are a lot of speeches they give __outlining__ what they plan to do when they get into the White House. It's their job to explain why they're better than their rivals.

When a candidate runs for office, they usually take a position on several issues relevant to the position for which they are running. A wide range of topics, such as education, clean water, taxation, war, and __healthcare__, are examples.

The debate is yet another aspect of running for office. At a debate, all of the candidates for a particular office sit down together to discuss their positions on a specific issue. Candidates take turns speaking and responding to each other's arguments during the debate. The outcome of a debate between two candidates can mean the difference between __victory__ and defeat.

After months of campaigning, the election is finally upon us. They'll cast their ballots and then get right back to work. Attending rallies or shaking hands with strangers on the street may be part of their campaign __strategy__. All the candidates can do is wait until the polls close. Family, friends, and campaign members usually gather to see how things turn out. If they are successful, they are likely to deliver a victory speech and then go to a party to celebrate.

Becoming Class President

Start working toward your goal of becoming class or high school president as soon as possible if you want to one day hold that position.

If you want to get involved in student __government__ your freshman year, go ahead and join, but don't hold your breath waiting to be elected president. Elections for the freshman class council are frequently a complete disaster. Since freshman elections are held within a month of the start of school, no one has had a chance to get to know one another. The person elected president is usually the one whose name has been mentioned the most by other students. A lot of the time, it's not based on competence or trust.

Building trust and __rapport__ with your classmates is essential from the beginning of the school year. This is the most crucial step in the process of becoming a Class Officer President.

Electing someone they like and trust is a top __priority__ for today's college students. Be a role model for your students. In order to demonstrate your competence, participate in class discussions and get good grades. Avoid being the class clown or the laziest or most absent-minded member of the group.

Become a part of the students' lives. Attend lunch with a variety of people from various backgrounds. Ask them about their __worries__ and their hopes for the school's future.

Make an effort to attend student __council__ meetings even if you aren't currently a member. If you're interested in joining the student council, you may be able to sit in on their meetings, or you may be able to attend an occasional meeting where non-council members can express their concerns and ideas.

Your Identity and Reputation Online

Your online identity grows every time you use a social network, send a text, or make a post on a website, for example. Your online __persona__ may be very different from your real-world persona – the way your friends, parents, and teachers see you.

One of the best things about having an online life is trying on different personas. If you want to change how you act and show up to people, you can. You can also learn more about things that you like. Steps to help you maintain control on the internet can be taken just like in real life.

Here are some things to think about to protect your online identity and reputation:

Nothing is temporary online. The worldwide web is full of opportunities to connect and share with other people. It's also a place with no " __take-backs__ " or "temporary" situations. It's easy for other people to copy, save, and forward your information even if you delete it.

Add a "private" option for your profiles. Anyone can copy or screen-grab things that you don't want the world to see using social __networking__ sites. Use caution when using the site's default settings. Each site has its own rules, so read them to ensure you're doing everything you can to keep your information safe.

Keep your passwords safe and change them often. Someone can ruin your __reputation__ by pretending to be you online. The best thing to do is pick passwords that no one can guess. The only people who should know about them are your parents or someone else who you can trust. Your best friend, boyfriend, or girlfriend should not know your passwords.

Don't put up pictures or comments that are __inappropriate__ or sexually provocative. In the future, things that are funny or cool to you now might not be so cool to someone else, like a teacher or admissions officer. If you don't want your grandmother, coach, or best friend's parents to see it, don't post it. Even on a private page, it could be hacked or copied and sent to someone else.

Don't give in to unwanted advances. There are a lot of inappropriate messages and requests for money that teenagers get when they're on the web. These things can be scary, weird, or even __embarrassing__ , but they can also be exciting and fun. Do not keep quiet about being bullied online. Tell an adult you trust right away if a stranger or someone you know is bullying you. It's never a good idea to answer. If you respond, you might say something that makes things even worse.

You can go to www.cybertipline.org to report bad behavior or other problems.

Avoid "flaming" by taking a break now and then. Do you want to send an angry text or comment to someone? Relax for a few minutes and realize that the __remarks__ will be there even if you have cooled off or change your mind about them.

People may feel free to write hurtful, __derogatory__ , or abusive remarks on the internet if they can remain anonymous. We can be painful to others if we share things or make angry comments when we aren't facing someone. If they find out, it could change how they see us. If you wouldn't say it, show it, or do it in person, don't do it online.

Make sure you don't break copyright laws. Don't upload, share, or distribute copyrighted photographs, sounds, or files. Be aware of copyright restrictions. Sharing them is great, but doing so illegally runs the risk of legal __repercussions__ down the road.

It's time for a self-evaluation. Take a look at your "digital footprint," which people can find out about you. When you search for your screen name or email address, see what comes up. That's one way to get a sense of what other people think of you online.

In the same way that your __real-life__ identity is formed, your online identity and reputation are also formed. It's different when you're on the internet because you don't always have the chance to explain how you feel or what you mean. Thinking about what you're going to say and being responsible can help you avoid leaving an online trail that you'll later be sorry about.

Proofreading Interpersonal
Skills: Peer Pressure

Tony is mingling with a large group of what he considers to be the school's cool kids. Suddenly, someone in the group begins mocking Tony's friend Rob, who walks with a limp due to a physical ~~dasability.~~ **disability.**

They begin to imitate ~~rob's~~ **Rob's** limping and ~~Call~~ **call** him 'lame cripple' and other derogatory terms. Although Tony disapproves of their behavior, he does not want to risk being excluded from the group, and thus joins them in mocking Rob.

Peer pressure is the influence exerted on us by ~~member's~~ **members** of our social group. It can manifest in a variety of ways and can lead to us engaging in behaviors we would not normally ~~consider~~ **consider,** such as Tony joining in and mocking his friend Rob.

However, peer pressure is not always detrimental. Positive peer pressure can motivate us to make better ~~chioces,~~ **choices,** such as studying harder, staying in school, or seeking a better job. ~~Whan~~ **When** others influence us to make poor ~~Choices,~~ **choices,** such as smoking, using illicit drugs, or bullying, we succumb to negative peer pressure. We all desire to belong to a group and fit in, so ~~Developing~~ **developing** strategies for resisting peer pressure when necessary can be beneficial.

Tony and his friends are engaging in bullying by ~~moking~~ **mocking** Rob. Bullying is defined as persistent, ~~unwanted.~~ **unwanted,** aggressive behavior directed toward another person. It is ~~moust~~ **most** prevalent in school-aged children but can also ~~aphfect~~ **affect** adults. Bullying can take on a variety of forms, including the following:

· ~~Verbil~~
· **Verbal** bullying is when someone is called names, threatened, or taunted verbally.
· Bullying is physical in nature - ~~hitting~~ **hitting,** spitting, tripping, or ~~poshing~~ **pushing** someone.
· Social ~~Bullying~~ **bullying** is intentionally excluding ~~Someone~~ **someone** from ~~activities~~ **activities,** spreading rumors, or embarrassing ~~sumeone.~~ **someone.**
· Cyberbullying is the act of verbally or socially bullying someone via the internet, such as through social media sites.

Peer pressure exerts a significant influence on an individual's decision to engage in bullying ~~behavoir.~~ **behavior.** In Tony's case, even though Rob is a friend and ~~tony~~ **Tony** would never consider mocking his disability, his desire to belong to a group outweighs his willingness to defend his ~~friend~~ **friend.**

Peer pressure is a strong force that is exerted on us by our social group members. Peer pressure is classified into two types: negative peer pressure, which results in poor decision-making, and positive peer pressure, which influences us to make the correct choices. Adolescents are particularly susceptible to peer pressure because of their desire to fit ~~in~~ **in.**

Peer pressure can motivate someone to engage in bullying behaviors such as mocking someone, threatening to harm them, taunting them online, or excluding them from an activity. Each year, bullying ~~affect's~~ **affects** an astounding 3.2 million school-aged children. ~~Severil~~ **Several** strategies for avoiding peer pressure bullying include the following:

- ~~consider~~ **Consider** your actions by surrounding yourself with good company.
- Acquiring the ability to say no to someone you trust.

Speak up - bullying is never acceptable and is taken ~~extramely~~ **extremely** ~~seroiusly~~ **seriously** in schools and the workplace. If someone is attempting to convince you to bully another person, speaking with a trusted adult such as a teacher, coach, counselor, or coworker can frequently help put ~~thing's~~ **things** into perspective and highlight the issue.

Proofreading Skills:
Volunteering

There are **10** mistakes in this passage. 3 capitals missing. 4 unnecessary capitals. 3 incorrect homophones.

Your own life can be changed and the lives of others, through volunteer work. ~~to~~ **To** cope with the news that there has been a disaster, you can volunteer to help those in need. Even if you can't contribute financially, you can donate ~~you're~~ **your** time instead.

Volunteering is such an integral part of the American culture that many high schools require their students to participate in community service to graduate.

When you volunteer, you have the freedom to choose what you'd like to do and who or what you think is most deserving of your time. Start with these ideas if you need a little inspiration. We've got just a few examples here.

Encourage the growth and development of young people. Volunteer as a ~~Camp~~ **camp** counselor, a Big Brother or Big Sister, or an after-school sports program. Special Olympics games and events are excellent opportunities to know children with special needs.

Spend the holidays doing good deeds for others. Volunteer at a food bank or distribute toys to children in need on Thanksgiving Day, and you'll be doing your part to help those in need. ~~your~~ **Your** church, temple, mosque, or another place of worship may also require your assistance.

You can visit an animal shelter and play with the ~~Animals.~~ **animals.** Volunteers are critical to the well-being of shelter animals. (You also get a good workout when you walk rescued dogs.)

Become a member of a political campaign. ~~Its~~ **It's** a great way to learn more about the inner workings of politics if ~~your~~ **you're** curious about it. If you are not able ~~To~~ **to** cast a ballot, you can still help elect your preferred candidate.

Help save the planet. Join a river preservation group and lend a hand. Participate in a park cleanup day in your community. Not everyone is cut out for the great outdoors; if you can't see yourself hauling trees up a hill, consider working in the park's office or education center instead.

Take an active role in promoting health-related causes. Many of us know someone afflicted with a medical condition (like cancer, HIV, or diabetes, for example). ~~a~~ **A** charity that helps people with a disease, such as delivering meals, raising money, or providing other assistance, can make you ~~Feel~~ **feel** good about yourself.

Find a way to combine your favorite things if you have more than one. For example, if you're a fan of kids and have a talent for arts and crafts, consider volunteering at a children's hospital.

Defensive Driving

1. You can reduce the likelihood of being involved in an accident by driving _____.
   - a. distinctly driving
   - b. defensively

2. Drivers may drive too closely behind, _____, or zigzag in and out of traffic without regard for safety.
   - a. make quick changes without signaling
   - b. make random rear mirrors adjustment

3. One-third of all traffic accidents are caused by _____drivers.
   - a. submissive
   - b. aggressive

4. A driver's ability to see and respond to possible difficulties is _____ by _____, such as talking on the phone or eating.
   - a. imperfect, distance
   - b. impaired, distractions

5. Drinking and using drugs (both prescription and _____ medications) both slow down reaction times and _____ judgment in drivers.
   - a. OTD, impulse
   - b. OTC, impair

6. Predicting what the other driver will do and making the necessary _____ can help lower your _____.
   - a. speed, adjust
   - b. adjustments, risk

7. Driver error is at blame for _____ of all _____, according to the Department of Transportation.
   - a. 90%, collisions
   - b. 80%, risks

8. Keep a safe _____ from the vehicle ahead of you.
   - a. densify
   - b. distance

9. Pay attention to your _____ and stay _____ at all times.
   - a. surroundings, alert
   - b. friends, risk

10. Do not make the mistake of assuming that another driver will move out of the way or enable you to _____ when you are driving.
    - a. stop
    - b. merge

11. A _____ is anything that takes your mind off of what you're doing.
    - a. distraction
    - b. dimensions

12. Having an alternative _____ of travel is also crucial.
    - a. speed limit
    - b. route

13. To maintain vehicle control, you must manage your _____.
    - a. speed
    - b. distance

14. When driving in _____ conditions, such as rain, fog, nighttime driving, or behind a huge truck or motorcycle, you should _____ the space between you and the vehicle in front of you by an additional second.
    - a. poor, increase
    - b. fair, decrease

Teen Drinking and Driving

1. Even just a few beers can put your life and the lives of others in jeopardy if you get behind the wheel of a vehicle while _____.
   - a. intoxicated
   - b. incinerated
   - c. indecencies

2. Teenagers, because of their lack of driving experience, are less skilled at recognizing and reacting to driving _____.
   - a. legislation
   - b. hazards
   - c. stressors

3. BAC stands for _____.
   - a. blood alcohol content
   - b. blood alcohology confinement
   - c. blood alcoholic nonattainment

4. Under the _____ law, which applies to drivers younger than 21, it is against the law to get behind the wheel with any amount of alcohol in your system, even traces of it.
   - a. zero-tolerance
   - b. zero-non-impaired
   - c. zero-alcohol and beverages

5. (BAC) of _____ per deciliter (g/dL) or higher is considered to be alcohol-impaired.
   - a. .02 grams
   - b. .08 grams
   - c. .3% grams

6. When a police officer has _____, a student's privilege to drive a vehicle can be instantly withdrawn and suspended.
   - a. parent's permission
   - b. a court order
   - c. sufficient evidence

7. If a student is found guilty of driving under the influence of alcohol or another controlled substance, the student faces the possibility of being _____ from school.
   - a. given a warning
   - b. enrolled
   - c. expelled

8. Driving under the influence of alcohol or drugs is referred to as driving _____.
   - a. DIU
   - b. DWI
   - c. DUI

9. Signs of legal impairment
   - a. Nausea, Diarrhea, Coughing
   - b. Nausea, Slur speech, Impaired vision
   - c. Slur speech, Workaholic, Laughing a lot

10. Always fasten your _____, no matter how _____ the drive may be.
    - a. seat belt, short
    - b. belt buckle, fast
    - c. seat belt, long

UNDERSTANDING RIDESHARE

The way in which people travel is undergoing significant change. Ride-sharing and ride-hailing services, such as Uber, provide an **alternative** to the taxi business.

When ridesharing startup Uber first debuted its services, the world of private transportation shifted radically. They offered a **luxury** black car service as an alternative to the usual taxi ride.

In the past, ridesharing was a lot like **carpooling** , where the person riding along often paid for half of the trip. Both the driver and passenger were traveling in the same direction, and the rider would contribute to the trip's cost.

Ridesharing today is for-profit, and the driver has no **destination** in mind rather than providing transportation services like a taxi. A third-party app or website charges a fee to connect riders and drivers.

It's common to see the term "rideshare" replaced with "ride-hail." However, this can be deceptive, as "hailing" usually refers to the act of **flagging** down a cab from a distance.

Hail requests can't be accepted by drivers for ridesharing services like Lyft, Uber, and TappCar because the companies don't support the feature. The **legislation** also prohibits drivers from receiving hails. Otherwise, the service would be categorized as a taxi service.

Instead, users must use their smartphone to "haul" a driver through their preferred ridesharing app.

Rideshare companies use a **smartphone** app to connect drivers with passengers in the local region. The driver opens the app and changes their status to "online" to show they are ready to take a ride.

Customer pick-up and drop-off requests are sent to the driver, who responds by accepting or **declining** the ride.

After accepting the trip and picking up the passenger, the driver proceeds to the passenger's destination.

The passenger will exit the vehicle once the driver reaches the final location.

Because payments for **fares** are processed within the app, no money exchange occurs between the driver and the passenger.

Additionally, the app enables passengers and drivers to provide **ratings** for one another. Both the driver and rider benefit from this grading system, which ensures a high level of service and respect for both parties.

Step 1: Double-check that the bottom numbers (the denominators) are the same.
Step 2: Add the top numbers (the numerators), then place that answer over the denominator
Step 3: Reduce the fraction to its simplest form (if possible)

Score : _____

Date : _____

Adding Fractions

1) $\dfrac{5}{7} + \dfrac{4}{7} = \dfrac{9}{7} = 1\dfrac{2}{7}$

2) $\dfrac{2}{8} + \dfrac{5}{8} =$

3) $\dfrac{6}{7} + \dfrac{4}{7} =$

4) $\dfrac{5}{4} + \dfrac{3}{4} =$

5) $\dfrac{1}{8} + \dfrac{3}{8} =$

6) $\dfrac{2}{6} + \dfrac{5}{6} =$

7) $\dfrac{2}{6} + \dfrac{2}{6} =$

8) $\dfrac{5}{4} + \dfrac{3}{4} =$

9) $\dfrac{8}{8} + \dfrac{6}{8} =$

10) $\dfrac{3}{7} + \dfrac{5}{7} =$

11) $\dfrac{7}{9} + \dfrac{1}{9} =$

12) $\dfrac{3}{9} + \dfrac{6}{9} =$

13) $\dfrac{2}{7} + \dfrac{4}{7} =$

14) $\dfrac{3}{6} + \dfrac{2}{6} =$

15) $\dfrac{3}{6} + \dfrac{5}{6} =$

The factors of a number are the numbers that add up to the original number when multiplied together. Factors of 8, for example, could be 2 and 4 because 2 * 4 equals 8.

Find the Greatest Common Factor for each number pair.

1) 15 , 3   __3__

2) 24 , 12   _____

3) 10 , 4   _____

4) 40 , 4   _____

5)   8 , 40   _____

6) 10 , 4   _____

7) 12 , 20   _____

8)   5 , 20   _____

9)   8 , 2   _____

10) 24 , 40 _____

11)   6 , 8   _____

12) 10 , 3   _____

13)   8 , 6   _____

14) 24 , 10 _____

15) 24 , 12 _____

16) 40 , 24 _____

17)   8 , 10 _____

18) 10 , 20 _____

19)   2 , 3   _____

20)   6 , 12 _____

Step 1: List or write ALL the factors of each number.

Step 2: Identify the common factors.

Step 3: After identifying the common factors, select or choose the number which has the largest value. This number will be your Greatest Common Factor (GCF).

Example:
12, 18

Factors of 12: 1, 2, 3, 4, 6, 12
Factors of 18: 1, 2, 3, 6, 9, 18

What is the Greatest Common Factor?
The GCF of 12 and 18 is 6. That's it!

The factors of a number are the numbers that add up to the original number when multiplied together. Factors of 8, for example, could be 2 and 4 because 2 * 4 equals 8.

Score : _____

Date : _____

List All of the Prime Factors for each number.

1) 38 __2, 19_____

2) 49 _____

3) 35 _____

4) 25 _____

5) 15 _____

6) 44 _____

7) 32 _____

8) 48 _____

9) 22 _____

10) 21 _____

11) 30 _____

12) 20 _____

13) 39 _____

14) 14 _____

15) 12 _____

16) 26 _____

17) 46 _____

18) 40 _____

19) 24 _____

20) 10 _____

The term "prime factorization" refers to the process of determining which prime numbers multiply to produce the original number.

Score : _____

Date : _____

Step 1 : Divide the given number in two factors.

Step 2 : Now divide these two factors into other two multiples.

Step 3 : Repeat the step 2 until we reach all prime factors.

Step 4 : All the prime factors so obtained collectively known as prime factors of given number. In order to cross check; multiply all the prime factors, you must get the given number.

Find the Prime Factors of the Numbers

1)
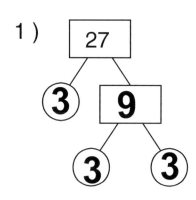

Prime Factors
_ x _ x _ = 27

2)
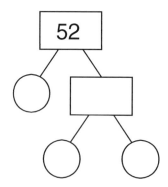

Prime Factors
_ x _ x _ = 52

3)
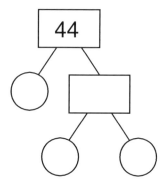

Prime Factors
_ x _ x _ = 44

4)
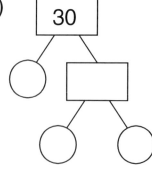

Prime Factors
_ x _ x _ = 30

5)
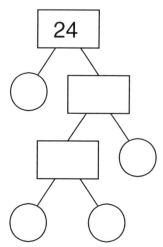

Prime Factors
_ x _ x _ x _ = 24

6)
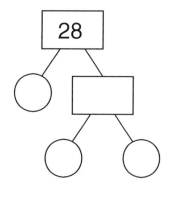

Prime Factors
_ x _ x _ = 28

Numerical Cognition Exercise
Rearranging Digits

Rearrange each set of numbers to produce the largest possible number.

1) 399 __**993**__   6) 846 _____

2) 744 _____   7) 844 _____

3) 488 _____   8) 345 _____

4) 616 _____   9) 959 _____

5) 734 _____   10) 559 _____

Rearrange each set of numbers to make the smallest number possible.

1) 897 __**789**__   6) 149 _____

2) 696 _____   7) 862 _____

3) 825 _____   8) 212 _____

4) 135 _____   9) 557 _____

5) 751 _____   10) 675 _____

Numerical Cognition Exercise
Rearranging Digits

Rearrange each set of numbers to produce the largest possible number.

1)   1,182   **8,211**   6)   7,769   _____

2)   1,549   _____   7)   7,521   _____

3)   5,366   _____   8)   8,146   _____

4)   3,869   _____   9)   8,161   _____

5)   2,853   _____   10)   7,769   _____

Rearrange each set of numbers to make the smallest number possible.

1)   7,816   **1,678**   6)   6,636   _____

2)   3,827   _____   7)   8,176   _____

3)   4,946   _____   8)   9,222   _____

4)   5,938   _____   9)   2,172   _____

5)   1,627   _____   10)   5,366   _____

TIME

What time is on the clock?   _____

What time was it 1 hour ago?   _____

What time was it 3 hours and 40 minutes ago?   _____

What time will it be in 4 hours and 20 minutes?   _____

What time is on the clock?   _____

What time was it 2 hours ago?   _____

What time will it be in 3 hours ?   _____

What time will it be in 4 hours and 20 minutes?   _____

What time is on the clock?   _____

What time was it 1 hour ago?   _____

What time was it 3 hours and 20 minutes ago?   _____

What time will it be in 2 hours ?   _____

What time is on the clock?   _____

What time will it be in 3 hours and 20 minutes?   _____

What time was it 2 hours ago?   _____

What time was it 1 hour ago?   _____

Find the Missing Addends.

1) $59 = \underline{\quad} + 40$

2) $19 + \underline{\quad} = 36$

3) $34 + \underline{\quad} = 51$

4) $14 + \underline{\quad} = 41$

5) $\underline{\quad} + 28 = 53$

6) $33 = \underline{\quad} + 18$

7) $57 = \underline{\quad} + 40$

8) $27 + \underline{\quad} = 42$

9) $\underline{\quad} + 10 = 45$

10) $65 = 34 + \underline{\quad}$

11) $27 + \underline{\quad} = 53$

12) $47 = \underline{\quad} + 27$

13) $43 = \underline{\quad} + 15$

14) $11 + \underline{\quad} = 24$

15) $40 = \underline{\quad} + 15$

16) $\underline{\quad} + 36 = 58$

17) $72 = 33 + \underline{\quad}$

18) $38 = 16 + \underline{\quad}$

19) $\underline{\quad} + 21 = 37$

20) $13 + \underline{\quad} = 50$

21) $\underline{\quad} + 23 = 51$

22) $\underline{\quad} + 18 = 46$

23) $\underline{\quad} + 32 = 52$

24) $57 = 22 + \underline{\quad}$

25) $37 + \underline{\quad} = 75$

26) $34 = \underline{\quad} + 19$

27) $28 = 10 + \underline{\quad}$

28) $66 = 33 + \underline{\quad}$

29) $20 + \underline{\quad} = 53$

30) $29 = 19 + \underline{\quad}$

```
  75_        57_        _69        _55        9_6
+ 9_4      + _25      + 9_1      + 4_5      + _6_
 1_95        9_2       168_       74_       1406
```

```
  _67        1_2        1_4        5_6        _74
+ 5_3      + _4_      + 79_      + 36_      + 4_3
 146_       860        _39        _92       139_
```

```
  _0_        6_9        _6_        _0_        65_
+ 860      + _3_      + 868      + 165      + _58
 12_5       851       11_0        2_9       11_0
```

```
  _89        39_        31_        263        _10
+ 5_8      + _75      + _92      + 1_1      + 1_8
 120_       13_6        5_3        _3_        35_
```

```
  806        _58        1_6        _45        _97
+ 6_8      + 2_7      + _87      + 4_5      + 8_9
 1_1_       57_        55_       130_       110_
```

$63.32 +$87.76	$57.23 +$25.66	$34.79 +$68.43	$84.62 +$23.84	$25.78 +$99.45
$72.59 +$19.64	$67.32 +$66.27	$85.42 +$11.33	$59.36 +$75.85	$73.25 +$71.12
$14.85 +$86.82	$48.57 +$56.12	$42.34 +$80.98	$76.39 +$45.96	$50.49 +$33.61
$13.83 +$34.61	$12.59 +$31.76	$80.57 +$84.11	$22.35 +$29.88	$95.62 +$64.31
$28.73 +$64.19	$19.33 +$83.11	$74.42 +$77.21	$28.39 +$32.36	$26.21 +$92.67

10122 + 86800	265710 + 883815	6900016 + 8967065	94785 + 51037
403123 + 535453	5061847 + 1878336	88389 + 38835	313963 + 824442
2936692 + 7549491	15234 + 29032	512353 + 139827	1923899 + 6762860
93107 + 15816	421331 + 962779	5141586 + 6071731	42257 + 96189

1) 1067 + 1078 =

2) 438 + 2611 =

3) -2831 + -2939 =

4) 2330 + -1901 =

5) 935 + 1991 =

6) 603 + 1073 =

7) -2280 + -393 =

8) -230 + -138 =

9) 1368 + 624 =

10) 1143 + -2262 =

11) 1708 + -337 =

12) 2667 + 2849 =

13) 2277 + -466 =

14) -2079 + -2586 =

15) 2966 + 2413 =

16) -1488 + 2557 =

17) 1087 + -2291 =

18) -2005 + 2153 =

19) 2125 + 2919 =

20) -270 + 2104 =

21) 2759 + 592 =

22) -1815 + 2739 =

23) 1956 + -560 =

24) 1569 + 2401 =

25) 2496 + 674 =

26) -2907 + 884 =

27) 1727 + 739 =

28) 125 + 783 =

29) 1602 + -1844 =

30) 2042 + -2763 =

Multiplying and Dividing Rational Numbers

Find each product or quotient. Round to the nearest ten-thousandth.

1) $\dfrac{3}{5} \div \dfrac{6}{4}$

8) $(-10) \bullet (-37) \bullet 33$

2) $\dfrac{-9}{8} \bullet \dfrac{-6}{5}$

9) $30 \div 26 \div 4$

3) $(-24) \bullet 18 \bullet 22$

10) $\dfrac{2}{8} \bullet \dfrac{-4}{9}$

4) $4.8 \bullet 6.0$

11) $\dfrac{8}{4} \div \dfrac{-2}{3}$

5) $5.0 \div (-3.4)$

12) $\dfrac{7}{2} \bullet \dfrac{9}{6}$

6) $2 \div (-29) \div (-27)$

13) $5.9 \div 3.5$

7) $2.4 \bullet 7.1 \bullet (-5.6)$

14) $(-24) \div 25 \div (-37)$

Score : _____

Date : _____

Combining Like Terms

1) p - 8p

2) q + 7q

3) -3 + 2(6k + 8)

4) 7 - 2z + 4z

5) -9 + 3r + 8 - 7r

6) 5 + 3z - 2z

7) -6(9 - 5c)

8) 6 + 2 + 9r + 3r

9) -7 - 3(-6 + 2f)

10) -8(3q + 4)

Domain and Range Mapping Diagrams

Determine whether each diagram depicts a function or not.

1)

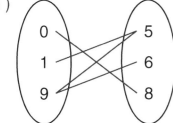

Function: _____

2)

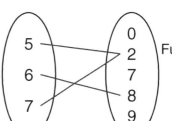

Function: _____

3)

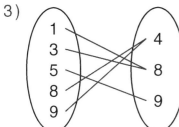

Function: _____

4)

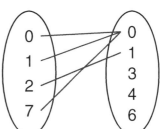

Function: _____

5)

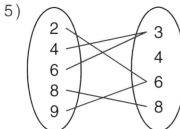

Function: _____

6)

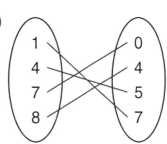

Function: _____

7)

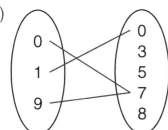

Function: _____

8)

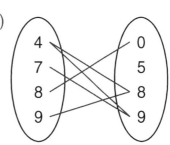

Function: _____

Ordered Pairs

Find the Domain and Range. Also, state whether each set of ordered pairs is a function or not.

1) { (1, 9), (3, -7), (-8, -4), (1, -3), (-3, 7) }

   Domain:

   Range:

   Function? : _____

2) { (-6, 1), (7, -3), (3, 5), (9, 6), (-2, 6) }

   Domain:

   Range:

   Function? : _____

3) { (4, 7), (7, -2), (-2, 6), (-7, -6), (-7, 9) }

   Domain:

   Range:

   Function? : _____

4) { (-8, 3), (3, 7), (6, -9), (-1, 3), (4, -8) }

   Domain:

   Range:

   Function? : _____

5) { (1, 2), (-1, -4), (3, 7), (9, -5), (-8, 8) }

   Domain:

   Range:

   Function? : _____

6) { (-1, -5), (4, -8), (-2, 4), (1, 9), (8, 1) }

   Domain:

   Range:

   Function? : _____

7) { (-3, 6), (0, -8), (-6, 1), (-1, 5), (-9, -9) }

   Domain:

   Range:

   Function? : _____

8) { (2, 0), (2, 6), (5, 8), (4, 1), (-1, -1) }

   Domain:

   Range:

   Function? : _____

9) { (3, 0), (0, -3), (4, -8), (2, 0), (7, -7) }

   Domain:

   Range:

   Function? : _____

10) { (4, 3), (3, -9), (7, -6), (4, -3), (-3, -8) }

   Domain:

   Range:

   Function? : _____

Word Problems

1) After eating at the restaurant, Sandy, Melanie, and Jason decided to divide the bill
   evenly. If each person paid eleven dollars, what was the total of the bill ?   _____

2) There were 17 bales of hay in the barn. Tom stacked more bales in the barn
   today. There are now 63 bales of hay in the barn. How many bales did
   he store in the barn ?   _____

3) Mike's high school played twelve soccer games this year. The team won most of
   their games. They were defeated during four games. How many games did they win ?_____

4) Jessica is baking a cake. The recipe calls for 7 cups of flour. She already put in
   3 cups. How many more cups does she need to add ?   _____

5) How many ink cartridges can you buy with 112 dollars if
   one cartridge costs 14 dollars ?   _____

6) Joan found ninety - three seashells on the beach, she gave Sam some of her
   seashells. She has thirty - nine seashell left. How many seashells did she give to Sam ? _____

7) Dan has twenty - two books in his library. He bought several books at a yard sale
   over the weekend. He now has seventy - eight books in his library. How many books
   did he buy at the yard sale ?   _____

8) After paying six dollars for the pie, Sam has fifty - five dollars left.
   How much money did he have before buying the pie ?   _____

9) There are 38 maple trees currently in the park. Park workers will plant more
   maple trees today. When the workers are finished there will be 67
   maple trees in the park. How many maple trees did the workers plant today ?_____

10) Fred had 47 peaches left at his roadside fruit stand. He went to the
    orchard and picked more peaches to stock up the stand. There are now 55
    peaches at the stand, how many did he pick ?   _____

Separable Equations

Find the general solution of each equation.

1) $\dfrac{dy}{dx} = e^{3x+y}$

2) $\dfrac{dy}{dx} = 2y(x + 8)$

3) $\dfrac{dy}{dx} = e^{x+3y}$

4) $\dfrac{dy}{dx} = \dfrac{2}{\sin(y)}$

5) $\dfrac{dy}{dx} = 4xe^{y}$

6) $\dfrac{dy}{dx} = \dfrac{e^{2x}}{4y}$

7) $\dfrac{dy}{dx} = \dfrac{x^{4}}{e^{4y}}$

8) $\dfrac{dy}{dx} = 11e^{x+y}$

9) $\dfrac{dy}{dx} = \dfrac{x}{12y}$

10) $\dfrac{dy}{dx} = \dfrac{2}{2\sin(y)}$

11) $\dfrac{dy}{dx} = \dfrac{-x}{10y}$

12) $\dfrac{dy}{dx} = 2xe^{2y}$

Logarithmic Differentiation

Differentiate each function using logarithmic differentiation.

1) $y = (-4x^3)(-3x^3)$

2) $y = (7x^2)(2x^4 + 2)$

3) $y = (3x^2 - 3)(-7x^2 - 1)$

4) $y = \dfrac{6x^2 +}{-4x - 7}$

5) $y = 5x^{3x}$

6) $y = -5x^{4x}$

7) $y = \dfrac{-2x^2 -}{6x - 6}$

8) $y = \dfrac{2x - 3}{7x^3 - 3x}$

9) $y = 8x^{6x}$

10) $y = (2x^4 + 7x - 1)(x^2)$

11) $y = \dfrac{x^3 -}{6x^2 - 1}$

12) $y = -8x^{6x}$

Product Rule

Differentiate each function with respect to the given variable, by using the power rule.

1) $y = (5x^2 + 5x + 3)(4x^3 - 3x - 1)$

2) $y = (-x^4 - x^2 + 5x)(x^3 - 3)$

3) $y = (-3x^2 + 2)(6x^3 - 3x^2)$

4) $y = (5x^2)(6x^2)$

5) $y = (-5x^3 - x - 4)(-x^5 - 7)$

6) $y = (-2x^2 + 2x + 6)(-7x^5)$

7) $y = (3x^5 - 6x^3 - 4x^2)(2x^5 + 2x^4 + 7x)$

8) $y = (-7x^2 + 2x)(6x^5 - 7)$

9) $y = (7x^5)(5x^5 + 2x^4)$

10) $y = (-2x^3 - 4x^2 - 3)(5x^3)$

Power, Constant, and Sum Rules

Differentiate each function with respect to the given variable.

1) $y = x^2 - 4x - 12$

2) $y = x^2 - 5x + 6$

3) $y = \dfrac{-7}{17} x^{\frac{-4}{11}}$

4) $y = \dfrac{3}{4} x^{\frac{-1}{2}}$

5) $y = 1$

6) $y = 13$

7) $y = x^3 + x^2 - 33x + 63$

8) $y = \dfrac{3}{x^7}$

9) $y = \dfrac{-16}{x^2}$

10) $y = \dfrac{-9}{x^6}$

Quotient Rule

Differentiate each function.

1) $y = \dfrac{-4x - 6}{3x^2 + 1}$

2) $y = \dfrac{6x - 5}{2x^3 - x}$

3) $y = \dfrac{2x^3 -}{4x - 5}$

4) $y = \dfrac{3x + 2}{-6x^2 - 6}$

5) $y = \dfrac{7x^3 -}{6x + 6}$

6) $y = \dfrac{-x - 1}{7x^3 - 7x}$

7) $y = \dfrac{5x + 1}{x^2 + 1}$

8) $y = \dfrac{6x^3 -}{3x - 7}$

9) $y = \dfrac{6x^2 -}{3x + 1}$

10) $y = \dfrac{5x^2 -}{-x - 3}$

11) $y = \dfrac{4x^2 -}{7x - 5}$

12) $y = \dfrac{-3x - 7}{-x^3 - 2x}$

Limits at Infinity

Find each limit. Round to two decimals if necessary.

1) $\lim\limits_{x \to \infty}$ $-x^2 - x - 3$

2) $\lim\limits_{x \to -\infty}$ $-\ln(-x - 3)$

3) $\lim\limits_{x \to -\infty}$ $\dfrac{2x^3 - 3x^2 - 3x - 3}{5x^2 - 5x - 1}$

4) $\lim\limits_{x \to \infty}$ $x - 3$

5) $\lim\limits_{x \to \infty}$ $-2e^{-3x} + 1$

6) $\lim\limits_{x \to -\infty}$ $\dfrac{-3x - 3}{5x^3 + 4x^2 + 4x + 2}$

7) $\lim\limits_{x \to -\infty}$ $\dfrac{4x^2 + 4x - 2}{4x - 3}$

8) $\lim\limits_{x \to \infty}$ $2x - 1$

9) $\lim\limits_{x \to -\infty}$ $\dfrac{-2\tan(-3x - 2) + 1}{4x^2 + 4x}$

10) $\lim\limits_{x \to \infty}$ $\dfrac{4x^2 + 4x + 4}{-3\tan(-2x + 3) + 3}$

3 Minute Drill

56 ÷ 8 =	12 ÷ 2 =	7 ÷ 1 =	18 ÷ 3 =	36 ÷ 4 =
33 ÷ 11 =	18 ÷ 6 =	22 ÷ 11 =	30 ÷ 6 =	10 ÷ 5 =
28 ÷ 7 =	6 ÷ 3 =	48 ÷ 6 =	2 ÷ 2 =	36 ÷ 9 =
3 ÷ 1 =	5 ÷ 1 =	15 ÷ 3 =	2 ÷ 1 =	5 ÷ 5 =
27 ÷ 9 =	1 ÷ 1 =	6 ÷ 3 =	20 ÷ 10 =	22 ÷ 11 =
2 ÷ 1 =	99 ÷ 11 =	15 ÷ 5 =	24 ÷ 8 =	14 ÷ 2 =
4 ÷ 2 =	28 ÷ 4 =	12 ÷ 4 =	35 ÷ 7 =	72 ÷ 8 =
27 ÷ 9 =	24 ÷ 6 =	30 ÷ 5 =	21 ÷ 7 =	6 ÷ 1 =
20 ÷ 5 =	24 ÷ 12 =	20 ÷ 10 =	4 ÷ 4 =	45 ÷ 9 =
55 ÷ 11 =	18 ÷ 6 =	81 ÷ 9 =	9 ÷ 3 =	24 ÷ 12 =
40 ÷ 5 =	42 ÷ 7 =	8 ÷ 8 =	70 ÷ 10 =	12 ÷ 12 =
3 ÷ 1 =	48 ÷ 8 =	11 ÷ 11 =	35 ÷ 5 =	18 ÷ 9 =

9) 218   6) 588   4) 104

4) 199   6) 171   5) 165

6) 507   9) 207   3) 276

Find the Missing Number

1) $N \div 13 = 35$ N = _____   2) $464 \div N = 16$ N = _____

3) $N \div 17 = 38$ N = _____   4) $N \div 16 = 27$ N = _____

5) $558 \div N = 18$ N = _____   6) $N \div 19 = 19$ N = _____

7) $N \div 17 = 27$ N = _____   8) $N \div 20 = 15$ N = _____

9) $570 \div N = 15$ N = _____   10) $N \div 24 = 30$ N = _____

11) $N \div 15 = 40$ N = _____   12) $680 \div N = 40$ N = _____

13) $N \div 31 = 40$ N = _____   14) $308 \div N = 28$ N = _____

15) $1482 \div N = 39$ N = _____   16) $323 \div N = 17$ N = _____

17) $N \div 32 = 36$ N = _____   18) $1280 \div N = 32$ N = _____

19) $N \div 31 = 25$ N = _____   20) $1330 \div N = 38$ N = _____

21) $310 \div N = 10$ N = _____   22) $532 \div N = 38$ N = _____

23) $N \div 40 = 35$ N = _____   24) $1520 \div N = 38$ N = _____

25) $N \div 33 = 40$ N = _____   26) $N \div 25 = 36$ N = _____

27) $N \div 16 = 27$ N = _____   28) $552 \div N = 23$ N = _____

29) $N \div 10 = 12$ N = _____   30) $272 \div N = 16$ N = _____

$4 \overline{)52}$ $7 \overline{)222}$ $3 \overline{)45}$ $9 \overline{)817}$

$6 \overline{)150}$ $2 \overline{)52}$ $6 \overline{)63}$ $9 \overline{)166}$

$2 \overline{)192}$ $7 \overline{)413}$ $7 \overline{)168}$ $5 \overline{)64}$

$2 \overline{)191}$ $3 \overline{)46}$ $4 \overline{)263}$ $6 \overline{)480}$

$5 \overline{)313}$ $8 \overline{)701}$ $3 \overline{)99}$ $8 \overline{)376}$

44 ÷ 4 =

11 ÷ 11 =

21 ÷ 3 =

32 ÷ 8 =

45 ÷ 9 =

60 ÷ 5 =

30 ÷ 3 =

120 ÷ 10 =

11 ÷ 11 =

8 ÷ 1 =

72 ÷ 6 =

45 ÷ 5 =

12 ÷ 2 =

88 ÷ 11 =

2 ÷ 1 =

36 ÷ 12 =

81 ÷ 9 =

20 ÷ 4 =

35 ÷ 5 =

100 ÷ 10 =

96 ÷ 12 =

24 ÷ 12 =

20 ÷ 10 =

6 ÷ 2 =

21 ÷ 7 =

22 ÷ 2 =

6 ÷ 1 =

27 ÷ 3 =

32 ÷ 8 =

60 ÷ 6 =

Solve each division problem. Write out any remainders in decimal form.

$4\overline{)7.54}$ $\qquad$ $4\overline{)2.92}$ $\qquad$ $4\overline{)5.95}$

$9\overline{)1.08}$ $\qquad$ $7\overline{)7.80}$ $\qquad$ $9\overline{)1.47}$

$2\overline{)3.72}$ $\qquad$ $5\overline{)6.43}$ $\qquad$ $9\overline{)9.81}$

$7\overline{)2.52}$ $\qquad$ $2\overline{)5.94}$ $\qquad$ $2\overline{)4.40}$

$6\overline{)8.69}$ $\qquad$ $7\overline{)7.35}$ $\qquad$ $8\overline{)1.52}$

$8\overline{)5.92}$ $\qquad$ $3\overline{)4.30}$ $\qquad$ $6\overline{)7.76}$

$5\overline{)4.65}$ $\qquad$ $3\overline{)6.06}$ $\qquad$ $5\overline{)6.44}$

What is the slope of each line ?

1) 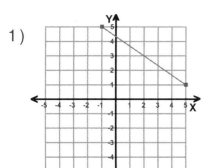   Slope = _____

2) 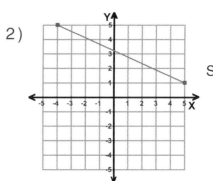   Slope = _____

3) 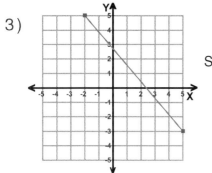   Slope = _____

4) 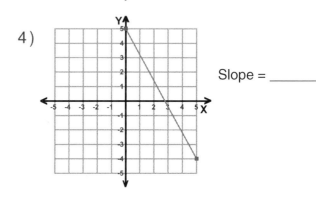   Slope = _____

5) $y = 1 x + 3$ Slope = _____

6) $y = -\frac{1}{2} x - 3$ Slope = _____

7) $y = \frac{3}{5} x - 2$ Slope = _____

8) $y = -\frac{7}{8} x + 1$ Slope = _____

Write the slope-intercept form and plot the equation of each line given the slope and y-interccept.

9) 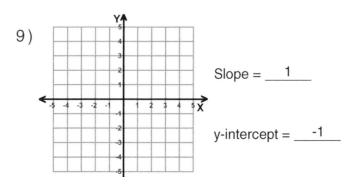   Slope = ___1___

y-intercept = ___-1___

Equation : _____

10)   Slope = ___3___

y-intercept = ___2___

Equation : _____

Equivalent Ratios

1)   5 : 8 = 10 : __ = __ :24   __ :32   25 : __ = 30 : __

2)   1 : 3 = 2 : __ = 3 : __ = __ :12 = __ :15 = __ :18

3)   2 : 3 = __ : 6 = 6 : __ = 8 : __ = 10 : __ = __ :18

4)   1 :10 = __ :20 = 3 : __ = __ :40 = __ :50 = __ :60

5)   3 : 5 = 6 : __ = __ :15   __ :20   __ :25   18 : __

6)   1 : 4 = __ : 8   3 : __ = __ :16   5 : __ = __ :24

7)   1 : 2 = __ : 4   __ : 6   __ : 8   __ :10   6 : __

8)   1 : 2 = __ : 4   __ : 6   __ : 8   __ :10   6 : __

9)   4 : 9 = __ :18   __ :27   __ :36   __ :45   24 : __

10)   1 : 7 = 2 : __ = 3 : __ = __ :28   __ :35   __ :42

Estimating Sums and Differences to the Nearest Tens

Estimate the sum or difference by rounding each number to the nearest ten.

1)   94 ———>
    - 11 ———>   - _____

2)   48 ———>
    + 24 ———>   + _____

3)   84 ———>
    - 16 ———>   - _____

4)   93 ———>
    + 49 ———>   + _____

5)   72 ———>
    + 62 ———>   + _____

6)   69 ———>
    - 38 ———>   - _____

7)   66 ———>
    - 55 ———>   - _____

8)   82 ———>
    - 18 ———>   - _____

9)   57 ———>
    + 14 ———>   + _____

10)   65 ———>
     + 34 ———>   + _____

11)   41 ———>
     - 22 ———>   - _____

12)   35 ———>
     + 28 ———>   + _____

13)   37 ———>
     - 36 ———>   - _____

14)   85 ———>
     + 54 ———>   + _____

Even and Odd Numbers with Tables

Color the odd numbers green.

890	822	920	994	508	662	535	679
843	691	711	835	966	539	668	933

Color the even numbers blue.

874	692	588	967	861	959	944	989
521	681	833	859	703	536	571	950

Color the even numbers blue, and color the odd numbers green.

748	608	577	885	558	838	900
976	646	659	982	922	623	863
914	917	607	551	972	797	697
718	901	819	765	739	715	529

Exponents with Multiplication and Division

Simplify. Your answer should contain only positive exponents.

1) $3ng^5 \cdot 2n^2g^3$

7) $\dfrac{k}{k^{-4}}$

2) $3y^6 \cdot 6y^{-2}$

8) $\dfrac{8r^{-5}g^{-4}}{5rg^{-3}}$

3) $2 \cdot 2^5$

9) $k \cdot k^{-6}$

4) $\dfrac{8w^6}{5w}$

10) $\left(\dfrac{1}{s}\right)^4 \cdot \left(\dfrac{1}{s}\right)^5$

5) $\dfrac{6^4}{6}$

11) $\dfrac{2d}{6d^{-6}}$

6) $\dfrac{6^5}{6^4}$

12) $s^3b^{-5} \cdot 2s^{-4}b^6 \cdot 3sb^2$

Evaluate the Exponents

1) $(12)^3$ = _____

2) $(9)^3$ = _____

3) $(-5)^2$ = _____

4) $(-8)^3$ = _____

5) $(-2)^2$ = _____

6) $(-12)^2$ = _____

7) $(3)^3$ = _____

8) $(6)^2$ = _____

9) $(-3)^3$ = _____

10) $(-6)^2$ = _____

11) $(-7)^3$ = _____

12) $(7)^2$ = _____

13) $(-9)^2$ = _____

14) $(10)^3$ = _____

15) $(-4)^3$ = _____

16) $(2)^2$ = _____

17) $(8)^3$ = _____

18) $(3)^3$ = _____

19) $(5)^2$ = _____

20) $(-2)^2$ = _____

Complete Each Family of Facts

1)
△ 19 / 11 8

☐ + ☐ = ☐
☐ + ☐ = ☐
☐ - ☐ = ☐
☐ - ☐ = ☐

4)
△ 12 / 7 5

☐ + ☐ = ☐
☐ + ☐ = ☐
☐ - ☐ = ☐
☐ - ☐ = ☐

2)
△ 12 / 11 1

☐ + ☐ = ☐
☐ + ☐ = ☐
☐ - ☐ = ☐
☐ - ☐ = ☐

5)
△ 14 / 4 10

☐ + ☐ = ☐
☐ + ☐ = ☐
☐ - ☐ = ☐
☐ - ☐ = ☐

3)
△ 15 / 6 9

☐ + ☐ = ☐
☐ + ☐ = ☐
☐ - ☐ = ☐
☐ - ☐ = ☐

6)
△ 19 / 9 10

☐ + ☐ = ☐
☐ + ☐ = ☐
☐ - ☐ = ☐
☐ - ☐ = ☐

Complete Each Family of Facts

1)
△ 15 / 3 5

☐ X ☐ = ☐
☐ X ☐ = ☐
☐ ÷ ☐ = ☐
☐ ÷ ☐ = ☐

4)

☐ X ☐ = ☐
☐ X ☐ = ☐
☐ ÷ ☐ = ☐
☐ ÷ ☐ = ☐

2)
△ 18 / 9 2

☐ X ☐ = ☐
☐ X ☐ = ☐
☐ ÷ ☐ = ☐
☐ ÷ ☐ = ☐

5)
△ 28 / 7 4

☐ X ☐ = ☐
☐ X ☐ = ☐
☐ ÷ ☐ = ☐
☐ ÷ ☐ = ☐

3)
△ 24 / 4 6

☐ X ☐ = ☐
☐ X ☐ = ☐
☐ ÷ ☐ = ☐
☐ ÷ ☐ = ☐

6)
△ 48 / 6 8

☐ X ☐ = ☐
☐ X ☐ = ☐
☐ ÷ ☐ = ☐
☐ ÷ ☐ = ☐

Find the Prime Factors of the Numbers

1)
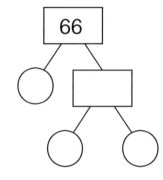

Prime Factors
_ X _ X _ = 66

2)
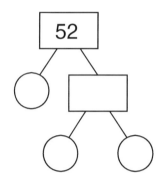

Prime Factors
_ X _ X _ = 52

3)
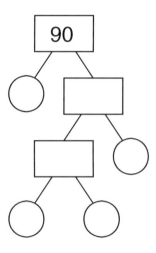

Prime Factors
_ X _ X _ X _ = 90

4)
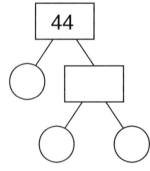

Prime Factors
_ X _ X _ = 44

5)
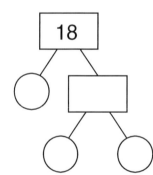

Prime Factors
_ X _ X _ = 18

6)
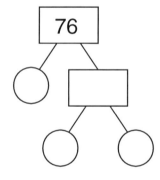

Prime Factors
_ X _ X _ = 76

Visually Adding Simple Fractions

1)

$$\frac{1}{11} + \frac{7}{11} = \underline{\qquad}$$

2)

$$\frac{1}{10} + \frac{7}{10} = \underline{\qquad}$$

3)

$$\frac{1}{5} + \frac{3}{5} = \underline{\qquad}$$

4)

$$\frac{2}{11} + \frac{6}{11} = \underline{\qquad}$$

5)

$$\frac{3}{7} + \frac{3}{7} = \underline{\qquad}$$

Score : _____

Date : _____

Write the Correct Comparison Symbol (>, < or =) in Each Box

1) $\dfrac{5}{7}$ ☐ $\dfrac{6}{7}$

2) $\dfrac{1}{5}$ ☐ $\dfrac{4}{6}$

3) $\dfrac{-2}{3}$ ☐ $\dfrac{-1}{9}$

4) $\dfrac{2}{5}$ ☐ $\dfrac{3}{5}$

5) $\dfrac{-3}{4}$ ☐ $\dfrac{-5}{7}$

6) $\dfrac{5}{6}$ ☐ $\dfrac{2}{8}$

7) $\dfrac{1}{2}$ ☐ $\dfrac{1}{6}$

8) $\dfrac{-1}{6}$ ☐ $\dfrac{-1}{2}$

9) $\dfrac{-1}{4}$ ☐ $\dfrac{-3}{7}$

10) $\dfrac{-4}{6}$ ☐ $\dfrac{-1}{4}$

11) $\dfrac{-8}{9}$ ☐ $\dfrac{-7}{9}$

12) $\dfrac{1}{2}$ ☐ $\dfrac{7}{8}$

13) $\dfrac{-2}{4}$ ☐ $\dfrac{-3}{5}$

14) $\dfrac{-6}{8}$ ☐ $\dfrac{-5}{6}$

15) $\dfrac{1}{3}$ ☐ $\dfrac{1}{9}$

16) $\dfrac{1}{2}$ ☐ $\dfrac{1}{3}$

17) $\dfrac{-3}{9}$ ☐ $\dfrac{-2}{3}$

18) $\dfrac{-4}{5}$ ☐ $\dfrac{-2}{9}$

19) $\dfrac{6}{7}$ ☐ $\dfrac{1}{7}$

20) $\dfrac{5}{8}$ ☐ $\dfrac{1}{2}$

Multiplying Fractions with Cross Canceling

1) $\dfrac{1}{3} \times \dfrac{1}{2} =$

2) $\dfrac{1}{4} \times \dfrac{1}{5} =$

3) $\dfrac{2}{5} \times \dfrac{2}{4} =$

4) $\dfrac{8}{10} \times \dfrac{2}{5} =$

5) $\dfrac{1}{2} \times \dfrac{1}{3} =$

6) $\dfrac{1}{3} \times \dfrac{1}{2} =$

7) $\dfrac{1}{3} \times \dfrac{2}{5} =$

8) $\dfrac{3}{4} \times \dfrac{1}{2} =$

9) $\dfrac{2}{3} \times \dfrac{1}{2} =$

10) $\dfrac{1}{2} \times \dfrac{4}{5} =$

11) $\dfrac{1}{2} \times \dfrac{2}{10} =$

12) $\dfrac{3}{5} \times \dfrac{3}{4} =$

13) $\dfrac{5}{10} \times \dfrac{1}{2} =$

14) $\dfrac{1}{3} \times \dfrac{7}{10} =$

15) $\dfrac{2}{4} \times \dfrac{2}{3} =$

Complete the function table for each equation.

1) $y = \frac{1}{5}x - 8$

x	y
2	
3	
-2	
6	
-3	

5) $y = -8x + 6$

x	y
3	
-6	
4	
9	
2	

9) $y = x + 7$

x	y
5	
0	
-8	
8	
-6	

2) $y = -9x + 4$

x	y
9	
6	
-1	
-4	
-6	

6) $y = x - 5$

x	y
-9	
-7	
0	
-1	
3	

10) $y = 9x - 4$

x	y
8	
-8	
-3	
5	
2	

3) $y = 6x$

x	y
8	
6	
-4	
4	
2	

7) $y = 3x$

x	y
8	
1	
-7	
7	
-3	

11) $y = \frac{1}{4}x + 2$

x	y
6	
7	
3	
4	
-7	

4) $y = x - 2$

x	y
6	
-5	
1	
-6	
-3	

8) $y = -4x$

x	y
-1	
-2	
-7	
4	
-9	

12) $y = \frac{1}{7}x + 9$

x	y
5	
7	
0	
1	
-1	

Double Line Graph Comprehension

Graph the given information as a line graph.

Time on Monday	Degrees Celsius	
	Richmond	Atlanta
6AM	16	12
10AM	28	8
2PM	24	16
6PM	32	32
10PM	8	4

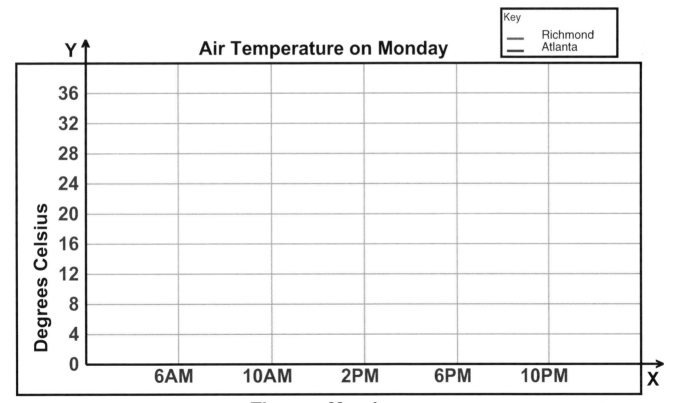

Reading Pie Graphs

John tracked the time he spent on homework per topic during one week. Answer the questions based on the pie graph below.

Time Spent on Homework

1) What percentage of time did John spend on the English and Art homework?   _____

2) If John spent 100 minutes on homework, how many minutes were spent on Health?   _____

3) Combined, which two topics required the greatest amount of time?   _____

4) Was the Math and Spanish work or the History and Health work longer; or were they equally time consuming?   _____

5) Between Math and Spanish which topic took longer; or did they require equal time?   _____

History 15%
Spanish 12%
Math 13%
Art 23%
English 27%
Health 10%

A local pizzeria tracked which pizza toppings customers purchased. Answer the questions based on the pie graph below.

Most Purchased Pizza Topping

1) Were onion and ham picked more than the bacon and sausage; or were they equally bought?   _____

2) Combined, which two toppings did the greatest number of customers choose?   _____

3) If there were 200 customers that were tracked, how many bought sausage?   _____

4) What percentage of customers chose either the beef or the olives?   _____

5) Between onion and ham which topping was more popular; or were they equally popular?   _____

olives 13%
onion 12%
ham 10%
bacon 28%
sausage 22%
beef 15%

Single Line Graphing

Graph the given information as a line graph.

Day	Eggs Laid
Mon	60
Tues	24
Wed	36
Thu	60
Fri	48
Sat	72
Sun	60

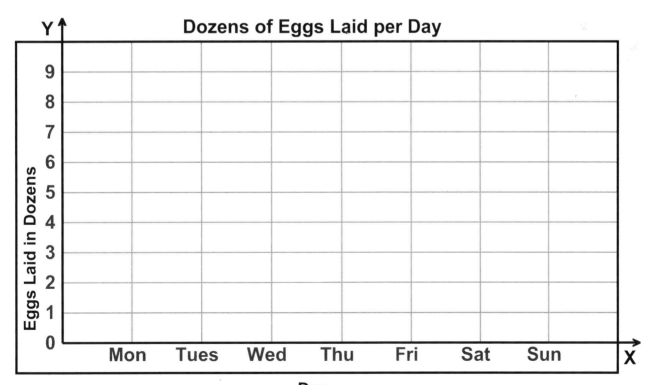

Dozens of Eggs Laid per Day

Ordering Whole Numbers

Order the numbers from greatest to least.

1)

981,073
621,733
845,052
188,220

	Thousands			Ones		
	Hundreds	Tens	Ones	Hundreds	Tens	Ones
greatest ->						
least ->						

Answer: _____

2)

560,733
891,665
455,665
811,511

	Thousands			Ones		
	Hundreds	Tens	Ones	Hundreds	Tens	Ones
greatest ->						
least ->						

Answer: _____

3)

564,909
537,062
322,823
374,785

	Thousands			Ones		
	Hundreds	Tens	Ones	Hundreds	Tens	Ones
greatest ->						
least ->						

Answer: _____

4)

145,499
607,787
109,559
842,522

	Thousands			Ones		
	Hundreds	Tens	Ones	Hundreds	Tens	Ones
greatest ->						
least ->						

Answer: _____

Find the Greatest Common Factor for each number pair.

1)   6 , 30   _____

2)   24 , 40   _____

3)   15 , 4   _____

4)   30 , 8   _____

5)   30 , 2   _____

6)   12 , 40   _____

7)   5 , 6   _____

8)   40 , 8   _____

9)   24 , 4   _____

10)   4 , 30   _____

11)   20 , 6   _____

12)   40 , 10   _____

13)   24 , 40   _____

14)   40 , 6   _____

15)   40 , 15   _____

16)   3 , 8   _____

17)   10 , 30   _____

18)   6 , 8   _____

19)   2 , 40   _____

20)   40 , 4   _____

Identify the Lines, Rays or Line Segments.

1)

_____

2)

_____

3)

_____

4)

_____

5)

_____

6)

_____

7)

_____

8)

_____

9)

_____

1) Absolute value of -5 is _____

2) Absolute value of 10 is _____

3) Absolute value of 10 is _____

4) Absolute value of -4 is _____

5) Absolute value of 6 is _____

6) Absolute value of -10 is _____

7) Absolute value of 7 is _____

8) Absolute value of -6 is _____

9) Absolute value of 8 is _____

10) Absolute value of -1 is _____

11) Absolute value of 9 is _____

12) Absolute value of 3 is _____

13) Absolute value of 2 is _____

14) Absolute value of 6 is _____

15) Absolute value of -5 is _____

16) Absolute value of -2 is _____

17) Absolute value of 2 is _____

18) Absolute value of 8 is _____

19) Absolute value of 1 is _____

20) Absolute value of 8 is _____

21) Absolute value of 2 is _____

22) Absolute value of 10 is _____

23) Absolute value of 7 is _____

24) Absolute value of -7 is _____

25) Absolute value of -5 is _____

26) Absolute value of -2 is _____

27) Absolute value of 1 is _____

28) Absolute value of -7 is _____

29) Absolute value of -5 is _____

30) Absolute value of 2 is _____

1) $(+7) + (-3) =$

2) $(+8) + (+3) =$

3) $(+8) + (+1) =$

4) $(+7) + (-7) =$

5) $(-2) + (-1) =$

6) $(-3) + (-3) =$

7) $(-2) + (-2) =$

8) $(+3) + (-4) =$

9) $(-3) + (+8) =$

10) $(+1) + (-9) =$

11) $(-5) + (+7) =$

12) $(-8) + (+5) =$

13) $(+9) + (-9) =$

14) $(-7) + (+4) =$

15) $(+1) + (-1) =$

16) $(+6) + (+6) =$

17) $(-9) + (-4) =$

18) $(-1) + (-1) =$

19) $(-3) + (-7) =$

20) $(-5) + (+7) =$

21) $(+3) + (+4) =$

22) $(-5) + (+7) =$

23) $(+8) + (+4) =$

24) $(+6) + (-3) =$

25) $(-4) + (+9) =$

26) $(-6) + (-4) =$

27) $(+4) + (+5) =$

28) $(+4) + (+7) =$

29) $(-2) + (-3) =$

30) $(+7) + (+2) =$

1) (+8) x (+4) =

2) (+6) x (+8) =

3) (+3) x (+8) =

4) (+2) x (+7) =

5) (0) x (+1) =

6) (0) x (+9) =

7) (+2) x (+7) =

8) (+8) x (+6) =

9) (+1) x (+4) =

10) (+5) x (0) =

11) (+7) x (+3) =

12) (0) x (+8) =

13) (+7) x (+8) =

14) (+5) x (0) =

15) (+8) x (+5) =

16) (+5) x (+4) =

17) (+6) x (+1) =

18) (+8) x (+2) =

19) (+3) x (+2) =

20) (+1) x (+6) =

21) (+7) x (+7) =

22) (+5) x (+9) =

23) (+7) x (0) =

24) (+6) x (+6) =

25) (+4) x (+6) =

26) (+4) x (+2) =

27) (+1) x (+1) =

28) (+3) x (+4) =

29) (0) x (+2) =

30) (+6) x (+1) =

Find the Least Common Multiple for each number pair.

1)   12 , 20   _____

2)   2 , 5   _____

3)   15 , 5   _____

4)   6 , 10   _____

5)   5 , 30   _____

6)   3 , 40   _____

7)   4 , 15   _____

8)   24 , 8   _____

9)   3 , 15   _____

10)   3 , 24   _____

11) 10 , 24   _____

12) 10 , 6   _____

13)   6 , 12   _____

14) 30 , 15   _____

15) 15 , 20   _____

16) 30 , 15   _____

17)   8 , 10   _____

18) 10 , 24   _____

19) 12 , 24   _____

20) 30 , 4   _____

Mean, Mode, Median, and Range

1) -6, -2, -7, 4, 3, -4

Mean _____ Median _____ Mode _____ Range _____

6) -9, 6, -7, -9, 9

Mean _____ Median _____ Mode _____ Range _____

2) -5, 6, 9, 2, -4, -7, -5, 8, 5

Mean _____ Median _____ Mode _____ Range _____

7) 1, -9, 3, 8, 7, 2

Mean _____ Median _____ Mode _____ Range _____

3) -1, -1, 4, 3, 3, 8, 8, 5, -7, -2

Mean _____ Median _____ Mode _____ Range _____

8) 2, -2, -6, -6, -10, 6, 5, 5, -4, 0

Mean _____ Median _____ Mode _____ Range _____

4) 1, 6, 7, -1, 6, 1, -7, 3

Mean _____ Median _____ Mode _____ Range _____

9) -6, 7, 4, -6, -1, 5, -3

Mean _____ Median _____ Mode _____ Range _____

5) 1, -2, 9, 5, -3

Mean _____ Median _____ Mode _____ Range _____

10) -3, 5, 7, 7, 9, -1, -2, 7, 7

Mean _____ Median _____ Mode _____ Range _____

Number Lines

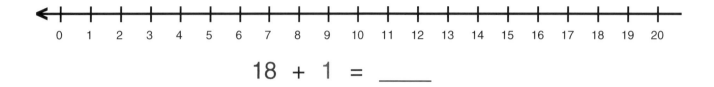

18 + 1 = _____

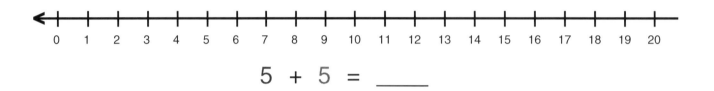

5 + 5 = _____

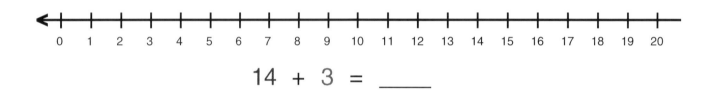

14 + 3 = _____

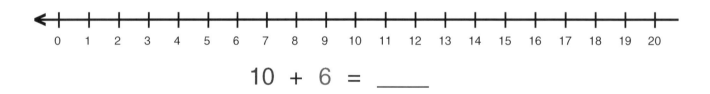

10 + 6 = _____

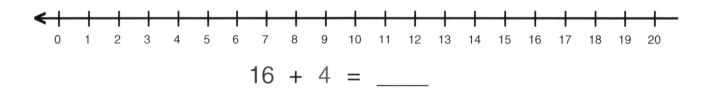

16 + 4 = _____

Order of Operations

1) 18 ÷ 6 x 5 - 2

2) 16 ÷ 2 +14 x 8

3) 11 x 5 - 3 +13

4) 6 x 11 +24 ÷ 3

5) 4 x 15 ÷ 5 +19

6) 6 - 1 x 12 + 7

7) 12 ÷ 4 x 2 - 1

8) 11 - 20 ÷ 5 x 17

9) 8 + 6 - 4 x 10

10) 16 - 16 ÷ 2 +16

Order of Operations

1) 6 + 4 - 1 x 12

2) 19 + 10 x 6 + 12

3) 18 + 7 + 18 x 4

4) 11 + 6 x 10 - 8

5) 9 x 9 - 2 + 18

6) 7 x 17 + 15 - 8

7) 7 - 1 x 6 + 3

8) 15 + 6 - 4 x 11

9) 11 - 4 + 4 x 13

10) 4 x 19 - 16 + 5

Percentage Calculations

Round your answer to two decimal places.

1) 0.65 x 98 = ____

6) 68 ÷ 93 = ___ %

2) 20 ÷ 18 % = ____

7) 0.62 x 71 = ____

3) 90% x 56 = ____

8) 95 ÷ 0.23 = ____

4) 60 ÷ 0.78 = ____

9) 90% x 81 = ____

5) 42 ÷ 49 = ___ %

10) 71 ÷ 61 % = ____

Identify and Calculate the Area and Perimeter for each Triangle.

1)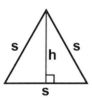

s = 7 cm

h = 6.1 cm

Area: _____

Perimeter: _____

Type: _____

2)

s = 5.1 cm

h = 4.4 cm

Area: _____

Perimeter: _____

Type: _____

3)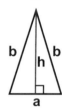

a = 4.4 ft   b = 8 ft

h = 7.4 ft

Area: _____

Perimeter: _____

Type: _____

4)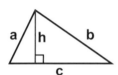

a = 4.92 ft

c = 8.7 ft

Area: _____

Perimeter: _____

Type: _____

5)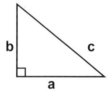

a = 7.5 inches   b = 6 inches

c = 9.6 inches

Area: _____

Perimeter: _____

Type: _____

6)

s = 7.1 mm

h = 6.1 mm

Area: _____

Perimeter: _____

Type: _____

7)

a = 4.2 inches   b = 6.6 inches

h = 6.1 inches

Area: _____

Perimeter: _____

Type: _____

8)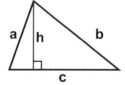

a = 6.05 mm   b = 9.31 mm

c = 9.4 mm   h = 5.7 mm

Area: _____

Perimeter: _____

Type: _____

9)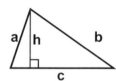

a = 5.18 yds   b = 8.65 yds

c = 8.8 yds   h = 4.9 yds

Area: _____

Perimeter: _____

Type: _____

Write the Names for the Numbers.

1)   7,397   _____

_____

2)   6,831   _____

_____

3)   3,887   _____

_____

4)   7,427   _____

_____

5)   9,885   _____

_____

6)   1,537   _____

_____

7)   5,924   _____

_____

8)   7,147   _____

_____

9)   4,718   _____

_____

10)   7,222   _____

_____

Write out the Correct Number Name.

1) 159,785,728,298 _____

2)   95,883,459 _____

3) 791,695,257,252 _____

4) 77,414,744,518 _____

5)   3,998,939,662 _____

6)   6,453,291 _____

7)   2,165,633 _____

8)   27,894,813 _____

9)   852,371,825 _____

10)   141,339,361 _____

Write the Numbers in Standard Form.

1) _____ 20 + 7

2) _____ 40 + 4

3) _____ 40 + 8

4) _____ 80 + 6

5) _____ 80 + 5

6) _____ 40 + 0

7) _____ 60 + 1

8) _____ 70 + 0

9) _____ 20 + 3

10) _____ 90 + 1

11) _____ 40 + 6

12) _____ 80 + 2

13) _____ 10 + 2

14) _____ 30 + 9

15) _____ 90 + 4

Solve and Graph the Inequalities

1) p - 7 > 10

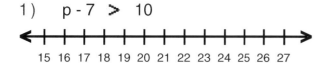

2) 5 + k ≥ 10

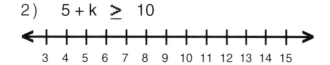

3) 4 + f < 15

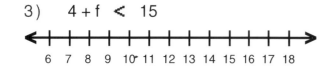

4) -2 + g ≤ 6

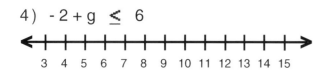

5) 14 ≥ s + 3

6) 10 ≤ - 4 +

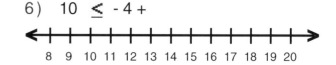

7) 14 ≥ 7 + x

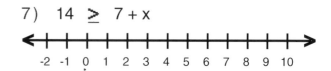

8) 2 + n ≤ 17

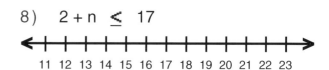

9) 4 + h > 12

10) y + 5 > 9

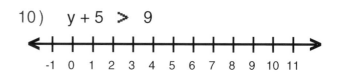

Identifying Polynomials

Identify the type for each.

1) $5k^3x - 6y$

2) $8xs^6b^4 - 6k^7 + 7r^5n^3 - 2n^5y^2$

3) $- 8s^2g^6 + 2r^5 - 5p^4c^7 - 7d^4q^2 + 9q^7h^3$

4) $- gc^3 - 2r^5 + 4x^6q^7 - 5h^2z^7$

5) $- b + p - y + k$

6) $- 6z^6q - 2r + 7c + 9s - 3n - 4g$

7) $rz^3k^5 + 6p^2 + 7n^6q^4 - 9q^5g^6 + 5b^2$

8) $2q^7x^5 + 9s^4 - 8g^3k^6 - 4n^3b^7 + 3b^6r^2 + 3r$

9) $4ph^3 - 8q^4 + 5y^2s^5 + 7k^3z^5$

10) $sn^6g^5 - 6z^4 + 4b^3y^2 + 3y^5p^3 + 9q^4 - 2q$

Translate Algebraic Expressions

1) Product of 2 and f   _____

2) Sum of 2 and c   _____

3) Take away 4 from s   _____

4) 7 less than 8 times w   _____

5) 5 is subtracted from b   _____

6) Two-thirds of b is added to the product of 5 and q   _____

7) 3 times the sum of m and 9   _____

8) Add 7 to 8 times w   _____

9) Subtract three-fifths from 2 times s   _____

10) 9 is added to three-fourths of y   _____

Score : _____

Date : _____

Working with Properties

1) Which of the following is an example of Commutative Property of Addition ?

    A. 4 + 6 = 6 + 4   **B.** 7 x 1 = 7   _____

    C. 2 + 3 = 5 + 2   **D.** (6 + 9) + 8 = 6 + (9 + 8)

2) Which Property of Multiplication is shown ?   (5 + 8) x 4 = 5 x 4 + 8 x 4

    A. Distributive Property   **B.** Commutative Property   _____

    C. Associative Property   **D.** Identity Property

3) Which is an example of Associative Property of Addition ?

    A. 3 + 5 = 5 + 3   **B.** (5 + 4) + 8 = 5 + (4 + 8)   _____

    C. 7 + (-7) = 0   **D.** 9 + 0 = 9

4) Which property would you use to simplify the following expression ?

    A. Multiplication Property of Zero   **B.** Commutative Property   _____

    C. Associative Property   **D.** Distributive Property

5) Which of the following does not show the Commutative Property of Addition ?

    A. 3x + 4y = 4y + 3x   **B.** ab = ba   _____

    C. 5 + x = x + 5   **D.** a + b = b + a

6) Which operation will not change the value of any nonzero number ?

    A. Adding One   **B.** Multiplying by One   _____

    C. Dividing by Zero   **D.** Multiplying by Zero

7) Which equation shows the Identity Property of Multiplication ?

    A. a(b + c) = ab + ac   **B.** a + a + a = 3 x a   _____

    C. (a + b) + 6 = a + (6 + b)   **D.** a x 1

8) Which property is used in the following expression ?   (a x b) x c = a x (b x c)

    A. Associative Property of Addition   **B.** Distributive Property   _____

    C. Associative Property of Multiplication   **D.** Commutative Property of Addition

9) Which property is used in the following ?

    A. Commutative Property   **B.** Distributive Property   _____

    C. Associative Property   **D.** None of the above

10) Which of the following does not show the Commutative Property ?

    A. x + y = y + x   **B.** 7 + y = y + 7   _____

    C. yx = xy   **D.** xy - 2 = xy

Working with the Properties of Mathematics

11) Which Property of Addition does 2 + 0 = 2 illustrate ?

    A. Identity Property   **B.** Zero Property

    C. Commutative Property   **D.** Distributive Property   ———

12) Which is an example of Identity Property of Addition ?

    A. 3 + 7 = 7 + 3   **B.** 4 x 1 = 4

    C. (7 + 6) + 8 = 7 + (6 + 8)   **D.** 2 + 0 = 2   ———

13) Which equation shows the Commutative Property of Multiplication ?

    A. 6 x 1 = 6   **B.** 3 x 3 = 3 + 3 + 3

    C. 4 x 9 = 9 x 4   **D.** 7 x 2 - 5 x 2 = (7 - 5) x 3   ———

14) Simplify this expression : 6(y + z)

    A. 6z + y   **B.** 6y + z

    C. 6yz   **D.** 6y + 6z   ———

15) Which property is used in the following expression ?   (3 x 6) x 9 = 6 x (9 x 3)

    A. Associative Property of Multiplication   **B.** Commutative Property of Addition   ———

    C. Associative Property of Addition   **D.** Distributive Property of Multiplication

16) Which property of addition is used in the following ?   (7 + 5) + 9 = 7 + (5 + 9)

    A. Identity Property   **B.** Distributive Property   ———

    C. Commutative Property   **D.** Associative Property

17) Which property is used in the following expression ?   2(5 + 4) = 10 + 8

    A. Distributive Property   **B.** Associative Property of Multiplication

    C. Associative Property of Addition   **D.** Commutative Property of Addition   ———

Equivalent Ratios

Write two equivalent ratios.

1) $\dfrac{7}{8}$ ⬚⬚

2) $\dfrac{5}{7}$ ⬚⬚

3) $\dfrac{9}{5}$ ⬚⬚

4) $\dfrac{11}{5}$ ⬚⬚

5) $\dfrac{10}{3}$ ⬚⬚

6) $\dfrac{11}{6}$ ⬚⬚

Determine whether the ratios are equivalent.

7) $\dfrac{5}{11}$ and $\dfrac{20}{44}$ _____

8) $\dfrac{2}{7}$ and $\dfrac{7}{10}$ _____

9) $\dfrac{3}{11}$ and $\dfrac{6}{5}$ _____

10) $\dfrac{12}{5}$ and $\dfrac{8}{3}$ _____

11) $\dfrac{3}{8}$ and $\dfrac{6}{16}$ _____

12) $\dfrac{7}{11}$ and $\dfrac{7}{3}$ _____

Use equivalent ratios to find the unknown value.

13) $\dfrac{n}{15} = \dfrac{7}{5}$ n = _____

14) $\dfrac{6}{7} = \dfrac{z}{49}$ z = _____

15) $\dfrac{2}{11} = \dfrac{4}{y}$ y = _____

16) $\dfrac{7}{2} = \dfrac{z}{12}$ z = _____

17) $\dfrac{5}{12} = \dfrac{25}{y}$ y = _____

18) $\dfrac{20}{r} = \dfrac{4}{7}$ r = _____

Scientific Notation

Write each number in standard format.

1) 5.525×10^{4} = _____

2) 3.7915×10^{-6} = _____

3) 2.57×10^{-9} = _____

4) 7.372×10^{-1} = _____

5) 3.34×10^{-8} = _____

6) 7.64×10^{-4} = _____

7) $7.52 \times {}^{4}$ = _____

8) 9.0674×10^{7} = _____

9) 9.508×10^{5} = _____

10) 8.384×10^{1} = _____

Write each number in scientific notation.

11)   9788000000   = _____

12)   0.0000003060   = _____

13)   0.005827   = _____

14)   8535.8   = _____

15)   851880000   = _____

16)   3550000   = _____

17)   945.4   = _____

18)   0.00087077   = _____

19)   0.00001820   = _____

20)   0.0984   = _____

Complete the Skip Counting Series

1) 71, 69, 67, ___, ___, ___, ___, ___, ___, ___

2) ___, 17, 7, -3, ___, ___, ___, ___, ___, ___

3) ___, ___, 53, ___, ___, -7, ___, ___, -67, ___

4) ___, 8, ___, ___, ___, 28, ___, ___, ___, 48

5) ___, ___, 34, ___, ___, 64, 74, ___, ___, ___

6) ___, ___, ___, ___, ___, 12, 14, ___, ___, 20

7) ___, 45, ___, ___, ___, ___, ___, ___, 59, 61

8) ___, 88, ___, ___, ___, ___, ___, 100, ___, 104

9) ___, ___, ___, 100, ___, ___, 106, ___, 110, ___

10) 36, ___, ___, 42, ___, 46, ___, ___, ___, ___

11) 65, ___, 69, ___, ___, ___, ___, 79, ___, ___

12) 89, ___, 93, ___, ___, ___, ___, ___, 105, ___

Complete the Skip Counting Series

1) 7 , 14 , 21 , __ , __ , __ , __ , __ , __ , __ , __ , __

2) 10 , 20 , 30 , __ , __ , __ , __ , __ , __ , __ , __ , __

3) 6 , 12 , 18 , __ , __ , __ , __ , __ , __ , __ , __ , __

4) 12 , 24 , 36 , __ , __ , __ , __ , __ , __ , __ , __ , __

5) 5 , 10 , 15 , __ , __ , __ , __ , __ , __ , __ , __ , __

6) 2 , 4 , 6 , __ , __ , __ , __ , __ , __ , __ , __ , __

7) 11 , 22 , 33 , __ , __ , __ , __ , __ , __ , __ , __ , __

8) 4 , 8 , 12 , __ , __ , __ , __ , __ , __ , __ , __ , __

9) 3 , 6 , 9 , __ , __ , __ , __ , __ , __ , __ , __ , __

10) 9 , 18 , 27 , __ , __ , __ , __ , __ , __ , __ , __ , __

11) 8 , 16 , 24 , __ , __ , __ , __ , __ , __ , __ , __ , __

Trigonometric Ratios

Find the given trigonometric ratio. The answer will be in fraction form.

1) cos B = _____

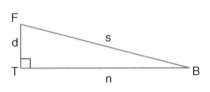

2) cos X = _____

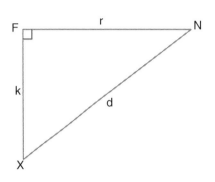

3) sin N = _____

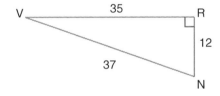

4) tan O = _____

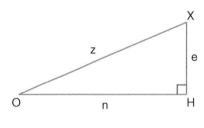

5) sin S = _____

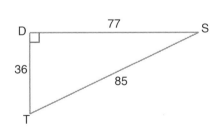

6) tan U = _____

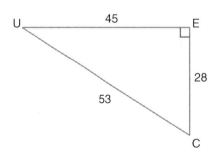

Word Problems

1) Tim worked on the farm storing bales of hay in the barn. The first day he stacked 40 bales and 20 bales on the second day. How many bales were stored in the barn?

_____

2) While fishing over the weekend Tim caught 12 and Mike caught 47 fish. How many fish were caught?

_____

3) The post office mails 74 letters each day, out of which 47 are addressed to foreign countries. How many letters are addressed domestically?

_____

4) Melanie is reading a book that contains 73 pages. She has read 27 pages. How many pages are unread?

_____

5) Sam painted his house with white and blue paint. He used a total of 76 gallons of paint. If he used 41 gallons of white paint, how many gallons of blue paint did he use?

_____

6) There are 79 lemons in the store, 31 lemon are sold by the end of the day. How many lemons are left in the store?

_____

7) Jessica and Mary decided to bake cookies for a family picnic. Jessica baked 38 raisin cookies and Mary baked 10 sugar cookies. How many cookies were baked?

_____

8) Benny scored 32 points in Monday's basketball game and 28 points in Friday's game. How many points did he score in the last two games?

_____

9) There are 22 scissors in the drawer. Fred placed 15 more scissors in the drawer. How many scissors are in the drawer?

_____

10) Tim's Cupcake Shop sold a total of 87 cupcakes yesterday, and 15 of those had sprinkles. How many cupcakes were sold without sprinkles?

_____

ANSWERS
Adding Fractions

1) $\dfrac{5}{7} + \dfrac{4}{7} = \dfrac{5}{7} + \dfrac{4}{7} = \dfrac{9}{7} = 1\dfrac{2}{7}$

2) $\dfrac{2}{8} + \dfrac{5}{8} = \dfrac{2}{8} + \dfrac{5}{8} = \dfrac{7}{8}$

3) $\dfrac{6}{7} + \dfrac{4}{7} = \dfrac{6}{7} + \dfrac{4}{7} = \dfrac{10}{7} = 1\dfrac{3}{7}$

4) $\dfrac{5}{4} + \dfrac{3}{4} = \dfrac{5}{4} + \dfrac{3}{4} = \dfrac{8}{4} = \dfrac{2}{1} = 2\dfrac{0}{1}$

5) $\dfrac{1}{8} + \dfrac{3}{8} = \dfrac{1}{8} + \dfrac{3}{8} = \dfrac{4}{8} = \dfrac{1}{2}$

6) $\dfrac{2}{6} + \dfrac{5}{6} = \dfrac{2}{6} + \dfrac{5}{6} = \dfrac{7}{6} = 1\dfrac{1}{6}$

7) $\dfrac{2}{6} + \dfrac{2}{6} = \dfrac{2}{6} + \dfrac{2}{6} = \dfrac{4}{6} = \dfrac{2}{3}$

8) $\dfrac{5}{4} + \dfrac{3}{4} = \dfrac{5}{4} + \dfrac{3}{4} = \dfrac{8}{4} = \dfrac{2}{1} = 2\dfrac{0}{1}$

9) $\dfrac{8}{8} + \dfrac{6}{8} = \dfrac{8}{8} + \dfrac{6}{8} = \dfrac{14}{8} = \dfrac{7}{4} = 1\dfrac{3}{4}$

10) $\dfrac{3}{7} + \dfrac{5}{7} = \dfrac{3}{7} + \dfrac{5}{7} = \dfrac{8}{7} = 1\dfrac{1}{7}$

11) $\dfrac{7}{9} + \dfrac{1}{9} = \dfrac{7}{9} + \dfrac{1}{9} = \dfrac{8}{9}$

12) $\dfrac{3}{9} + \dfrac{6}{9} = \dfrac{3}{9} + \dfrac{6}{9} = \dfrac{9}{9} = 1$

13) $\dfrac{2}{7} + \dfrac{4}{7} = \dfrac{2}{7} + \dfrac{4}{7} = \dfrac{6}{7}$

14) $\dfrac{3}{6} + \dfrac{2}{6} = \dfrac{3}{6} + \dfrac{2}{6} = \dfrac{5}{6}$

15) $\dfrac{3}{6} + \dfrac{5}{6} = \dfrac{3}{6} + \dfrac{5}{6} = \dfrac{8}{6} = \dfrac{4}{3} = 1\dfrac{1}{3}$

Greatest Common Factor ANSWERS

1) 15 , 3 _3_

2) 24 , 12 _12_

3) 10 , 4 _2_

4) 40 , 4 _4_

5) 8 , 40 _8_

6) 10 , 4 _2_

7) 12 , 20 _4_

8) 5 , 20 _5_

9) 8 , 2 _2_

10) 24 , 40 _8_

11) 6 , 8 _2_

12) 10 , 3 _1_

13) 8 , 6 _2_

14) 24 , 10 _2_

15) 24 , 12 _12_

16) 40 , 24 _8_

17) 8 , 10 _2_

18) 10 , 20 _10_

19) 2 , 3 _1_

20) 6 , 12 _6_

Prime Factors ANSWERS

1) 38   2 , 19

2) 49   7

3) 35   5 , 7

4) 25   5

5) 15   3 , 5

6) 44   2 , 11

7) 32   2

8) 48   2 , 3

9) 22   2 , 11

10) 21   3 , 7

11) 30   2 , 3 , 5

12) 20   2 , 5

13) 39   3 , 13

14) 14   2 , 7

15) 12   2 , 3

16) 26   2 , 13

17) 46   2 , 23

18) 40   2 , 5

19) 24   2 , 3

20) 10   2 , 5

ANSWERS

Find the Prime Factors of the Numbers

1)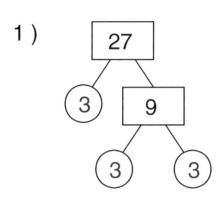

2)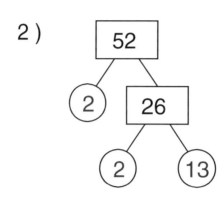

3)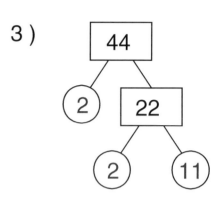

Factors
3 x 3 x 3 = 27

Factors
2 x 2 x 13 = 52

Factors
2 x 2 x 11 = 44

---

4)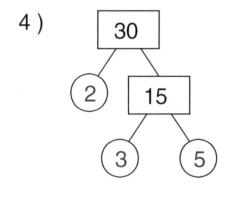

5)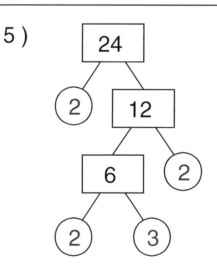

6)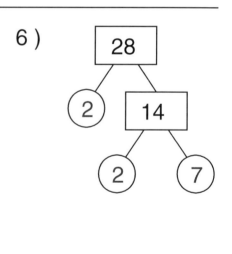

Factors
2 x 3 x 5 = 30

Factors
2 x 2 x 2 x 3 = 24

Factors
2 x 2 x 7 = 28

ANSWERS
Rearranging Digits

1) 399   993

2) 744   744

3) 488   884

4) 616   661

5) 734   743

6) 846   864

7) 844   844

8) 345   543

9) 959   995

10) 559   955

1) 897   789

2) 696   669

3) 825   258

4) 135   135

5) 751   157

6) 149   149

7) 862   268

8) 212   122

9) 557   557

10) 675   567

ANSWERS
Rearranging Digits

1) 1,182   <u>8,211</u>   6) 7,769   <u>9,776</u>

2) 1,549   <u>9,541</u>   7) 7,521   <u>7,521</u>

3) 5,366   <u>6,653</u>   8) 8,146   <u>8,641</u>

4) 3,869   <u>9,863</u>   9) 8,161   <u>8,611</u>

5) 2,853   <u>8,532</u>   10) 7,769   <u>9,776</u>

1) 7,816   <u>1,678</u>   6) 6,636   <u>3,666</u>

2) 3,827   <u>2,378</u>   7) 8,176   <u>1,678</u>

3) 4,946   <u>4,469</u>   8) 9,222   <u>2,229</u>

4) 5,938   <u>3,589</u>   9) 2,172   <u>1,227</u>

5) 1,627   <u>1,267</u>   10) 5,366   <u>3,566</u>

TIME ANSWERS

What time is on the clock?   6:00

What time was it 1 hour ago?   5:00

What time was it 3 hours and 40 minutes ago?   2:20

What time will it be in 4 hours and 20 minutes?   10:20

What time is on the clock?   7:40

What time was it 2 hours ago?   5:40

What time will it be in 3 hours ?   10:40

What time will it be in 4 hours and 20 minutes?   12:00

What time is on the clock?   10:20

What time was it 1 hour ago?   9:20

What time was it 3 hours and 20 minutes ago?   7:00

What time will it be in 2 hours ?   12:20

What time is on the clock?   10:00

What time will it be in 3 hours and 20 minutes?   1:20

What time was it 2 hours ago?   8:00

What time was it 1 hour ago?   9:00

ANSWER SHEET
Find the Missing Addends.

1) $59 = 19 + 40$

2) $19 + 17 = 36$

3) $34 + 17 = 51$

4) $14 + 27 = 41$

5) $25 + 28 = 53$

6) $33 = 15 + 18$

7) $57 = 17 + 40$

8) $27 + 15 = 42$

9) $35 + 10 = 45$

10) $65 = 34 + 31$

11) $27 + 26 = 53$

12) $47 = 20 + 27$

13) $43 = 28 + 15$

14) $11 + 13 = 24$

15) $40 = 25 + 15$

16) $22 + 36 = 58$

17) $72 = 33 + 39$

18) $38 = 16 + 22$

19) $16 + 21 = 37$

20) $13 + 37 = 50$

21) $28 + 23 = 51$

22) $28 + 18 = 46$

23) $20 + 32 = 52$

24) $57 = 22 + 35$

25) $37 + 38 = 75$

26) $34 = 15 + 19$

27) $28 = 10 + 18$

28) $66 = 33 + 33$

29) $20 + 33 = 53$

30) $29 = 19 + 10$

ANSWER SHEET

751	577	769	255	946
+ 944	+ 325	+ 911	+ 485	+ 460
1695	902	1680	740	1406

867	112	144	526	974
+ 593	+ 748	+ 795	+ 366	+ 423
1460	860	939	892	1397

405	619	262	104	652
+ 860	+ 232	+ 868	+ 165	+ 458
1265	851	1130	269	1110

689	391	311	263	210
+ 518	+ 975	+ 192	+ 171	+ 148
1207	1366	503	434	358

806	358	166	845	297
+ 608	+ 217	+ 387	+ 455	+ 809
1414	575	553	1300	1106

ANSWER SHEET

$63.32	$57.23	$34.79	$84.62	$25.78
+$87.76	+$25.66	+$68.43	+$23.84	+$99.45
$151.08	$82.89	$103.22	$108.46	$125.23
$72.59	$67.32	$85.42	$59.36	$73.25
+$19.64	+$66.27	+$11.33	+$75.85	+$71.12
$92.23	$133.59	$96.75	$135.21	$144.37
$14.85	$48.57	$42.34	$76.39	$50.49
+$86.82	+$56.12	+$80.98	+$45.96	+$33.61
$101.67	$104.69	$123.32	$122.35	$84.10
$13.83	$12.59	$80.57	$22.35	$95.62
+$34.61	+$31.76	+$84.11	+$29.88	+$64.31
$48.44	$44.35	$164.68	$52.23	$159.93
$28.73	$19.33	$74.42	$28.39	$26.21
+$64.19	+$83.11	+$77.21	+$32.36	+$92.67
$92.92	$102.44	$151.63	$60.75	$118.88

ANSWER SHEET

10122	265710	6900016	94785
+ 86800	+ 883815	+ 8967065	+ 51037
96922	1149525	15867081	145822

403123	5061847	88389	313963
+ 535453	+ 1878336	+ 38835	+ 824442
938576	6940183	127224	1138405

2936692	15234	512353	1923899
+ 7549491	+ 29032	+ 139827	+ 6762860
10486183	44266	652180	8686759

93107	421331	5141586	42257
+ 15816	+ 962779	+ 6071731	+ 96189
108923	1384110	11213317	138446

ANSWER SHEET

1) $1067 + 1078 = 2145$

2) $438 + 2611 = 3049$

3) $-2831 + -2939 = -5770$

4) $2330 + -1901 = 429$

5) $935 + 1991 = 2926$

6) $603 + 1073 = 1676$

7) $-2280 + -393 = -2673$

8) $-230 + -138 = -368$

9) $1368 + 624 = 1992$

10) $1143 + -2262 = -1119$

11) $1708 + -337 = 1371$

12) $2667 + 2849 = 5516$

13) $2277 + -466 = 1811$

14) $-2079 + -2586 = -4665$

15) $2966 + 2413 = 5379$

16) $-1488 + 2557 = 1069$

17) $1087 + -2291 = -1204$

18) $-2005 + 2153 = 148$

19) $2125 + 2919 = 5044$

20) $-270 + 2104 = 1834$

21) $2759 + 592 = 3351$

22) $-1815 + 2739 = 924$

23) $1956 + -560 = 1396$

24) $1569 + 2401 = 3970$

25) $2496 + 674 = 3170$

26) $-2907 + 884 = -2023$

27) $1727 + 739 = 2466$

28) $125 + 783 = 908$

29) $1602 + -1844 = -242$

30) $2042 + -2763 = -721$

ANSWER SHEET
Multiplying and Dividing Rational Numbers

Find each product or quotient. Round to the nearest ten-thousandth.

1) $\frac{3}{5} \div \frac{6}{4}$

   0.4000

2) $\frac{-9}{8} \bullet \frac{-6}{5}$

   1.3500

3) $(-24) \bullet 18 \bullet 22$

   -9504

4) $4.8 \bullet 6.0$

   28.8000

5) $5.0 \div (-3.4)$

   -1.4706

6) $2 \div (-29) \div (-27)$

   0.0026

7) $2.4 \bullet 7.1 \bullet (-5.6)$

   -95.4240

8) $(-10) \bullet (-37) \bullet 33$

   12210

9) $30 \div 26 \div 4$

   0.2885

10) $\frac{2}{8} \bullet \frac{-4}{9}$

   -0.1111

11) $\frac{8}{4} \div \frac{-2}{3}$

   -3.0000

12) $\frac{7}{2} \bullet \frac{9}{6}$

   5.2500

13) $5.9 \div 3.5$

   1.6857

14) $(-24) \div 25 \div (-37)$

   0.0259

ANSWER SHEET

Combining Like Terms

1) $p - 8p$

    $-7p$

2) $q + 7q$

    $8q$

3) $-3 + 2(6k + 8)$

    $12k + 13$

4) $7 - 2z + 4z$

    $2z + 7$

5) $-9 + 3r + 8 - 7r$

    $-4r - 1$

6) $5 + 3z - 2z$

    $z + 5$

7) $-6(9 - 5c)$

    $30c - 54$

8) $6 + 2 + 9r + 3r$

    $12r + 8$

9) $-7 - 3(-6 + 2f)$

    $-6f + 11$

10) $-8(3q + 4)$

    $-24q - 32$

ANSWER SHEET
Domain and Range Mapping Diagrams

Determine whether each diagram depicts a function or not.

1) 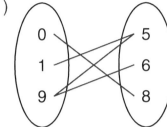 Function: __No__

2) 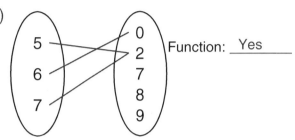 Function: __Yes__

3) 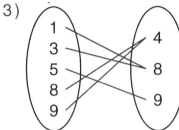 Function: __Yes__

4) 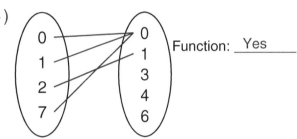 Function: __Yes__

5) 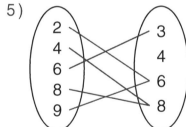 Function: __Yes__

6) 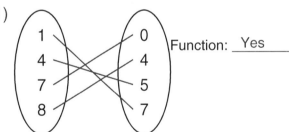 Function: __Yes__

7) 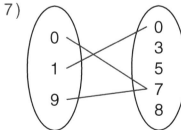 Function: __Yes__

8) 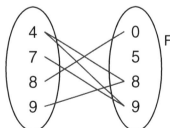 Function: __No__

ANSWER SHEET
Ordered Pairs

Find the Domain and Range. Also, state whether each set of ordered pairs is a function or not.

1) { (1, 9), (3, -7), (-8, -4), (1, -3), (-3, 7) }

Domain: { -8, -3, 1, 3 }
Range: { -7, -4, -3, 7, 9 }
No, this isn't a function.

2) { (-6, 1), (7, -3), (3, 5), (9, 6), (-2, 6) }

Domain: { -6, -2, 3, 7, 9 }
Range: { -3, 1, 5, 6 }
Yes, this is a function.

3) { (4, 7), (7, -2), (-2, 6), (-7, -6), (-7, 9) }

Domain: { -7, -2, 4, 7 }
Range: { -6, -2, 6, 7, 9 }
No, this isn't a function.

4) { (-8, 3), (3, 7), (6, -9), (-1, 3), (4, -8) }

Domain: { -8, -1, 3, 4, 6 }
Range: { -9, -8, 3, 7 }
Yes, this is a function.

5) { (1, 2), (-1, -4), (3, 7), (9, -5), (-8, 8) }

Domain: { -8, -1, 1, 3, 9 }
Range: { -5, -4, 2, 7, 8 }
Yes, this is a function.

6) { (-1, -5), (4, -8), (-2, 4), (1, 9), (8, 1) }

Domain: { -2, -1, 1, 4, 8 }
Range: { -8, -5, 1, 4, 9 }
Yes, this is a function.

7) { (-3, 6), (0, -8), (-6, 1), (-1, 5), (-9, -9) }

Domain: { -9, -6, -3, -1, 0 }
Range: { -9, -8, 1, 5, 6 }
Yes, this is a function.

8) { (2, 0), (2, 6), (5, 8), (4, 1), (-1, -1) }

Domain: { -1, 2, 4, 5 }
Range: { -1, 0, 1, 6, 8 }
No, this isn't a function.

9) { (3, 0), (0, -3), (4, -8), (2, 0), (7, -7) }

Domain: { 0, 2, 3, 4, 7 }
Range: { -8, -7, -3, 0 }
Yes, this is a function.

10) { (4, 3), (3, -9), (7, -6), (4, -3), (-3, -8) }

Domain: { -3, 3, 4, 7 }
Range: { -9, -8, -6, -3, 3 }
No, this isn't a function.

ANSWER SHEET
Word Problems

1) After eating at the restaurant, Sandy, Melanie, and Jason decided to divide the bill evenly. If each person paid eleven dollars, what was the total of the bill ?

33 dollars

2) There were 17 bales of hay in the barn. Tom stacked more bales in the barn today. There are now 63 bales of hay in the barn. How many bales did he store in the barn ?

46 bales of hay

3) Mike's high school played twelve soccer games this year. The team won most of their games. They were defeated during four games. How many games did they win ?

8 games

4) Jessica is baking a cake. The recipe calls for 7 cups of flour. She already put in 3 cups. How many more cups does she need to add ?

4 cups of flour

5) How many ink cartridges can you buy with 112 dollars if one cartridge costs 14 dollars ?

8 cartridges

6) Joan found ninety - three seashells on the beach, she gave Sam some of her seashells. She has thirty - nine seashell left. How many seashells did she give to Sam ?

54 seashells

7) Dan has twenty - two books in his library. He bought several books at a yard sale over the weekend. He now has seventy - eight books in his library. How many books did he buy at the yard sale ?

56 books

8) After paying six dollars for the pie, Sam has fifty - five dollars left. How much money did he have before buying the pie ?

61 dollars

9) There are 38 maple trees currently in the park. Park workers will plant more maple trees today. When the workers are finished there will be 67 maple trees in the park. How many maple trees did the workers plant today ?

29 maple trees

10) Fred had 47 peaches left at his roadside fruit stand. He went to the orchard and picked more peaches to stock up the stand. There are now 55 peaches at the stand, how many did he pick ?

8 peaches

Separable Equations

Find the general solution of each equation.

1) $\dfrac{dy}{dx} = e^{3x+y}$

$y = -\ln(\dfrac{-1}{3} e^{3x} - C)$

2) $\dfrac{dy}{dx} = 2y(x + 8)$

$y = Ce^{(x^2 + 16x)}$

3) $\dfrac{dy}{dx} = e^{x+3y}$

$y = \dfrac{-1}{3} \ln(-3e^{x} - C)$

4) $\dfrac{dy}{dx} = \dfrac{2}{\sin(y)}$

$y = \cos^{-1}(-2x + C)$

5) $\dfrac{dy}{dx} = 4xe^{y}$

$y = -\ln(\dfrac{-4x^2}{2} + C)$

6) $\dfrac{dy}{dx} = \dfrac{e^{2x}}{4y}$

$y = \sqrt{\dfrac{1}{4} (e^{2x} + C)}$

7) $\dfrac{dy}{dx} = \dfrac{x^4}{e^{4y}}$

$y = \dfrac{1}{4} \ln(\dfrac{4}{5} x^5 + C)$

8) $\dfrac{dy}{dx} = 11e^{x+y}$

$y = -\ln(-11e^{x} - C)$

9) $\dfrac{dy}{dx} = \dfrac{x}{12y}$

$y = \sqrt{12x^2 + C}$

10) $\dfrac{dy}{dx} = \dfrac{2}{2\sin(y)}$

$y = \cos^{-1}(-1x + C)$

11) $\dfrac{dy}{dx} = \dfrac{-x}{10y}$

$y = \sqrt{\dfrac{-1}{10} x^2 + C}$

12) $\dfrac{dy}{dx} = 2xe^{2y}$

$y = \dfrac{-1}{2} \ln(-2x^2 + C)$

ANSWER SHEET
Logarithmic Differentiation

Differentiate each function using logarithmic differentiation.

1) $y = (-4x^3)(-3x^3)$

$$\frac{dy}{dx} = 72x^5$$

2) $y = (7x^2)(2x^4 + 2)$

$$\frac{dy}{dx} = 84x^5 + 28x$$

3) $y = (3x^2 - 3)(-7x^2 - 1)$

$$\frac{dy}{dx} = -84x^3 + 36x$$

4) $y = \dfrac{6x^2 + 2}{-4x - 7}$

$$\frac{dy}{dx} = \frac{-24x^2 - 84x +}{16x^2 + 56x + 49}$$

5) $y = 5x^{3x}$

$$\frac{dy}{dx} = 15x^{3x}(\ln x + 1)$$

6) $y = -5x^{4x}$

$$\frac{dy}{dx} = -20x^{4x}(\ln x + 1)$$

7) $y = \dfrac{-2x^2 -}{6x - 6}$

$$\frac{dy}{dx} = \frac{-12x^2 + 24x +}{36x^2 - 72x + 36}$$

8) $y = \dfrac{2x - 3}{7x^3 - 3x}$

$$\frac{dy}{dx} = \frac{-28x^3 + 6 \quad ^2 - 9}{49x^6 - 42x^4 + 9x^2}$$

9) $y = 8x^{6x}$

$$\frac{dy}{dx} = 48x^{6x}(\ln x + 1)$$

10) $y = (2x^4 + 7x - 1)(x^2)$

$$\frac{dy}{dx} = 12x^5 + 21x^2 - 2x$$

11) $y = \dfrac{x^3 -}{6x^2 - 1}$

$$\frac{dy}{dx} = \frac{6x^4 + \quad ^2 + 1}{36x^4 - 12x^2 + 1}$$

12) $y = -8x^{6x}$

$$\frac{dy}{dx} = -48x^{6x}(\ln x + 1)$$

ANSWER SHEET
Product Rule

Differentiate each function with respect to the given variable, by using the power rule.

1) $y = (5x^2 + 5x + 3)(4x^3 - 3x - 1)$

$\dfrac{dy}{dx} = 100x^4 + 80x^3 - 9x^2 - 40x - 14$

2) $y = (-x^4 - x^2 + 5x)(x^3 - 3)$

$\dfrac{dy}{dx} = -7x^6 - 5x^4 + 32x^3 + 6x$

3) $y = (-3x^2 + 2)(6x^3 - 3x^2)$

$\dfrac{dy}{dx} = -90x^4 + 36x^3 + 36x^2 - 12x$

4) $y = (5x^2)(6x^2)$

$\dfrac{dy}{dx} = 120x^3$

5) $y = (-5x^3 - x - 4)(-x^5 - 7)$

$\dfrac{dy}{dx} = 40x^7 + 6x^5 + 20x^4 + 105x^2$
$\quad +$

6) $y = (-2x^2 + 2x + 6)(-7x^5)$

$\dfrac{dy}{dx} = 98x^6 - 84x^5 - 210x^4$

7) $y = (3x^5 - 6x^3 - 4x^2)(2x^5 + 2x^4 + 7x)$

$\dfrac{dy}{dx} = 60x^9 + 54x^8 - 96x^7 - 140x^6$
$\quad + \quad {}^5 - 168x^3 - 84x^2$

8) $y = (-7x^2 + 2x)(6x^5 - 7)$

$\dfrac{dy}{dx} = -294x^6 + 72x^5 + 98x - 14$

9) $y = (7x^5)(5x^5 + 2x^4)$

$\dfrac{dy}{dx} = 350x^9 + 126x^8$

10) $y = (-2x^3 - 4x^2 - 3)(5x^3)$

$\dfrac{dy}{dx} = -60x^5 - 100x^4 - 45x^2$

Power, Constant, and Sum Rules

Differentiate each function with respect to the given variable.

1) $y = x^2 - 4x - 12$

$\frac{dy}{dx} = 2x - 4$

2) $y = x^2 - 5x + 6$

$\frac{dy}{dx} = 2x - 5$

3) $y = \frac{-7}{17} x^{\frac{-4}{11}}$

$\frac{dy}{dx} = \frac{28}{187x^{\frac{15}{11}}}$

4) $y = \frac{3}{4} x^{\frac{-1}{2}}$

$\frac{dy}{dx} = \frac{-3}{8x^{\frac{3}{2}}}$

5) $y = 1$

$\frac{dy}{dx} = 0$

6) $y = 13$

$\frac{dy}{dx} = 0$

7) $y = x^3 + x^2 - 33x + 63$

$\frac{dy}{dx} = 3x^2 + 2x - 33$

8) $y = \frac{3}{x^7}$

$\frac{dy}{dx} = \frac{-21}{x^8}$

9) $y = \frac{-16}{x^2}$

$\frac{dy}{dx} = \frac{32}{x^3}$

10) $y = \frac{-9}{x^6}$

$\frac{dy}{dx} = \frac{54}{x^7}$

ANSWER SHEET
Quotient Rule

Differentiate each function.

1) $y = \dfrac{-4x - 6}{3x^2 + 1}$

$\dfrac{dy}{dx} = \dfrac{12x^2 + 36x -}{9x^4 + 6x^2 + 1}$

2) $y = \dfrac{6x - 5}{2x^3 - x}$

$\dfrac{dy}{dx} = \dfrac{-24x^3 + 3 \quad ^2 - 5}{4x^6 - 4x^4 + x^2}$

3) $y = \dfrac{2x^3 -}{4x - 5}$

$\dfrac{dy}{dx} = \dfrac{16x^3 - 3 \quad ^2 + 35}{16x^2 - 40x + 25}$

4) $y = \dfrac{3x + 2}{-6x^2 - 6}$

$\dfrac{dy}{dx} = \dfrac{18x^2 + 24x -}{36x^4 + 72x^2 + 36}$

5) $y = \dfrac{7x^3 -}{6x + 6}$

$\dfrac{dy}{dx} = \dfrac{84x^3 + 12 \quad ^2 - 6}{36x^2 + 72x + 36}$

6) $y = \dfrac{-x - 1}{7x^3 - 7x}$

$\dfrac{dy}{dx} = \dfrac{14x^3 + 21x^2 - 7}{49x^6 - 98x^4 + 49x^2}$

7) $y = \dfrac{5x + 1}{x^2 + 1}$

$\dfrac{dy}{dx} = \dfrac{-5x^2 - 2x +}{x^4 + 2x^2 + 1}$

8) $y = \dfrac{6x^3 -}{3x - 7}$

$\dfrac{dy}{dx} = \dfrac{36x^3 - 12 \quad ^2 + 35}{9x^2 - 42x + 49}$

9) $y = \dfrac{6x^2 -}{3x + 1}$

$\dfrac{dy}{dx} = \dfrac{18x^2 + 12x +}{9x^2 + 6x + 1}$

10) $y = \dfrac{5x^2 - 4}{-x - 3}$

$\dfrac{dy}{dx} = \dfrac{-5x^2 - 30x -}{x^2 + 6x + 9}$

11) $y = \dfrac{4x^2 -}{7x - 5}$

$\dfrac{dy}{dx} = \dfrac{28x^2 - 40x +}{49x^2 - 70x + 25}$

12) $y = \dfrac{-3x - 7}{-x^3 - 2x}$

$\dfrac{dy}{dx} = \dfrac{-6x^3 - 21x^2 - 14}{x^6 + 4x^4 + 4x^2}$

ANSWER SHEET
Limits at Infinity

Find each limit. Round to two decimals if necessary.

1) $\lim\limits_{x \to \infty}$ $-x^2 - x - 3$

$-\infty$

2) $\lim\limits_{x \to -\infty}$ $-\ln(-x - 3)$

$-\infty$

3) $\lim\limits_{x \to -\infty} \dfrac{2x^3 - 3x^2 - 3x - 3}{5x^2 - 5x - 1}$

$-\infty$

4) $\lim\limits_{x \to \infty}$ $x - 3$

∞

5) $\lim\limits_{x \to \infty}$ $-2e^{-3x} + 1$

1

6) $\lim\limits_{x \to -\infty} \dfrac{-3x - 3}{5x^3 + 4x^2 + 4x + 2}$

0

7) $\lim\limits_{x \to -\infty} \dfrac{4x^2 + 4x - 2}{4x - 3}$

$-\infty$

8) $\lim\limits_{x \to \infty}$ $2x - 1$

∞

9) $\lim\limits_{x \to -\infty} \dfrac{-2\tan(-3x - 2) + 1}{4x^2 + 4x}$

Diverges

10) $\lim\limits_{x \to \infty} \dfrac{4x^2 + 4x + 4}{-3\tan(-2x + 3) + 3}$

Diverges

ANSWER SHEET
3 Minute Drill

$56 \div 8 = 7$	$12 \div 2 = 6$	$7 \div 1 = 7$	$18 \div 3 = 6$	$36 \div 4 = 9$
$33 \div 11 = 3$	$18 \div 6 = 3$	$22 \div 11 = 2$	$30 \div 6 = 5$	$10 \div 5 = 2$
$28 \div 7 = 4$	$6 \div 3 = 2$	$48 \div 6 = 8$	$2 \div 2 = 1$	$36 \div 9 = 4$
$3 \div 1 = 3$	$5 \div 1 = 5$	$15 \div 3 = 5$	$2 \div 1 = 2$	$5 \div 5 = .1$
$27 \div 9 = 3$	$1 \div 1 = 1$	$6 \div 3 = 2$	$20 \div 10 = 2$	$22 \div 11 = 2$
$2 \div 1 = 2$	$99 \div 11 = 9$	$15 \div 5 = 3$	$24 \div 8 = 3$	$14 \div 2 = 7$
$4 \div 2 = 2$	$28 \div 4 = 7$	$12 \div 4 = 3$	$35 \div 7 = 5$	$72 \div 8 = 9$
$27 \div 9 = 3$	$24 \div 6 = 4$	$30 \div 5 = 6$	$21 \div 7 = 3$	$6 \div 1 = 6$
$20 \div 5 = 4$	$24 \div 12 = 2$	$20 \div 10 = 2$	$4 \div 4 = 1$	$45 \div 9 = 5$
$55 \div 11 = 5$	$18 \div 6 = 3$	$81 \div 9 = 9$	$9 \div 3 = 3$	$24 \div 12 = 2$
$40 \div 5 = 8$	$42 \div 7 = 6$	$8 \div 8 = 1$	$70 \div 10 = 7$	$12 \div 12 = 1$
$3 \div 1 = 3$	$48 \div 8 = 6$	$11 \div 11 = 1$	$35 \div 5 = 7$	$18 \div 9 = 2$

ANSWER SHEET

$$\begin{array}{r} 24 \text{ r } 2 \\ 9\overline{)218} \end{array}$$

$$\begin{array}{r} 98 \\ 6\overline{)588} \end{array}$$

$$\begin{array}{r} 26 \\ 4\overline{)104} \end{array}$$

$$\begin{array}{r} 49 \text{ r } 3 \\ 4\overline{)199} \end{array}$$

$$\begin{array}{r} 28 \text{ r } 3 \\ 6\overline{)171} \end{array}$$

$$\begin{array}{r} 33 \\ 5\overline{)165} \end{array}$$

$$\begin{array}{r} 84 \text{ r } 3 \\ 6\overline{)507} \end{array}$$

$$\begin{array}{r} 23 \\ 9\overline{)207} \end{array}$$

$$\begin{array}{r} 92 \\ 3\overline{)276} \end{array}$$

ANSWER SHEET

1) $N \div 13 = 35$ N = <u>455</u>   2) $464 \div N = 16$ N = <u>29</u>

3) $N \div 17 = 38$ N = <u>646</u>   4) $N \div 16 = 27$ N = <u>432</u>

5) $558 \div N = 18$ N = <u>31</u>   6) $N \div 19 = 19$ N = <u>361</u>

7) $N \div 17 = 27$ N = <u>459</u>   8) $N \div 20 = 15$ N = <u>300</u>

9) $570 \div N = 15$ N = <u>38</u>   10) $N \div 24 = 30$ N = <u>720</u>

11) $N \div 15 = 40$ N = <u>600</u>   12) $680 \div N = 40$ N = <u>17</u>

13) $N \div 31 = 40$ N = <u>1240</u>   14) $308 \div N = 28$ N = <u>11</u>

15) $1482 \div N = 39$ N = <u>38</u>   16) $323 \div N = 17$ N = <u>19</u>

17) $N \div 32 = 36$ N = <u>1152</u>   18) $1280 \div N = 32$ N = <u>40</u>

19) $N \div 31 = 25$ N = <u>775</u>   20) $1330 \div N = 38$ N = <u>35</u>

21) $310 \div N = 10$ N = <u>31</u>   22) $532 \div N = 38$ N = <u>14</u>

23) $N \div 40 = 35$ N = <u>1400</u>   24) $1520 \div N = 38$ N = <u>40</u>

25) $N \div 33 = 40$ N = <u>1320</u>   26) $N \div 25 = 36$ N = <u>900</u>

27) $N \div 16 = 27$ N = <u>432</u>   28) $552 \div N = 23$ N = <u>24</u>

29) $N \div 10 = 12$ N = <u>120</u>   30) $272 \div N = 16$ N = <u>17</u>

ANSWER SHEET

$$\begin{array}{r} 13 \\ 4\overline{)52} \end{array}$$
$$\begin{array}{r} 31\ r\ 5 \\ 7\overline{)222} \end{array}$$
$$\begin{array}{r} 15 \\ 3\overline{)45} \end{array}$$
$$\begin{array}{r} 90\ r\ 7 \\ 9\overline{)817} \end{array}$$

$$\begin{array}{r} 25 \\ 6\overline{)150} \end{array}$$
$$\begin{array}{r} 26 \\ 2\overline{)52} \end{array}$$
$$\begin{array}{r} 10\ r\ 3 \\ 6\overline{)63} \end{array}$$
$$\begin{array}{r} 18\ r\ 4 \\ 9\overline{)166} \end{array}$$

$$\begin{array}{r} 96 \\ 2\overline{)192} \end{array}$$
$$\begin{array}{r} 59 \\ 7\overline{)413} \end{array}$$
$$\begin{array}{r} 24 \\ 7\overline{)168} \end{array}$$
$$\begin{array}{r} 12\ r\ 4 \\ 5\overline{)64} \end{array}$$

$$\begin{array}{r} 95\ r\ 1 \\ 2\overline{)191} \end{array}$$
$$\begin{array}{r} 15\ r\ 1 \\ 3\overline{)46} \end{array}$$
$$\begin{array}{r} 65\ r\ 3 \\ 4\overline{)263} \end{array}$$
$$\begin{array}{r} 80 \\ 6\overline{)480} \end{array}$$

$$\begin{array}{r} 62\ r\ 3 \\ 5\overline{)313} \end{array}$$
$$\begin{array}{r} 87\ r\ 5 \\ 8\overline{)701} \end{array}$$
$$\begin{array}{r} 33 \\ 3\overline{)99} \end{array}$$
$$\begin{array}{r} 47 \\ 8\overline{)376} \end{array}$$

ANSWER SHEET

$44 \div 4 = 11$

$72 \div 6 = 12$

$96 \div 12 = 8$

$11 \div 11 = 1$

$45 \div 5 = 9$

$24 \div 12 = 2$

$21 \div 3 = 7$

$12 \div 2 = 6$

$20 \div 10 = 2$

$32 \div 8 = 4$

$88 \div 11 = 8$

$6 \div 2 = 3$

$45 \div 9 = 5$

$2 \div 1 = 2$

$21 \div 7 = 3$

$60 \div 5 = 12$

$36 \div 12 = 3$

$22 \div 2 = 11$

$30 \div 3 = 10$

$81 \div 9 = 9$

$6 \div 1 = 6$

$120 \div 10 = 12$

$20 \div 4 = 5$

$27 \div 3 = 9$

$11 \div 11 = 1$

$35 \div 5 = 7$

$32 \div 8 = 4$

$8 \div 1 = 8$

$100 \div 10 = 10$

$60 \div 6 = 10$

ANSWER SHEET

Solve each division problem. Write out any remainders in decimal form.

$$\overset{1.88 \text{ r } 0.02}{4\overline{)7.54}}$$

$$\overset{0.73}{4\overline{)2.92}}$$

$$\overset{1.48 \text{ r } 0.03}{4\overline{)5.95}}$$

$$\overset{0.12}{9\overline{)1.08}}$$

$$\overset{1.11 \text{ r } 0.03}{7\overline{)7.80}}$$

$$\overset{0.16 \text{ r } 0.03}{9\overline{)1.47}}$$

$$\overset{1.86}{2\overline{)3.72}}$$

$$\overset{1.28 \text{ r } 0.03}{5\overline{)6.43}}$$

$$\overset{1.09}{9\overline{)9.81}}$$

$$\overset{0.36}{7\overline{)2.52}}$$

$$\overset{2.97}{2\overline{)5.94}}$$

$$\overset{2.20}{2\overline{)4.40}}$$

$$\overset{1.44 \text{ r } 0.05}{6\overline{)8.69}}$$

$$\overset{1.05}{7\overline{)7.35}}$$

$$\overset{0.19}{8\overline{)1.52}}$$

$$\overset{0.74}{8\overline{)5.92}}$$

$$\overset{1.43 \text{ r } 0.01}{3\overline{)4.30}}$$

$$\overset{1.29 \text{ r } 0.02}{6\overline{)7.76}}$$

$$\overset{0.93}{5\overline{)4.65}}$$

$$\overset{2.02}{3\overline{)6.06}}$$

$$\overset{1.28 \text{ r } 0.04}{5\overline{)6.44}}$$

ANSWER SHEET

What is the slope of each line ?

1)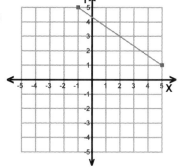

Slope = $-\dfrac{2}{3}$

2)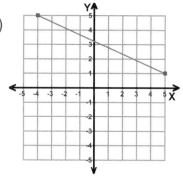

Slope = $-\dfrac{4}{9}$

3)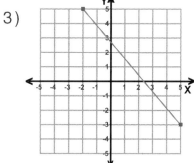

Slope = $-\dfrac{8}{7}$

4)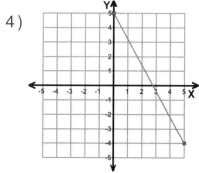

Slope = $-\dfrac{9}{5}$

5) $y = 1\,x + 3$ Slope = __1__

6) $y = -\dfrac{1}{2}\,x - 3$ Slope = $-\dfrac{1}{2}$

7) $y = \dfrac{3}{5}\,x - 2$ Slope = $\dfrac{3}{5}$

8) $y = -\dfrac{7}{8}\,x + 1$ Slope = $-\dfrac{7}{8}$

Write the slope-intercept form and plot the equation of each line given the slope and y-intercept.

9)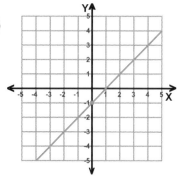

Slope = __1__

y-intercept = __-1__

Equation : $y = 1\,x - 1$

10)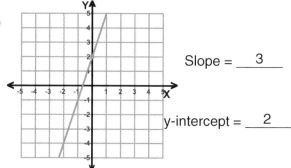

Slope = __3__

y-intercept = __2__

Equation : $y = 3\,x + 2$

ANSWER SHEET
Equivalent Ratios

1) $5:8 = 10:16 = 15:24 = 20:32 = 25:40 = 30:48$

2) $1:3 = 2:6 = 3:9 = 4:12 = 5:15 = 6:18$

3) $2:3 = 4:6 = 6:9 = 8:12 = 10:15 = 12:18$

4) $1:10 = 2:20 = 3:30 = 4:40 = 5:50 = 6:60$

5) $3:5 = 6:10 = 9:15 = 12:20 = 15:25 = 18:30$

6) $1:4 = 2:8 = 3:12 = 4:16 = 5:20 = 6:24$

7) $1:2 = 2:4 = 3:6 = 4:8 = 5:10 = 6:12$

8) $1:2 = 2:4 = 3:6 = 4:8 = 5:10 = 6:12$

9) $4:9 = 8:18 = 12:27 = 16:36 = 20:45 = 24:54$

10) $1:7 = 2:14 = 3:21 = 4:28 = 5:35 = 6:42$

ANSWER SHEET
Estimating Sums and Differences to the Nearest Tens

Estimate the sum or difference by rounding each number to the nearest ten.

1)
$$
\begin{array}{r}
94 \\
- 11 \\
\hline
83
\end{array}
\longrightarrow
\begin{array}{r}
90 \\
- 10 \\
\hline
80
\end{array}
$$

2)
$$
\begin{array}{r}
48 \\
+ 24 \\
\hline
72
\end{array}
\longrightarrow
\begin{array}{r}
50 \\
+ 20 \\
\hline
70
\end{array}
$$

3)
$$
\begin{array}{r}
84 \\
- 16 \\
\hline
68
\end{array}
\longrightarrow
\begin{array}{r}
80 \\
- 20 \\
\hline
60
\end{array}
$$

4)
$$
\begin{array}{r}
93 \\
+ 49 \\
\hline
142
\end{array}
\longrightarrow
\begin{array}{r}
90 \\
+ 50 \\
\hline
140
\end{array}
$$

5)
$$
\begin{array}{r}
72 \\
+ 62 \\
\hline
134
\end{array}
\longrightarrow
\begin{array}{r}
70 \\
+ 60 \\
\hline
130
\end{array}
$$

6)
$$
\begin{array}{r}
69 \\
- 38 \\
\hline
31
\end{array}
\longrightarrow
\begin{array}{r}
70 \\
- 40 \\
\hline
30
\end{array}
$$

7)
$$
\begin{array}{r}
66 \\
- 55 \\
\hline
11
\end{array}
\longrightarrow
\begin{array}{r}
70 \\
- 60 \\
\hline
10
\end{array}
$$

8)
$$
\begin{array}{r}
82 \\
- 18 \\
\hline
64
\end{array}
\longrightarrow
\begin{array}{r}
80 \\
- 20 \\
\hline
60
\end{array}
$$

9)
$$
\begin{array}{r}
57 \\
+ 14 \\
\hline
71
\end{array}
\longrightarrow
\begin{array}{r}
60 \\
+ 10 \\
\hline
70
\end{array}
$$

10)
$$
\begin{array}{r}
65 \\
+ 34 \\
\hline
99
\end{array}
\longrightarrow
\begin{array}{r}
70 \\
+ 30 \\
\hline
100
\end{array}
$$

11)
$$
\begin{array}{r}
41 \\
- 22 \\
\hline
19
\end{array}
\longrightarrow
\begin{array}{r}
40 \\
- 20 \\
\hline
20
\end{array}
$$

12)
$$
\begin{array}{r}
35 \\
+ 28 \\
\hline
63
\end{array}
\longrightarrow
\begin{array}{r}
40 \\
+ 30 \\
\hline
70
\end{array}
$$

13)
$$
\begin{array}{r}
37 \\
- 36 \\
\hline
1
\end{array}
\longrightarrow
\begin{array}{r}
40 \\
- 40 \\
\hline
0
\end{array}
$$

14)
$$
\begin{array}{r}
85 \\
+ 54 \\
\hline
139
\end{array}
\longrightarrow
\begin{array}{r}
90 \\
+ 50 \\
\hline
140
\end{array}
$$

ANSWER SHEET
Even and Odd Numbers with Tables

Color the odd numbers green.

890	822	920	994	508	662	535	679
843	691	711	835	966	539	668	933

Color the even numbers blue.

874	692	588	967	861	959	944	989
521	681	833	859	703	536	571	950

Color the even numbers blue, and color the odd numbers green.

748	608	577	885	558	838	900
976	646	659	982	922	623	863
914	917	607	551	972	797	697
718	901	819	765	739	715	529

ANSWER SHEET
Exponents with Multiplication and Division

Simplify. Your answer should contain only positive exponents.

1) $3ng^5 \cdot 2n^2g^3$

$6n^3g^8$

2) $3y^6 \cdot 6y^{-2}$

$18y^4$

3) $2 \cdot 2^5$

2^6

4) $\dfrac{8w^6}{5w}$

$\dfrac{8w^5}{5}$

5) $\dfrac{6^4}{6}$

6^3

6) $\dfrac{6^5}{6^4}$

6

7) $\dfrac{k}{k^{-4}}$

k^5

8) $\dfrac{8r^{-5}g^{-4}}{5rg^{-3}}$

$\dfrac{8}{5r^6g}$

9) $k \cdot k^{-6}$

$\dfrac{1}{k^5}$

10) $\left(\dfrac{1}{s}\right)^4 \cdot \left(\dfrac{1}{s}\right)^5$

$\left(\dfrac{1}{s}\right)^9$

11) $\dfrac{2d}{6d^{-6}}$

$\dfrac{d^7}{3}$

12) $s^3b^{-5} \cdot 2s^{-4}b^6 \cdot 3sb^2$

$6\,b^3$

ANSWER SHEET
Evaluate the Exponents

1) $(12)^3$ = __1728__

2) $(9)^3$ = __729__

3) $(-5)^2$ = __25__

4) $(-8)^3$ = __-512__

5) $(-2)^2$ = __4__

6) $(-12)^2$ = __144__

7) $(3)^3$ = __27__

8) $(6)^2$ = __36__

9) $(-3)^3$ = __-27__

10) $(-6)^2$ = __36__

11) $(-7)^3$ = __-343__

12) $(7)^2$ = __49__

13) $(-9)^2$ = __81__

14) $(10)^3$ = __1000__

15) $(-4)^3$ = __-64__

16) $(2)^2$ = __4__

17) $(8)^3$ = __512__

18) $(3)^3$ = __27__

19) $(5)^2$ = __25__

20) $(-2)^2$ = __4__

ANSWER SHEET
Complete Each Family of Facts

1)

$$11 + 8 = 19$$
$$8 + 11 = 19$$
$$19 - 8 = 11$$
$$19 - 11 = 8$$

4)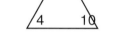

$$7 + 5 = 2$$
$$5 + 7 = 2$$
$$12 - 5 = 7$$
$$12 - 7 = 5$$

2)

$$11 + 1 = 12$$
$$1 + 11 = 12$$
$$12 - 1 = 11$$
$$12 - 11 = 1$$

5)

$$4 + 10 = 14$$
$$10 + 4 = 14$$
$$14 - 10 = 4$$
$$14 - 4 = 10$$

3)

$$6 + 9 = 5$$
$$9 + 6 = 5$$
$$15 - 9 = 6$$
$$15 - 6 = 9$$

6)

$$9 + 10 = 19$$
$$10 + 9 = 19$$
$$19 - 10 = 9$$
$$19 - 9 = 10$$

ANSWER SHEET
Complete Each Family of Facts

1)

3	x	5	=	5
5	x	3	=	5
15	÷	5	=	3
15	÷	3	=	5

4)

8	x	3	=	4
3	x	8	=	4
24	÷	3	=	8
24	÷	8	=	3

2)

9	x	2	=	8
2	x	9	=	8
18	÷	2	=	9
18	÷	9	=	2

5)

7	x	4	=	8
4	x	7	=	8
28	÷	4	=	7
28	÷	7	=	4

3)

4	x	6	=	4
6	x	4	=	4
24	÷	6	=	4
24	÷	4	=	6

6)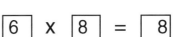

6	x	8	=	8
8	x	6	=	8
48	÷	8	=	6
48	÷	6	=	8

ANSWER SHEET
Find the Prime Factors of the Numbers

1)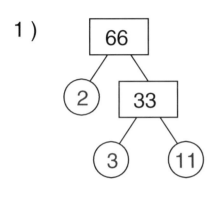

Factors
2 x 3 x 11 = 66

2)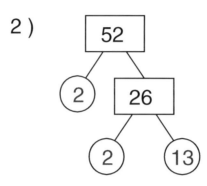

Factors
2 x 2 x 13 = 52

3)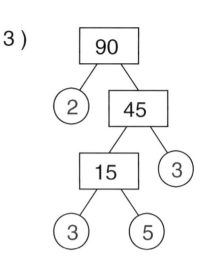

Factors
2 x 3 x 3 x 5 = 90

---

4)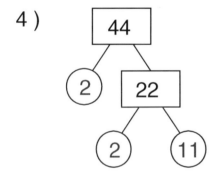

Factors
2 x 2 x 11 = 44

5)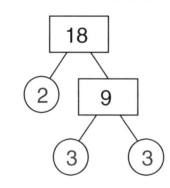

Factors
2 x 3 x 3 = 18

6)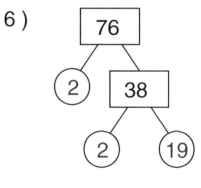

Factors
2 x 2 x 19 = 76

ANSWER SHEET
Visually Adding Simple Fractions

1)

$$\frac{1}{11} + \frac{7}{11} = \frac{8}{11}$$

2)

$$\frac{1}{10} + \frac{7}{10} = \frac{8}{10}$$

3)

$$\frac{1}{5} + \frac{3}{5} = \frac{4}{5}$$

4)

$$\frac{2}{11} + \frac{6}{11} = \frac{8}{11}$$

5)

$$\frac{3}{7} + \frac{3}{7} = \frac{6}{7}$$

ANSWER SHEET

Write the Correct Comparison Symbol (>, < or =) in Each Box

1) $\dfrac{5}{7}$ $\boxed{<}$ $\dfrac{6}{7}$

2) $\dfrac{1}{5}$ $\boxed{<}$ $\dfrac{4}{6}$

3) $\dfrac{-2}{3}$ $\boxed{<}$ $\dfrac{-1}{9}$

4) $\dfrac{2}{5}$ $\boxed{<}$ $\dfrac{3}{5}$

5) $\dfrac{-3}{4}$ $\boxed{<}$ $\dfrac{-5}{7}$

6) $\dfrac{5}{6}$ $\boxed{>}$ $\dfrac{2}{8}$

7) $\dfrac{1}{2}$ $\boxed{>}$ $\dfrac{1}{6}$

8) $\dfrac{-1}{6}$ $\boxed{>}$ $\dfrac{-1}{2}$

9) $\dfrac{-1}{4}$ $\boxed{>}$ $\dfrac{-3}{7}$

10) $\dfrac{-4}{6}$ $\boxed{<}$ $\dfrac{-1}{4}$

11) $\dfrac{-8}{9}$ $\boxed{<}$ $\dfrac{-7}{9}$

12) $\dfrac{1}{2}$ $\boxed{<}$ $\dfrac{7}{8}$

13) $\dfrac{-2}{4}$ $\boxed{>}$ $\dfrac{-3}{5}$

14) $\dfrac{-6}{8}$ $\boxed{>}$ $\dfrac{-5}{6}$

15) $\dfrac{1}{3}$ $\boxed{>}$ $\dfrac{1}{9}$

16) $\dfrac{1}{2}$ $\boxed{>}$ $\dfrac{1}{3}$

17) $\dfrac{-3}{9}$ $\boxed{>}$ $\dfrac{-2}{3}$

18) $\dfrac{-4}{5}$ $\boxed{<}$ $\dfrac{-2}{9}$

19) $\dfrac{6}{7}$ $\boxed{>}$ $\dfrac{1}{7}$

20) $\dfrac{5}{8}$ $\boxed{>}$ $\dfrac{1}{2}$

ANSWER SHEET
Multiplying Fractions with Cross Canceling

1) $\dfrac{1}{3} \times \dfrac{1}{2} = \dfrac{1 \times 1}{3 \times 2} = \dfrac{1}{6}$

2) $\dfrac{1}{4} \times \dfrac{1}{5} = \dfrac{1 \times 1}{4 \times 5} = \dfrac{1}{20}$

3) $\dfrac{2}{5} \times \dfrac{2}{4} = \dfrac{{}^1\cancel{2} \times \cancel{2}^{\,1}}{5 \times \cancel{\cancel{4}}\,{}_1} = \dfrac{1}{5}$

4) $\dfrac{8}{10} \times \dfrac{2}{5} = \dfrac{8 \times \cancel{2}^{\,1}}{{}_5\cancel{10} \times 5} = \dfrac{8}{25}$

5) $\dfrac{1}{2} \times \dfrac{1}{3} = \dfrac{1 \times 1}{2 \times 3} = \dfrac{1}{6}$

6) $\dfrac{1}{3} \times \dfrac{1}{2} = \dfrac{1 \times 1}{3 \times 2} = \dfrac{1}{6}$

7) $\dfrac{1}{3} \times \dfrac{2}{5} = \dfrac{1 \times 2}{3 \times 5} = \dfrac{2}{15}$

8) $\dfrac{3}{4} \times \dfrac{1}{2} = \dfrac{3 \times 1}{4 \times 2} = \dfrac{3}{8}$

9) $\dfrac{2}{3} \times \dfrac{1}{2} = \dfrac{{}^1\cancel{2} \times 1}{3 \times \cancel{2}\,{}_1} = \dfrac{1}{3}$

10) $\dfrac{1}{2} \times \dfrac{4}{5} = \dfrac{1 \times \cancel{4}^{\,2}}{{}_1\cancel{2} \times 5} = \dfrac{2}{5}$

11) $\dfrac{1}{2} \times \dfrac{2}{10} = \dfrac{1 \times \cancel{2}^{\,1}}{{}_1\cancel{2} \times 10} = \dfrac{1}{10}$

12) $\dfrac{3}{5} \times \dfrac{3}{4} = \dfrac{3 \times 3}{5 \times 4} = \dfrac{9}{20}$

13) $\dfrac{5}{10} \times \dfrac{1}{2} = \dfrac{{}^1\cancel{5} \times 1}{{}_2\cancel{10} \times 2} = \dfrac{1}{4}$

14) $\dfrac{1}{3} \times \dfrac{7}{10} = \dfrac{1 \times 7}{3 \times 10} = \dfrac{7}{30}$

15) $\dfrac{2}{4} \times \dfrac{2}{3} = \dfrac{{}^1\cancel{2} \times \cancel{2}^{\,1}}{{}_1{}_2\cancel{4} \times 3} = \dfrac{1}{3}$

ANSWER SHEET
Complete the function table for each equation.

1) $y = \dfrac{1}{5}x - 8$

x	y
2	-7.6
3	-7.4
-2	-8.4
6	-6.8
-3	-8.6

5) $y = -8x + 6$

x	y
3	-18
-6	54
4	-26
9	-66
2	-10

9) $y = x + 7$

x	y
5	12
0	7
-8	-1
8	15
-6	1

2) $y = -9x + 4$

x	y
9	-77
6	-50
-1	13
-4	40
-6	58

6) $y = x - 5$

x	y
-9	-14
-7	-12
0	-5
-1	-6
3	-2

10) $y = 9x - 4$

x	y
8	68
-8	-76
-3	-31
5	41
2	14

3) $y = 6x$

x	y
8	48
6	36
-4	-24
4	24
2	12

7) $y = 3x$

x	y
8	24
1	3
-7	-21
7	21
-3	-9

11) $y = \dfrac{1}{4}x + 2$

x	y
6	3.5
7	3.75
3	2.75
4	3
-7	0.25

4) $y = x - 2$

x	y
6	4
-5	-7
1	-1
-6	-8
-3	-5

8) $y = -4x$

x	y
-1	4
-2	8
-7	28
4	-16
-9	36

12) $y = \dfrac{1}{7}x + 9$

x	y
5	9.714
7	10
0	9
1	9.143
-1	8.857

ANSWER SHEET
Double Line Graph Comprehension

Graph the given information as a line graph.

Time on Monday	Degrees Celsius	
	Richmond	Atlanta
6AM	16	12
10AM	28	8
2PM	24	16
6PM	32	32
10PM	8	4

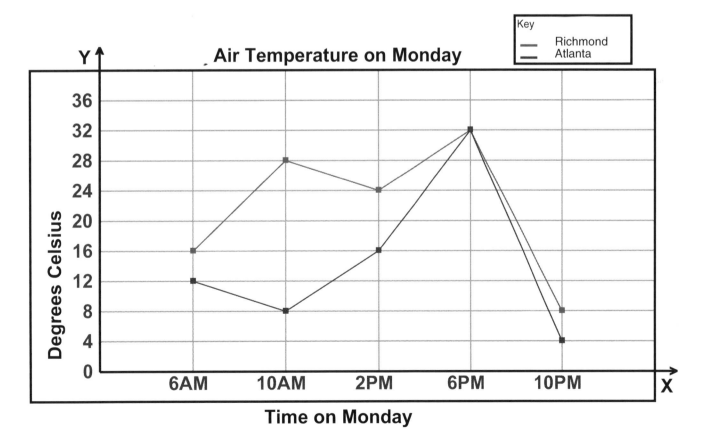

ANSWER SHEET
Reading Pie Graphs

John tracked the time he spent on homework per topic during one week.
Answer the questions based on the pie graph below.

Time Spent on Homework

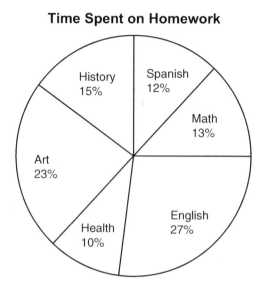

1) What percentage of time did John spend on the English and Art homework? _____50%_____

2) If John spent 100 minutes on homework, how many minutes were spent on Health? _____10_____

3) Combined, which two topics required the greatest amount of time? _English & Art_

4) Was the Math and Spanish work or the History and Health work longer; or were they equally time consuming? _Equal Amounts_

5) Between Math and Spanish which topic took longer; or did they require equal time? _____Math_____

A local pizzeria tracked which pizza toppings customers purchased.
Answer the questions based on the pie graph below.

Most Purchased Pizza Topping

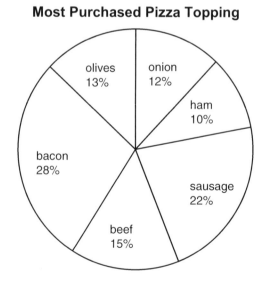

1) Were onion and ham picked more than the bacon and sausage; or were they equally bought? _bacon & sausage_

2) Combined, which two toppings did the greatest number of customers choose? _bacon & sausage_

3) If there were 200 customers that were tracked, how many bought sausage? _____44_____

4) What percentage of customers chose either the beef or the olives? _____28%_____

5) Between onion and ham which topping was more popular; or were they equally popular? _____onion_____

ANSWER SHEET
Single Line Graphing

Graph the given information as a line graph.

Day	Eggs Laid
Mon	60
Tues	24
Wed	36
Thu	60
Fri	48
Sat	72
Sun	60

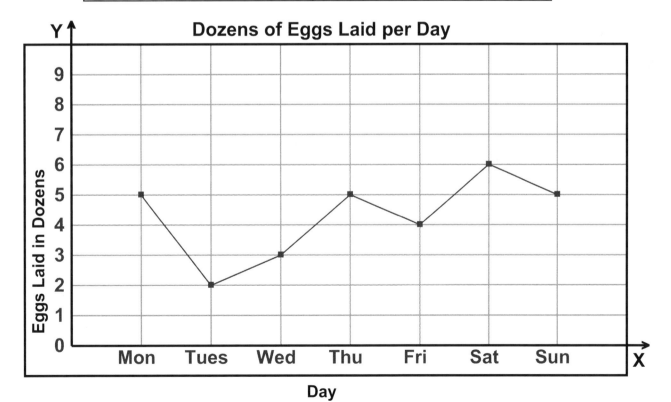

Dozens of Eggs Laid per Day

ANSWER SHEET
Ordering Whole Numbers

Order the numbers from greatest to least.

1)

981,073
621,733
845,052
188,220

Thousands			Ones		
Hundreds	Tens	Ones	Hundreds	Tens	Ones
greatest -> 9	8				
8	4				
6	2				
least -> 1	8				

Answer: 981,073 845,052 621,733 188,220

2)

560,733
891,665
455,665
811,511

Thousands			Ones		
Hundreds	Tens	Ones	Hundreds	Tens	Ones
greatest -> 8	9				
8	1				
5	6				
least -> 4	5				

Answer: 891,665 811,511 560,733 455,665

3)

564,909
537,062
322,823
374,785

Thousands			Ones		
Hundreds	Tens	Ones	Hundreds	Tens	Ones
greatest -> 5	6				
5	3				
3	7				
least -> 3	2				

Answer: 564,909 537,062 374,785 322,823

4)

145,499
607,787
109,559
842,522

Thousands			Ones		
Hundreds	Tens	Ones	Hundreds	Tens	Ones
greatest -> 8	4				
6	0				
1	4				
least -> 1	0				

Answer: 842,522 607,787 145,499 109,559

ANSWER SHEET
Find the Greatest Common Factor for each number pair.

1)   6 , 30   <u>6</u>

2)   24 , 40   <u>8</u>

3)   15 , 4   <u>1</u>

4)   30 , 8   <u>2</u>

5)   30 , 2   <u>2</u>

6)   12 , 40   <u>4</u>

7)   5 , 6   <u>1</u>

8)   40 , 8   <u>8</u>

9)   24 , 4   <u>4</u>

10)   4 , 30   <u>2</u>

11)   20 , 6   <u>2</u>

12)   40 , 10   <u>10</u>

13)   24 , 40   <u>8</u>

14)   40 , 6   <u>2</u>

15)   40 , 15   <u>5</u>

16)   3 , 8   <u>1</u>

17)   10 , 30   <u>10</u>

18)   6 , 8   <u>2</u>

19)   2 , 40   <u>2</u>

20)   40 , 4   <u>4</u>

ANSWER SHEET
Identify the Lines, Rays or Line Segments.

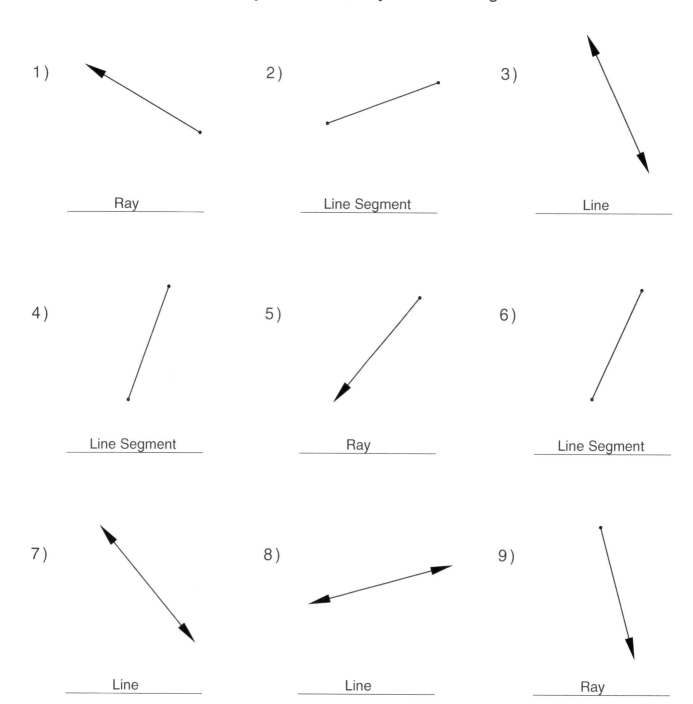

1) <u>Ray</u>

2) <u>Line Segment</u>

3) <u>Line</u>

4) <u>Line Segment</u>

5) <u>Ray</u>

6) <u>Line Segment</u>

7) <u>Line</u>

8) <u>Line</u>

9) <u>Ray</u>

ANSWER SHEET

1) Absolute value of -5 is 5

2) Absolute value of 10 is 10

3) Absolute value of 10 is 10

4) Absolute value of -4 is 4

5) Absolute value of 6 is 6

6) Absolute value of -10 is 10

7) Absolute value of 7 is 7

8) Absolute value of -6 is 6

9) Absolute value of 8 is 8

10) Absolute value of -1 is 1

11) Absolute value of 9 is 9

12) Absolute value of 3 is 3

13) Absolute value of 2 is 2

14) Absolute value of 6 is 6

15) Absolute value of -5 is 5

16) Absolute value of -2 is 2

17) Absolute value of 2 is 2

18) Absolute value of 8 is 8

19) Absolute value of 1 is 1

20) Absolute value of 8 is 8

21) Absolute value of 2 is 2

22) Absolute value of 10 is 10

23) Absolute value of 7 is 7

24) Absolute value of -7 is 7

25) Absolute value of -5 is 5

26) Absolute value of -2 is 2

27) Absolute value of 1 is 1

28) Absolute value of -7 is 7

29) Absolute value of -5 is 5

30) Absolute value of 2 is 2

ANSWER SHEET

1) $(+7) + (-3) = 4$

2) $(+8) + (+3) = 11$

3) $(+8) + (+1) = 9$

4) $(+7) + (-7) = 0$

5) $(-2) + (-1) = -3$

6) $(-3) + (-3) = -6$

7) $(-2) + (-2) = -4$

8) $(+3) + (-4) = -1$

9) $(-3) + (+8) = 5$

10) $(+1) + (-9) = -8$

11) $(-5) + (+7) = 2$

12) $(-8) + (+5) = -3$

13) $(+9) + (-9) = 0$

14) $(-7) + (+4) = -3$

15) $(+1) + (-1) = 0$

16) $(+6) + (+6) = 12$

17) $(-9) + (-4) = -13$

18) $(-1) + (-1) = -2$

19) $(-3) + (-7) = -10$

20) $(-5) + (+7) = 2$

21) $(+3) + (+4) = 7$

22) $(-5) + (+7) = 2$

23) $(+8) + (+4) = 12$

24) $(+6) + (-3) = 3$

25) $(-4) + (+9) = 5$

26) $(-6) + (-4) = -10$

27) $(+4) + (+5) = 9$

28) $(+4) + (+7) = 11$

29) $(-2) + (-3) = -5$

30) $(+7) + (+2) = 9$

ANSWER SHEET

1) $(+8) \times (+4) = 32$

2) $(+6) \times (+8) = 48$

3) $(+3) \times (+8) = 24$

4) $(+2) \times (+7) = 14$

5) $(0) \times (+1) = 0$

6) $(0) \times (+9) = 0$

7) $(+2) \times (+7) = 14$

8) $(+8) \times (+6) = 48$

9) $(+1) \times (+4) = 4$

10) $(+5) \times (0) = 0$

11) $(+7) \times (+3) = 21$

12) $(0) \times (+8) = 0$

13) $(+7) \times (+8) = 56$

14) $(+5) \times (0) = 0$

15) $(+8) \times (+5) = 40$

16) $(+5) \times (+4) = 20$

17) $(+6) \times (+1) = 6$

18) $(+8) \times (+2) = 16$

19) $(+3) \times (+2) = 6$

20) $(+1) \times (+6) = 6$

21) $(+7) \times (+7) = 49$

22) $(+5) \times (+9) = 45$

23) $(+7) \times (0) = 0$

24) $(+6) \times (+6) = 36$

25) $(+4) \times (+6) = 24$

26) $(+4) \times (+2) = 8$

27) $(+1) \times (+1) = 1$

28) $(+3) \times (+4) = 12$

29) $(0) \times (+2) = 0$

30) $(+6) \times (+1) = 6$

ANSWER SHEET

Find the Least Common Multiple for each number pair.

1) 12 , 20   60

2) 2 , 5   10

3) 15 , 5   15

4) 6 , 10   30

5) 5 , 30   30

6) 3 , 40   120

7) 4 , 15   60

8) 24 , 8   24

9) 3 , 15   15

10) 3 , 24   24

11) 10 , 24   120

12) 10 , 6   30

13) 6 , 12   12

14) 30 , 15   30

15) 15 , 20   60

16) 30 , 15   30

17) 8 , 10   40

18) 10 , 24   120

19) 12 , 24   24

20) 30 , 4   60

ANSWER SHEET
Mean, Mode, Median, and Range

1)   -6, -2, -7, 4, 3, -4
     -7, -6, -4, -2, 3, 4

Mean _-2_   Median _-3_   Mode _None_   Range _11_

6)   -9, 6, -7, -9, 9
     -9, -9, -7, 6, 9

Mean _-2_   Median _-7_   Mode _-9_   Range _18_

2)   -5, 6, 9, 2, -4, -7, -5, 8, 5
     -7, -5, -5, -4, 2, 5, 6, 8, 9

Mean _1_   Median _2_   Mode _-5_   Range _16_

7)   1, -9, 3, 8, 7, 2
     -9, 1, 2, 3, 7, 8

Mean _2_   Median _2.5_   Mode _None_   Range _17_

3)   -1, -1, 4, 3, 3, 8, 8, 5, -7, -2
     -7, -2, -1, -1, 3, 3, 4, 5, 8, 8

Mean _2_   Median _3_   Mode _-1, 3, 8_   Range _15_

8)   2, -2, -6, -6, -10, 6, 5, 5, -4, 0
     -10, -6, -6, -4, -2, 0, 2, 5, 5, 6

Mean _-1_   Median _-1_   Mode _-6, 5_   Range _16_

4)   1, 6, 7, -1, 6, 1, -7, 3
     -7, -1, 1, 1, 3, 6, 6, 7

Mean _2_   Median _2_   Mode _1, 6_   Range _14_

9)   -6, 7, 4, -6, -1, 5, -3
     -6, -6, -3, -1, 4, 5, 7

Mean _0_   Median _-1_   Mode _-6_   Range _13_

5)   1, -2, 9, 5, -3
     -3, -2, 1, 5, 9

Mean _2_   Median _1_   Mode _None_   Range _12_

10)   -3, 5, 7, 7, 9, -1, -2, 7, 7
      -3, -2, -1, 5, 7, 7, 7, 7, 9

Mean _4_   Median _7_   Mode _7_   Range _12_

ANSWER SHEET
Number Lines

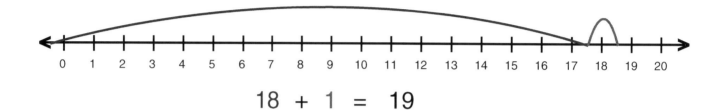

$$18 + 1 = 19$$

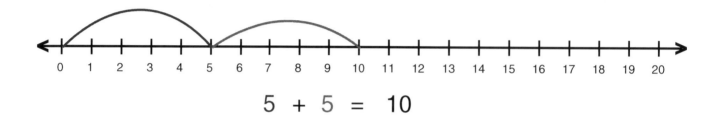

$$5 + 5 = 10$$

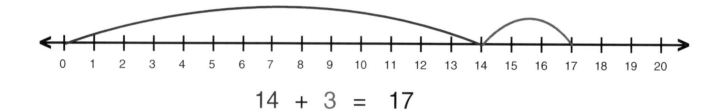

$$14 + 3 = 17$$

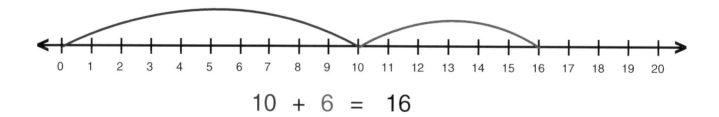

$$10 + 6 = 16$$

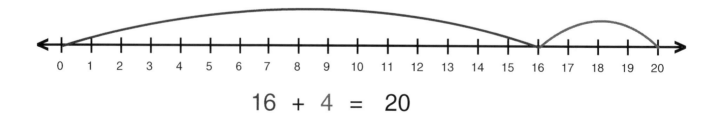

$$16 + 4 = 20$$

ANSWER SHEET
Order of Operations

1) 18 ÷ 6 x 5 - 2
       3 x 5 - 2
         15 - 2
            13

2) 16 ÷ 2 + 14 x 8
      8 + 14 x 8
      8 + · 112
         120

3) 11 x 5 - 3 + 13
     55 - 3 + 13
        65

4) 6 x 11 + 24 ÷ 3
    66 + 24 ÷ 3
    66 +   8
       74

5) 4 x 15 ÷ 5 + 19
    60 ÷ 5 + 19
     12 + 19
       31

6) 6 - 1 x 12 + 7
    6 -   12 + 7
         1

7) 12 ÷ 4 x 2 - 1
     3 x 2 - 1
       6 - 1
        5

8) 11 - 20 ÷ 5 x 17
   11 -   4 x 17
   11 -   68
       -57

9) 8 + 6 - 4 x 10
   8 + 6 -   40
       -26

10) 16 - 16 ÷ 2 + 16
    16 -   8 + 16
       24

ANSWER SHEET
Order of Operations

1) 6 + 4 - 1 x 12
    6 + 4 -   12
            -2

6) 7 x 17 + 15 - 8
    119 + 15 - 8
          126

2) 19 + 10 x 6 + 12
    19 +   60 + 12
          91

7) 7 - 1 x 6 + 3
    7 -   6 + 3
          4

3) 18 + 7 + 18 x 4
    18 + 7 +   72
          97

8) 15 + 6 - 4 x 11
    15 + 6 -   44
          -23

4) 11 + 6 x 10 - 8
    11 +   60 - 8
          63

9) 11 - 4 + 4 x 13
    11 - 4 +   52
          59

5) 9 x 9 - 2 + 18
    81 - 2 + 18
          97

10) 4 x 19 - 16 + 5
    76 - 16 + 5
          65

ANSWER SHEET

Percentage Calculations

Round your answer to two decimal places.

1) $0.65 \times 98 = 63.70$

2) $20 \div 18\% = 111.11$

3) $90\% \times 56 = 50.40$

4) $60 \div 0.78 = 76.92$

5) $42 \div 49 = 85.71\%$

6) $68 \div 93 = 73.12\%$

7) $0.62 \times 71 = 44.02$

8) $95 \div 0.23 = 413.04$

9) $90\% \times 81 = 72.90$

10) $71 \div 61\% = 116.39$

ANSWER SHEET
Identify and Calculate the Area and Perimeter for each Triangle.

1)

s = 7 cm

h = 6.1 cm

Area: _____21.35 sq cm_____

Perimeter: _21 cm_____

Type: _Equilateral Triangle_

2)

s = 5.1 cm

h = 4.4 cm

Area: _____11.22 sq cm_____

Perimeter: _15.3 cm_____

Type: _Equilateral Triangle_

3)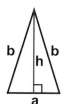

a = 4.4 ft   b = 8 ft

h = 7.4 ft

Area: _____16.28 sq ft_____

Perimeter: _20.4 ft_____

Type: _Isosceles Triangle_

4)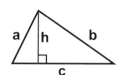

a = 4.92 ft

c = 8.7 ft

Area: _____19.14 sq ft_____

Perimeter: _21.47 ft_____

Type: _Common Triangle_

5)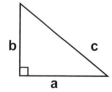

a = 7.5 inches   b = 6 inches

c = 9.6 inches

Area: _____22.5 sq inches_____

Perimeter: _23.1 inches_____

Type: _Right Triangle_

6)

s = 7.1 mm

h = 6.1 mm

Area: _____21.66 sq mm_____

Perimeter: _21.3 mm_____

Type: _Equilateral Triangle_

7)

a = 4.2 inches   b = 6.6 inches

h = 6.1 inches

Area: _____12.81 sq inches_____

Perimeter: _17.4 inches_____

Type: _Isosceles Triangle_

8)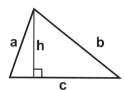

a = 6.05 mm   b = 9.31 mm

c = 9.4 mm

Area: _____26.79 sq mm_____

Perimeter: _24.76 mm_____

Type: _Common Triangle_

9)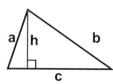

a = 5.18 yds   b = 8.65 yds

c = 8.8 yds   h = 4.9 yds

Area: _____21.56 sq yds_____

Perimeter: _22.63 yds_____

Type: _Common Triangle_

ANSWER SHEET
Write the Names for the Numbers.

1) 7,397 Seven Thousand, Three Hundred Ninety - Seven

2) 6,831 Six Thousand, Eight Hundred Thirty - One

3) 3,887 Three Thousand, Eight Hundred Eighty - Seven

4) 7,427 Seven Thousand, Four Hundred Twenty - Seven

5) 9,885 Nine Thousand, Eight Hundred Eighty - Five

6) 1,537 One Thousand, Five Hundred Thirty - Seven

7) 5,924 Five Thousand, Nine Hundred Twenty - Four

8) 7,147 Seven Thousand, One Hundred Forty - Seven

9) 4,718 Four Thousand, Seven Hundred Eighteen

10) 7,222 Seven Thousand, Two Hundred Twenty - Two

ANSWER SHEET
Write out the Correct Number Name.

1) 159,785,728,298   one hundred fifty-nine billion, seven hundred eighty-five million, seven hundred twenty-eight thousand, two hundred ninety-eight

2)   95,883,459   ninety-five million, eight hundred eighty-three thousand, four hundred fifty-nine

3) 791,695,257,252   seven hundred ninety-one billion, six hundred ninety-five million, two hundred fifty-seven thousand, two hundred fifty-two

4) 77,414,744,518   seventy-seven billion, four hundred fourteen million, seven hundred forty-four thousand, five hundred eighteen

5)   3,998,939,662   three billion, nine hundred ninety-eight million, nine hundred thirty-nine thousand, six hundred sixty-two

6)   6,453,291   six million, four hundred fifty-three thousand, two hundred ninety-one

7)   2,165,633   two million, one hundred sixty-five thousand, six hundred thirty-three

8)   27,894,813   twenty-seven million, eight hundred ninety-four thousand, eight hundred thirteen

9)   852,371,825   eight hundred fifty-two million, three hundred seventy-one thousand, eight hundred twenty-five

10)   141,339,361   one hundred forty-one million, three hundred thirty-nine thousand, three hundred sixty-one

ANSWER SHEET
Write the Numbers in Standard Form.

1) __27__   20 + 7

2) __44__   40 + 4

3) __48__   40 + 8

4) __86__   80 + 6

5) __85__   80 + 5

6) __40__   40 + 0

7) __61__   60 + 1

8) __70__   70 + 0

9) __23__   20 + 3

10) __91__   90 + 1

11) __46__   40 + 6

12) __82__   80 + 2

13) __12__   10 + 2

14) __39__   30 + 9

15) __94__   90 + 4

ANSWER SHEET
Solve and Graph the Inequalities

1) p > 17

2) k ≥ 5

3) f < 11

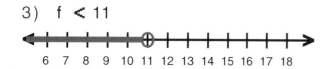

4) g ≤ 8

5) s ≤ 11

6) w ≥ 14

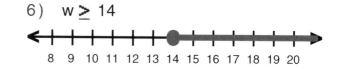

7) x ≤ 7

8) n ≤ 15

9) h > 8

10) y > 4

ANSWER SHEET
Identifying Polynomials

Identify the type for each.

1) $5k^3x - 6y$

   Binomial

2) $8xs^6b^4 - 6k^7 + 7r^5n^3 - 2n^5y^2$

   Polynomials - 4 Terms

3) $-8s^2g^6 + 2r^5 - 5p^4c^7 - 7d^4q^2 + 9q^7h^3$

   Polynomials - 5 Terms

4) $-gc^3 - 2r^5 + 4x^6q^7 - 5h^2z^7$

   Polynomials - 4 Terms

5) $-b + p - y + k$

   Polynomials - 4 Terms

6) $-6z^6q - 2r + 7c + 9s - 3n - 4g$

   Polynomials - 6 Terms

7) $rz^3k^5 + 6p^2 + 7n^6q^4 - 9q^5g^6 + 5b^2$

   Polynomials - 5 Terms

8) $2q^7x^5 + 9s^4 - 8g^3k^6 - 4n^3b^7 + 3b^6r^2 + 3r$

   Polynomials - 6 Terms

9) $4ph^3 - 8q^4 + 5y^2s^5 + 7k^3z^5$

   Polynomials - 4 Terms

10) $sn^6g^5 - 6z^4 + 4b^3y^2 + 3y^5p^3 + 9q^4 - 2q$

    Polynomials - 6 Terms

ANSWER SHEET
Translate Algebraic Expressions

1) Product of 2 and f $\qquad$ 2f

2) Sum of 2 and c $\qquad$ 2+c

3) Take away 4 from s $\qquad$ s-4

4) 7 less than 8 times w $\qquad$ 8w - 7

5) 5 is subtracted from b $\qquad$ b-5

6) Two-thirds of b is added to the product of 5 and q $\qquad$ $\frac{2}{3}b + 5q$

7) 3 times the sum of m and 9 $\qquad$ 3(m+9)

8) Add 7 to 8 times w $\qquad$ 8w + 7

9) Subtract three-fifths from 2 times s $\qquad$ $2s - \frac{3}{5}$

10) 9 is added to three-fourths of y $\qquad$ $9 + \frac{3}{4}y$

ANSWER SHEET

Working with the Properties of Mathematics

1) Which of the following is an example of Commutative Property of Addition ?

    A. 4 + 6 = 6 + 4   **B.** 7 x 1 = 7   _A_

    C. 2 + 3 = 5 + 2   **D.** (6 + 9) + 8 = 6 + (9 + 8)

2) Which Property of Multiplication is shown ?   (5 + 8) x 4 = 5 x 4 + 8 x 4

    A. Distributive Property   **B.** Commutative Property   _A_

    C. Associative Property   **D.** Identity Property

3) Which is an example of Associative Property of Addition ?

    A. 3 + 5 = 5 + 3   **B.** (5 + 4) + 8 = 5 + (4 + 8)   _B_

    C. 7 + (-7) = 0   **D.** 9 + 0 = 9

4) Which property would you use to simplify the following expression ?

    A. Multiplication Property of Zero   **B.** Commutative Property   _D_

    C. Associative Property   **D.** Distributive Property

5) Which of the following does not show the Commutative Property of Addition ?

    A. 3x + 4y = 4y + 3x   **B.** ab = ba   _B_

    C. 5 + x = x + 5   **D.** a + b = b + a

6) Which operation will not change the value of any nonzero number ?

    A. Adding One   **B.** Multiplying by One   _B_

    C. Dividing by Zero   **D.** Multiplying by Zero

7) Which equation shows the Identity Property of Multiplication ?

    A. a(b + c) = ab + ac   **B.** a + a + a = 3 x a   _D_

    C. (a + b) + 6 = a + (6 + b)   **D.** a x 1

8) Which property is used in the following expression ?   (a x b) x c = a x (b x c)

    A. Associative Property of Addition   **B.** Distributive Property   _C_

    C. Associative Property of Multiplication   **D.** Commutative Property of Addition

9) Which property is used in the following ?   8 x (4 + 2) = 8 x 4 + 8 x 2

    A. Commutative Property   **B.** Distributive Property   _B_

    C. Associative Property   **D.** None of the above

10) Which of the following does not show the Commutative Property ?

    A. x + y = y + x   **B.** 7 + y = y + 7   _D_

    C. yx = xy   **D.** xy - 2 = xy

ANSWER SHEET
Working with the Properties of Mathematics

11) Which Property of Addition does 2 + 0 = 2 illustrate ?

    A. Identity Property   **B.** Zero Property   <u>A</u>

    C. Commutative Property   **D.** Distributive Property

12) Which is an example of Identity Property of Addition ?

    A. 3 + 7 = 7 + 3   **B.** 4 x 1 = 4   <u>D</u>

    C. (7 + 6) + 8 = 7 + (6 + 8)   **D.** 2 + 0 = 2

13) Which equation shows the Commutative Property of Multiplication ?

    A. 6 x 1 = 6   **B.** 3 x 3 = 3 + 3 + 3   <u>C</u>

    C. 4 x 9 = 9 x 4   **D.** 7 x 2 - 5 x 2 = (7 - 5) x 3

14) Simplify this expression : 6(y + z)

    A. 6z + y   **B.** 6y + z   <u>D</u>

    C. 6yz   **D.** 6y + 6z

15) Which property is used in the following expression ?   (3 x 6) x 9 = 6 x (9 x 3)

    A. Associative Property of Multiplication   **B.** Commutative Property of Addition   <u>A</u>

    C. Associative Property of Addition   **D.** Distributive Property of Multiplication

16) Which property of addition is used in the following ?   (7 + 5) + 9 = 7 + (5 + 9)

    A. Identity Property   **B.** Distributive Property   <u>D</u>

    C. Commutative Property   **D.** Associative Property

17) Which property is used in the following expression ?   2(5 + 4) = 10 + 8

    A. Distributive Property   **B.** Associative Property of Multiplication   <u>A</u>

    C. Associative Property of Addition   **D.** Commutative Property of Addition

ANSWER SHEET
Equivalent Ratios

Write two equivalent ratios.

1)
7	14	21
8	16	24

2)
5	10	15
7	14	21

3)
9	18	27
5	10	15

4)
11	22	33
5	10	15

5)
10	20	30
3	6	9

6)
11	22	33
6	12	18

Determine whether the ratios are equivalent.

7) $\frac{5}{11}$ and $\frac{20}{44}$ ___Yes___

8) $\frac{2}{7}$ and $\frac{7}{10}$ ___No___

9) $\frac{3}{11}$ and $\frac{6}{5}$ ___No___

10) $\frac{12}{5}$ and $\frac{8}{3}$ ___No___

11) $\frac{3}{8}$ and $\frac{6}{16}$ ___Yes___

12) $\frac{7}{11}$ and $\frac{7}{3}$ ___No___

Use equivalent ratios to find the unknown value.

13) $\frac{n}{15} = \frac{7}{5}$ n = ___21___

14) $\frac{6}{7} = \frac{z}{49}$ z = ___42___

15) $\frac{2}{11} = \frac{4}{y}$ y = ___22___

16) $\frac{7}{2} = \frac{z}{12}$ z = ___42___

17) $\frac{5}{12} = \frac{25}{y}$ y = ___60___

18) $\frac{20}{r} = \frac{4}{7}$ r = ___35___

ANSWER SHEET
Scientific Notation

Write each number in standard format.

1) 5.525×10^{4} = 55250

2) 3.7915×10^{-6} = 0.00000379150

3) 2.57×10^{-9} = 0.000000002570

4) 7.372×10^{-1} = 0.7372

5) 3.34×10^{-8} = 0.00000003340

6) 7.64×10^{-4} = 0.000764

7) $7.52 \times {}^{4}$ = 75200

8) 9.0674×10^{7} = 90674000

9) 9.508×10^{5} = 950800

10) 8.384×10^{1} = 83.84

Write each number in scientific notation.

11) 9788000000 = $9.788 \times {}^{9}$

12) 0.0000003060 = 3.06×10^{-7}

13) 0.005827 = 5.827×10^{-3}

14) 8535.8 = $8.5358 \times {}^{3}$

15) 851880000 = $8.5188 \times {}^{8}$

16) 3550000 = $3.55 \times {}^{6}$

17) 945.4 = $9.454 \times {}^{2}$

18) 0.00087077 = 8.7077×10^{-4}

19) 0.00001820 = 1.82×10^{-5}

20) 0.0984 = 9.84×10^{-2}

ANSWER SHEET
Complete the Skip Counting Series

1)   71,   69,   67,   65,   63,   61,   59,   57,   55,   53

2)   27,   17,   7,   -3,   -13,   -23,   -33,   -43,   -53,   -63

3)   93,   73,   53,   33,   13,   -7,   -27,   -47,   -67,   -87

4)   3,   8,   13,   18,   23,   28,   33,   38,   43,   48

5)   14,   24,   34,   44,   54,   64,   74,   84,   94,   104

6)   2,   4,   6,   8,   10,   12,   14,   16,   18,   20

7)   43,   45,   47,   49,   51,   53,   55,   57,   59,   61

8)   86,   88,   90,   92,   94,   96,   98,   100,   102,   104

9)   94,   96,   98,   100,   102,   104,   106,   108,   110,   112

10)   36,   38,   40,   42,   44,   46,   48,   50,   52,   54

11)   65,   67,   69,   71,   73,   75,   77,   79,   81,   83

12)   89,   91,   93,   95,   97,   99,   101,   103,   105,   107

ANSWER SHEET
Complete the Skip Counting Series

1) 7, 14, 21, 28, 35, 42, 49, 56, 63, 70, 77, 84

2) 10, 20, 30, 40, 50, 60, 70, 80, 90, 100, 110, 120

3) 6, 12, 18, 24, 30, 36, 42, 48, 54, 60, 66, 72

4) 12, 24, 36, 48, 60, 72, 84, 96, 108, 120, 132, 144

5) 5, 10, 15, 20, 25, 30, 35, 40, 45, 50, 55, 60

6) 2, 4, 6, 8, 10, 12, 14, 16, 18, 20, 22, 24

7) 11, 22, 33, 44, 55, 66, 77, 88, 99, 110, 121, 132

8) 4, 8, 12, 16, 20, 24, 28, 32, 36, 40, 44, 48

9) 3, 6, 9, 12, 15, 18, 21, 24, 27, 30, 33, 36

10) 9, 18, 27, 36, 45, 54, 63, 72, 81, 90, 99, 108

11) 8, 16, 24, 32, 40, 48, 56, 64, 72, 80, 88, 96

ANSWER SHEET
Trigonometric Ratios
Find the given trigonometric ratio. The answer will be in fraction form.

1) cos B = $\frac{n}{s}$

2) cos X = $\frac{k}{d}$

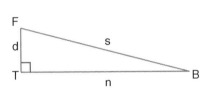

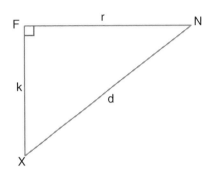

3) sin N = $\frac{35}{37}$

4) tan O = $\frac{e}{n}$

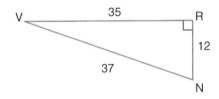

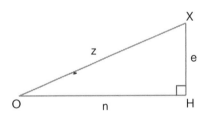

5) sin S = $\frac{36}{85}$

6) tan U = $\frac{28}{45}$

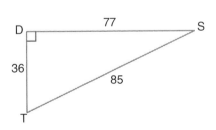

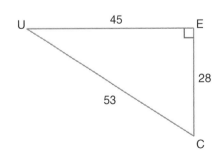

ANSWER SHEET
Word Problems

1) Tim worked on the farm storing bales of hay in the barn. The first day he stacked 40 bales and 20 bales on the second day. How many bales were stored in the barn?   60 bales

2) While fishing over the weekend Tim caught 12 and Mike caught 47 fish. How many fish were caught?   60 fish

3) The post office mails 74 letters each day, out of which 47 are addressed to foreign countries. How many letters are addressed domestically?   20 letters

4) Melanie is reading a book that contains 73 pages. She has read 27 pages. How many pages are unread?   40 pages

5) Sam painted his house with white and blue paint. He used a total of 76 gallons of paint. If he used 41 gallons of white paint, how many gallons of blue paint did he use?   40 gallons

6) There are 79 lemons in the store, 31 lemon are sold by the end of the day. How many lemons are left in the store?   50 lemons

7) Jessica and Mary decided to bake cookies for a family picnic. Jessica baked 38 raisin cookies and Mary baked 10 sugar cookies. How many cookies were baked?   50 cookies

8) Benny scored 32 points in Monday's basketball game and 28 points in Friday's game. How many points did he score in the last two games?   60 points

9) There are 22 scissors in the drawer. Fred placed 15 more scissors in the drawer. How many scissors are in the drawer?   40 scissors

10) Tim's Cupcake Shop sold a total of 87 cupcakes yesterday, and 15 of those had sprinkles. How many cupcakes were sold without sprinkles?   70 cupcakes

* English: Apostrophe

An apostrophe is a punctuation mark used to indicate where something has been removed. It can be used in contractions, to show possession, to replace a phrase, for the plural form of family names, for irregular plural possessives, and, on rare occasions, to provide clarity for a non-possessive plural. Avoid common apostrophe mistakes, such as using 'it's' for the possessive 'its,' which should be 'its.' Omitting the apostrophe, putting it in the wrong place for a possessive plural, and using 'of' when you mean to contract a word with 'have' are other common errors.

Apostrophes, like any other aspect of language, are prone to errors. The omission of the apostrophe is one of the most common.

Here are some examples:

'Let's go to McDonalds.' Correct: 'McDonald's'
'Whos responsible for the bill?' Correct: 'Who's'
'Its about five o'clock.' Correct: 'It's.' We are saying 'it is' here, so we need the apostrophe.

1. Where should the apostrophe go in didnt?
   a. didn't
   b. did'nt

2. How do you make the contraction for was not?
   a. was'nt
   b. wasn't

3. How do you make Jimmy possessive?
   a. Jimmy's
   b. Jimmys

4. Where should the apostrophe go in shouldnt?
   a. should'nt
   b. shouldn't

5. How do you make the contraction for she would?
   a. she'd
   b. sh'ed

6. What is the correct use of the apostrophe?
   a. brother's toys
   b. brother'is toys

7. Which of the following is the correct way to show possession with a plural noun ending in 's'?
   a. Add an apostrophe at the end.
   b. No apostrophe is required.

8. How would you express the plural possessive of the word 'child'?
   a. Child's
   b. Children's

9. What is the proper way to contract the possessive form of 'it'?
   a. Its
   b. It's

10. The _____ awfully good today.
    a. weather
    b. weather's

11. Adam believes _____ going to snow later.
    a. it's
    b. its

12. The dog was wagging _____ tail excitedly.
    a. its
    b. it's

13. Where did you leave _____ book?
    a. your
    b. you're

14. _____ going to Ms. Katy's room.
    a. Wer'e
    b. We're

15. Bobby always kicks _____ dolls around.
    a. Kim and Sandy's
    b. Jennifer and Katie

16. _____ not allowed to listen to music while they read.
    a. They're
    b. Their're

* ELA: Informational Text

An informational text is a nonfiction piece of writing that aims to educate or inform the reader about a specific topic. An informational text, unlike fiction or some other types of nonfiction texts, does not contain any characters. It presents information in a way that allows the reader to learn more about something of interest to them.

Informational text is a type of nonfiction that is intended to convey factual information about a specific topic. The purpose of informational text is to deliver information about a topic, and it is distinguished by its formatting, which includes organization, written cues (visual variations in text), and visuals/graphics.

Literary nonfiction, expository writing, persuasive/argumentative writing, and procedural writing are the four basic types of informational text. Examples of informational text can be found in a variety of formats both online and in print.

Select the best answer for each question.

1. Identify the main idea: "You wouldn't use a nail file to peel carrots. You can't tune an engine with a cheese grater, either. So why would you buy a wrench to do the job of a screwdriver?"
   a. Always use the right tool.
   b. Wrench and screwdrivers are basically the same.
   c. Use nail file for your fingernails.

2. Autobiographies are written in which point of view?
   a. second
   b. third
   c. first

3. Differentiate between a plot and a theme.
   a. A plot is the ending in a story, a theme conveys the message in first person
   b. A theme is a collection of the main idea, while a plot conveys the point of the ending
   c. A plot is more of what happens in a story, whereas a theme conveys the message of the story

4. Which is not an article in a reference book?
   a. thesaurus entry for the word army
   b. encyclopedia article on World War II
   c. a review of a novel

5. When creating summaries, it's important to _____.
   a. tell the ending of the story
   b. Write down the main points in your own words
   c. Use the first person exact words

6. Which type of literary nonfiction is not meant to be published or shared?
   a. biography
   b. diary
   c. memoir

7. Which of the following should you do as you read an informational text?
   a. Take notes
   b. find clue words and text
   c. read as quickly as possible

8. What makes a speech different from an article?
   a. speeches are meant to be spoken aloud to an audience
   b. speeches do not inform about a topic
   c. articles can persuade a reader

9. Which type of literary nonfiction is a short piece on a single topic?
   a. essay
   b. letter
   c. memoir

10. Procedural writing example:
    a. letter to the editor, blog entry
    b. textbook, travel brochure
    c. cookbooks, how-to articles, instruction manuals

* English: Nouns, Verbs, Adjectives, Adverbs

A noun is defined as a person, place, thing, or idea that has been used for thousands of years in all spoken languages.

An action verb is a word that shows action. 'What did they do in the sentence?' is one way to find the action verb. Action verbs are necessary for descriptive and informative writing.

Adjectives are descriptive words for nouns. We use them to provide our audience with a more complete and detailed picture of the noun we are describing. What words would you use to describe yourself? Would you describe yourself as intelligent or amusing? Is your room cluttered or neat? When describing something, adjectives are used.

An adverb is a word that modifies another word, such as a verb, adjective, or adverb. Adverbs improve the precision and interest of writing. Adverbs answer these questions:

- When?
- Where?
- In what manner?
- To what extent?

1. Which of the following is NOT a noun?
   a. place
   b. person
   c. action

2. A verb is a(n) _____.
   a. action
   b. word that describes a noun
   c. person, place, thing, or idea

3. True or False: An adjective describes a verb.
   a. True
   b. False

4. Adverbs describe or modify _____.
   a. adverbs
   b. adjectives
   c. verbs

5. What is the adverb in the sentence? Peter neatly wrote a shopping list.
   a. Peter
   b. wrote
   c. neatly

6. Which sentence shows the proper use of an adverb?
   a. Jim quick walked.
   b. Jim walked quickly.
   c. Jim walked quick.

7. Which of the following words is a common noun identifying a person?
   a. Dr. Jones
   b. doctor
   c. Mr. Jones

8. Which of the following nouns is a proper noun?
   a. Cat
   b. Central Park
   c. Fireman

9. Which sentence part contains an action verb?
   a. baseball or soccer
   b. eat an ice cream cone
   c. to the top of the hill and back

10. Adjectives are words that describe what?
    a. nouns
    b. other adjectives
    c. verbs

11. Which adjective would best describe a cat?
    a. sharp
    b. furry
    c. cold

12. Which sentence gives the clearest picture using adjectives?
    a. The tall, fast lady runs.
    b. The lady runs fast.
    c. The sleek, slender, funny little lady runs.

* Science: Coral Reefs

First, read the entire passage. After that, go back and fill in the blanks. You can skip the blanks you're unsure about and finish them later.

biomes	rocks	Photosynthesis	Barrier	25%
living	harden	shallow	habitation	atoll
Fringe	survive	Australia	Great	algae

One of the most important marine _____ is the coral reef. Coral reefs are home to approximately _____ of all known marine species, despite being a relatively small biome.

Coral reefs may appear to be made of _____ at first glance, but they are actually _____ organisms. These organisms are polyps, which are tiny little animals. Polyps live on the reef's periphery. When polyps die, they _____ and new polyps grow on top of them, causing the reef to expand.

Because polyps must eat to _____, you can think of the coral reef as eating as well. They eat plankton and _____, which are small animals. _____ is how algae get their food from the sun. This is why coral reefs form near the water's surface and in clear water where the algae can be fed by the sun.

To form, coral reefs require warm, _____ water. They form near the equator, near coastlines, and around islands all over the world. Southeast Asia and the region around _____ are home to a sizable portion of the world's coral reefs. The Great Barrier Reef, located off the coast of Queensland, Australia, is the world's largest coral reef. The _____ Barrier Reef is 2,600 miles long.

Coral reefs are classified into three types:

_____ reefs are reefs that grow close to the shore. It may be attached to the shore, or there may be a narrow swath of water known as a lagoon or channel between the land and the coral reef.

_____ reef - Barrier reefs grow away from the shoreline, sometimes for several miles.

An _____ is a coral ring that surrounds a lagoon of water. It begins as a fringe reef surrounding a volcanic island. As the coral grows, the island sinks into the ocean, leaving only the coral ring. Some atolls are large enough to support human _____. The Maldives is an example of this.

* Science: Ecosystem

First, read the entire passage. After that, go back and fill in the blanks. You can skip the blanks you're unsure about and finish them later.

sunlight	grass	another	chain	decaying
running	photosynthesis	living	herbivores	zebra

To survive, every _____ plant and animal requires energy. Plants get their energy from the soil, water, and the sun. Plants and other animals provide energy to animals. Plants and animals in an ecosystem rely on one _____ to survive. Scientists may use a food chain or a food web to describe this dependence.

A food chain describes how various organisms eat one another, beginning with a plant and ending with an animal.

For example, the food chain for a lion could be written as follows: grass ---> zebra ---> lion
The lion eats the _____, which consumes the _____.

The grasshopper consumes grass, the frog consumes the grasshopper, the snake consumes the frog, and the eagle consumes the snake. Each link in the food _____ has a name to help describe it. The terms are determined mainly by what the organism eats and how it contributes to the ecosystem's energy.

Producers - Plants are creators. This is because they generate energy for the ecosystem. They do this because _____ absorbs energy from the sun. They require water and nutrients from the soil as well, but plants are the only source of new energy.

Consumers - Consumers include animals. This is because they do not generate energy; instead, they consume it. Primary consumers, also known as _____, are animals that eat plants. Secondary consumers or carnivores are animals that eat other animals. A carnivore is referred to as a tertiary consumer when it consumes another carnivore. Some animals perform both functions, eating both plants and animals. They are known as omnivores.

Decomposers are organisms that consume _____ matter (like dead plants and animals). They aid in the reintroduction of nutrients into the soil for plant consumption. Worms, bacteria, and fungi are examples of decomposers.

As previously stated, all energy produced in the food chain is produced by producers or plants, who convert _____ into energy through photosynthesis. The rest of the food chain merely consumes energy. As a result, as you move up the food chain, less and less energy is available. As a result, as you move up the food chain, there are fewer and fewer organisms. In the preceding example, there is more grass than zebras and more zebras than lions. The zebras and lions expend energy by _____, hunting, and breathing.

19. You can not build on that _____. [cite / sight / site]

20. The _____ [cite / site / sight] of land is refreshing.

21. I _____ [complimented / complemented / discouraged] my wife on her cooking.

22. We all have a _____ [conscience / mind / conscious] of right and wrong.

23. The boxer is still _____. [conscience / conscious / knocked out]

24. I went to the city _____ [municipal / counsel / council] meeting.

25. My accountant _____ [directed / counciled / counseled] me on spending habits.

26. The teacher _____ [brought out / illicit / elicited] the correct response.

27. The criminal was arrested for _____ [elicit / illicit / illegal] activities.

28. The baby will cry as soon as _____ [its' / it's / its] mother leaves.

29. _____ [It's / It is / Its] a beautiful day

30. I have a headache, so I'm going to _____ [lay / lain / lie] down.

31. You should never tell a _____. [lay / lie / lye]

32. If you _____ [lose / find / loose] your phone, I will not buy a new one!

33. My pants feel _____, [loose / tight / lose] I need a belt.

34. I _____ [kindly / kind / a bit] of like spicy food.

35. He is a very _____ [kind of / mean / kind] teacher.

* English: Personal Pronouns

Score: _____

Date: _____

Personal pronouns are words that are used to replace the subject or object of a sentence to make it easier for readers to understand.

To give a brief, personal pronouns are:

1. Replace nouns and other pronouns to make sentences easier to read and understand.

2. A sentence's subject or object can be either. For example, 'I' is the first-person subject pronoun, whereas 'me' is the first-person object pronoun.

3. It is possible to use the singular or plural form.

4. They must agree on gender and number with the words they are substituting.

1. Which of the following sentences has a plural subject pronoun and a plural object pronoun?
   a. She wants to live as long as she can, as long as she have someone by her side.
   b. While Tom believe everything will be fine, many don't agree with him.
   c. Whether we lived or died, it didn't matter to us either way.

2. Which of the following words would make the following sentence grammatically correct? '6th graders should check with their teachers before you leave the classroom.'
   a. Replace 'their' with 'they'
   b. Replace 'you' with 'they'
   c. Replace '6th graders' with 'they'

3. The pronoun 'my' is a . . .
   a. 1st person possessive pronoun
   b. 3rd person nominative pronoun
   c. 2nd person possessive pronoun

4. Which of the following correctly identifies the subjective and objective pronouns in the sentence here? 'Run away from the dinosaurs with the giant feet?' she asked. 'You don't have to tell me twice.'
   a. she - subject pronoun; you - subject pronoun; me - object pronoun
   b. she - object pronoun; you - object pronoun; me - object pronoun
   c. she - object pronoun; you - subject pronoun; me - object pronoun

5. The pronoun 'your' is a . . .
   a. 2nd person possessive pronoun
   b. 1st person possessive pronoun
   c. 2nd person objective pronoun

6. Which pronouns are found in the following sentence? 'I kept telling her that we would go back for John, but I knew we had left him behind. '
   a. I, we, knew, we, him
   b. I, her, we, I, we, him
   c. I, we, I, we, him

7. Kevin likes playing basketball. _____ is a very good player.
   a. Him
   b. He
   c. Their

8. The pronoun 'its' is a . . .
   a. 3rd person possessive pronoun
   b. 2nd person possessive pronoun
   c. 3rd person objective pronoun

9. The pronoun 'their' is a . . .
   a. 2nd person possessive pronoun
   b. 3rd person objective pronoun
   c. 3rd person possessive pronoun

10. Kimmy is a very good cook. _____ can cook any kind of food.
   a. She
   b. Hey
   c. Their

* Reading Comprehension: Social Media Safety

Score: _____

Date: _____

Tip: After you've answered the easy ones, go back and work the harder ones.

Interactions	policies	relationship	post	pop-ups
incidents	identity	connect	Personal	logins
negative	harmful	restrictive	steal	privacy
passwords	viruses	platform	abuse	security

In the last 20 years, socializing has evolved dramatically. _____ between people are referred to as socializing. At one time, socializing meant getting together with family and friends. It now frequently refers to accessing the Internet via social media or websites that allow you to _____ and interact with other people.

One of the first things you can do to protect yourself while online occurs before you even visit a social media website. Ascertain that your computer is outfitted with up-to-date computer _____ software. This software detects and removes _____ that are harmful to your computer. When you use your computer, these viruses can sometimes hack into it and _____ your information, such as _____. Create strong _____ for all of your social media accounts. This is necessary to prevent others from accessing your social media account.

Internet security settings are pre-installed on all computers. These can be as loose or as _____ as you want them to be. To be safe, it is recommended that the Internet security settings be set to medium or higher. This enables your computer to block _____ and warn you when you are about to visit a potentially harmful website.

Two things to keep in mind

- Don't _____ anything you wouldn't want broadcast to the entire world.

- The 'Golden Rule' of life is to treat others as you would like to be treated.

LIFE SKILLS PRACTICE ONLY
Checks are pieces of paper used to make payments.

AWESOME BANK

DATE: _____

PAY TO THE
ORDER OF: _____ $ _____

_____ DOLLARS

FOR: _____

00000000 156   00000000 296 456

AWESOME BANK

DATE: _____

PAY TO THE
ORDER OF: _____ $ _____

_____ DOLLARS

FOR: _____

00000000 156   00000000 296 456

AWESOME BANK

DATE: _____

PAY TO THE
ORDER OF: _____ $ _____

_____ DOLLARS

FOR: _____

00000000 156   00000000 296 456

AWESOME BANK

DATE: _____

PAY TO THE
ORDER OF: _____ $ _____

_____ DOLLARS

FOR: _____

00000000 156   00000000 296 456

* Art: Mary Cassatt

First, read the entire passage. After that, go back and fill in the blanks. You can skip the blanks you're unsure about and finish them later.

influenced	private	Fine	museums	techniques
pastels	Pittsburgh	Japanese	childhood	enrolled

Mary Cassatt was born on May 22, 1844, into a prosperous family near _____, Pennsylvania. She spent a significant portion of her _____ in France and Germany, where she learned French and German. She developed an interest in art while in Europe and decided that she wanted to be a professional artist early on.

Despite her parents' reservations about Mary pursuing a career as an artist, she _____ in the Pennsylvania Academy of _____ Arts in 1860. Mary studied art at the academy for several years but became dissatisfied with the instruction and limitations on female students. Mary moved to Paris in 1866 and began taking _____ lessons from art instructor Jean-Leon Gerome. She also studied paintings in museums such as the Louvre on her own. One of her paintings (A Mandolin Player) was accepted for exhibition at the prestigious Paris Salon in 1868. Cassatt continued to paint with some success over the next few years.

By 1877, Mary Cassatt had grown dissatisfied with Paris's traditional art scene. Fortunately, Mary became close friends with Impressionist painter Edgar Degas around this time. She began to experiment with new painting _____ and discovered a whole new world of art in Impressionism. She began to exhibit her paintings alongside the Impressionists and gained further acclaim in the art world.

Early on, Cassatt's artistic style was _____ by European masters, and later, by the Impressionist art movement (especially Edgar Degas). Mary also studied _____ art, which is evident in many of her paintings. Mary wanted to use her art to express light and color. She frequently used _____. The majority of her paintings depict people. She primarily painted her family for many years. Later, scenes depicting a mother and child together became a major theme in her paintings.

Mary Cassatt is widely regarded as one of America's greatest artists. She rose to prominence in the art world at a time when it was extremely difficult for women to do so. Many of her paintings are currently on display at _____ such as the National Gallery of Art, The Metropolitan Museum of Art, and the National Portrait Gallery.

* Music: History of the Violin

Score: _____

Date: _____

First, read the entire passage. After that, go back and fill in the blanks. You can skip the blanks you're unsure about and finish them later.

strings	France	soundhole	bowed	ages
introduced	Italy	Baroque	existence	existence

Stringed instruments that use a bow to produce sound, such as the violin, are referred to as _____ stringed instruments. The ancestors of the violin are said to be the Arabian rabab and the rebec, which came from the Orient in the middle _____ and were popular in Spain and _____ in the fifteenth century. A bowed stringed instrument known as a fiddle first appeared in Europe near the end of the Middle Ages.

In terms of completeness, the violin is in a class by itself when compared to its forefathers. Furthermore, it did not evolve gradually over time but instead appeared in its current form abruptly around 1550. However, none of these early violins are still in _____ today. The violin's history is inferred from paintings from this era that depicts violins.

The two earliest recorded violin makers are from northern _____: Andre Amati of Cremona and Gasparo di Bertolotti of Salone (Gasparo di Salon). The history of the violin emerges from the fog of legend to hard fact thanks to these two violin makers. These two's violins are still in use today. The oldest violin still in _____ today is one built around 1565 by Andre Amati.

Though the violin was _____ to the world in the middle of the sixteenth century, a similar-looking instrument called the viol was made around the fourteenth century.

The viol flourished in the sixteenth and seventeenth centuries, and the violin and viol coexisted during the _____ period.

The viol family's instruments did not have the f-shaped _____ of the violin, but rather a C-shaped soundhole or a more decorative shape. The viol differs from the violin in that it has six, seven, or more _____ tuned in fourths (as opposed to the violin's four strings tuned in fifths), a fretted fingerboard, and a relatively thick body due to the sloping shoulder shape at the neck-body joint. There are several sizes, but the Viola da Gamba, which has a lower register similar to the cello, is the most well-known.

* Geography: Himalayas

Score: _____

Date: _____

Jurassic	Mount	earthquake	tallest	mountains
grasslands	Sheep	Abominable	oxygen	surface

The Himalayas are an Asian mountain range. The Himalayan region includes Nepal, Tibet, Bhutan, India, Afghanistan, and Pakistan. The Himalayas are home to the majority of the world's _____ mountains.

I'm almost sure you've heard of _____ Everest, the world's tallest mountain. Climbers train for years to scale this massive chunk of rock and ice. Because Everest is so high, most climbers require _____, which is a pure component of the air we breathe, to reach the summit, and many climbers must abandon their efforts before reaching the summit.

Plate tectonics created the Himalayas, which may sound like a technical term, but it's quite simple. Large swaths of land make up the earth's _____. Plate tectonics is basically what happens when the pieces move slightly and collide with each other. When these plates collide, one piece of land is forced beneath the other, raising the piece on top and eventually forming _____. Everest grew to a height of 29,000 feet as a result of this process!

The shifting that formed the Himalayas began during the _____ period; I wonder what the dinosaurs thought of the earth moving beneath their feet? But, just like us, they probably couldn't feel anything because plate tectonics is invisible to anyone living on the earth's surface - that is, until an _____ occurs, which is an extreme example of how plate tectonics work.

The name Himalayas means "home of snow," but most of the Himalayas are lower than the parts always covered in snow. The Himalayas are home to forests and _____ as well as ice. As you descend the mountains, the temperatures rise, and the snow melts. The Himalayas are the source (beginning point) of many important rivers in Asia, including the Ganges and the Yangtze. Many different kinds of animals and plants live in the forests and grasslands.

It's challenging to get past the image of bare mountains, but some areas of the Himalayas have fertile soil. The majority of farmable land in Nepal is in the foothills or lower hilly parts of the mountains. The majority of Nepal's rice is grown there. Apple, cherry, and grape orchards can be found in the Vale of the Kashmir region. _____, goats, and yaks are also raised. When the weather is warm, the animals graze higher in the mountains, but they move to lower pastures like snowfalls.

Have you ever heard of a Yeti? The Yeti, also known as the _____ Snowman, is a mythical creature that roams the Himalayas and resembles a giant hairy man. It is said to have shaggy, white fur and sharp teeth ready to devour anyone who comes into contact with it! According to monks, there are the remains of a Yeti hand in a Buddhist monastery in Pangboche, Nepal. Scientists believe they have proof that the Yeti is a rare type of polar bear, but others are skeptical. What are your thoughts? Is the Yeti a bear or a previously unknown monster?

* Geography: The North Pole

Score: _____

Date: _____

First, read the entire passage. After that, go back and fill in the blanks. You can skip the blanks you're unsure about and finish them later.

historians	cold	frozen	solar	survive
Frederick	Arctic	bears	axis	fish

What is the world's most northern location? You may be familiar with it as the location of Santa's workshop, but let's take a look at the North Pole's history, environment, and wildlife. It is situated in the middle of the _____ Ocean, which is almost entirely _____ all year. The only direction you could travel if you stood precisely on the North Pole is south!

For hundreds of years, explorers have attempted to reach the North Pole. Many exploration trips ended in disaster or with the explorers turning around and returning home due to inclement weather. _____ Cook was an American explorer who claimed to have discovered the North Pole for the first time in 1908. A year later, another American explorer, Robert Peary, made the same claim. Scientists and _____ have not been able to back up these claims. There are currently numerous expeditions to the North Pole, many traveling by airplane, boat, or submarine.

We all know the North Pole is _____, but compared to the South Pole, the weather is like summer. That is if you consider average winter temperatures of -22 degrees Fahrenheit to be comparable to summer temperatures! Summer temperatures hover around 32 degrees Fahrenheit on average. Pack your shorts and flip-flops for a trip to the North Pole!

There aren't many animals that can _____ in this environment because it's so cold all year. Many people believe that polar _____ live in the North Pole, but they do not travel that far north. Several bird species, including the Arctic snow bunting and the Arctic tern, travel to the North Pole. Every year, the tern travels to and from the South and North Poles!

Sealife is also scarce. Scientists discovered shrimp and _____, including Arctic cod, in the Arctic Ocean near the North Pole. Many sea animals, however, do not travel far enough north to reach the North Pole.

At the North Pole, day and night are very different. Because the Earth's _____ is tilted and the North Pole is at the top of the world, there is only one sunrise and one sunset each year. In the winter, there is constant darkness, whereas, in the summer, there is daylight all day and night!

An aurora is a unique event that occurs in polar areas, both north and south. These are brilliant colorful flashes of light in the night sky that are commonly referred to as polar lights. Auroras are caused by _____ winds and electromagnetic activity in the atmosphere.

* History Research: President Andrew Johnson

Primary sources to help with your research: Online research articles, Books, Historical documents and Autobiographies

Andrew Johnson is best known as the president who took over after Abraham Lincoln was assassinated. He is also well-known for being one of three presidents to have been impeached.

Andrew was born and raised in Raleigh, North Carolina. His parents were impoverished, and his father died when he was three years old. He was unable to attend school as a child because of his poverty, so his mother found him work as an apprentice to a tailor. Andrew could learn a trade this way. His family relocated to Tennessee when he was a teenager. Andrew established his own successful tailoring business here. Eliza McCardle, whom he married, was also someone he met and married. Eliza assisted Andrew with his education by teaching him math and assisting him in improving his reading and writing skills. Andrew developed an interest in debate and politics. His first political position was as a town alderman, and he was elected mayor in 1834.

What makes Andrew Jackson a hero?

What are 3 good things Andrew Jackson did?

Why was he the target of the first attempted presidential assassination.

Extra Credit Question:

Andrew Jackson first appeared on the $20 bill in what year?

_____

* History Research: The Pilgrims

Primary sources to help with your research: Online research articles, Books, Historical documents and Autobiographies

The Pilgrims were a group of English settlers who emigrated to the Americas in search of religious freedom. In 1620, they founded the Plymouth Colony.

The Pilgrims came to America in search of a better life. Many of the Pilgrims belonged to a religious sect known as Separatists. They were given this name because they desired to "separate" themselves from the Church of England and worship God in their own way. They could not do so in England, where they were persecuted and sometimes imprisoned for their beliefs. Other Pilgrims came to the New World in search of adventure or a better life.

In 1621, the Pilgrims celebrated their first harvest with a feast. They invited some Wampanoag people from the area to join them. This feast is sometimes referred to as the "First Thanksgiving." They kept this tradition going, and in 1623, when they were celebrating the end of a long drought, they coined the term "Thanksgiving."

What are 3 reasons the Pilgrims came to America?

What ships did the Pilgrims sail on?

What was the Mayflower voyage like?

What did pilgrims do when they arrived?

* History Research: California Gold Rush

Primary sources to help with your research: Online research articles, Books, Historical documents and Autobiographies

The California Gold Rush lasted from 1848 to 1855. Gold was discovered in California around this time. Over 300,000 people flocked to California in search of gold and a chance to "strike it rich."

James Marshall discovered gold in California at Sutter's Mill, near the town of Coloma. James was constructing a sawmill for John Sutter when he found gleaming flakes of gold in the river. He informed John Sutter of the discovery, which they attempted to keep secret. However, word quickly spread, and prospectors flocked to California in search of gold.

The California Gold Rush lasted from 1848 to 1855. Gold was discovered in California around this time. Over 300,000 people flocked to California in search of gold and a chance to "strike it rich."

Many of the early prospectors did well financially. They frequently made ten times what they could in a day working a regular job. The original gold miners would pan for it. Later, more complex methods were used to allow multiple miners to search for gold in more significant amounts of gravel.

Who got rich during the California gold rush?

When was gold found at Sutter's Mill in California?

Why were the gold rush people called the 49ers?

What California city became a boomtown? Why?

Why did towns become ghost towns?

* Reading Comprehension: Marco Polo

Marco Polo was a merchant and explorer who spent much of his life traveling throughout the Far East and China. For many years, his stories were the foundation of what much of Europe knew about Ancient China. He lived between 1254 and 1324.

Marco was born in 1254 in Venice, Italy. Marco's father was a merchant in Venice, a prosperous trading city.

The Silk Road was a network of trade routes that connected major cities and trading posts from Eastern Europe to Northern China. The Silk Road was named because silk cloth was China's main export. Few people completed the entire route. Trading was mostly done between cities or small sections of the route, and goods would slowly make their way from one end to the other, changing hands several times along the way. Marco Polo's father and uncle desired to try something new. They intended to travel all the way to China and return the goods to Venice. They believed that by doing so, they would be able to make a fortune. It took them nine years, but they eventually returned home.

Marco left for China for the first time when he was 17 years old. He accompanied his father and uncle on the trip. During their first trip to China, his father and uncle met the Mongol Emperor Kublai Khan and promised him they would return. At the time, Kublai was the ruler of all of China.

Marco Polo traveled to China for three years. Along the way, he visited many great cities and sites, including the holy city of Jerusalem, the Hindu Kush mountains, Persia, and the Gobi Desert. He met a wide range of people and had numerous adventures.

Marco spent many years in China, where he learned the language. As a messenger and spy for Kublai Khan, he traveled throughout China. He even went as far south as Myanmar and Vietnam are today. He learned about different cultures, foods, cities, and people during these visits. He saw places and things that no European had ever seen before.

Marco was captivated by the wealth and luxury of Chinese cities and the court of Kublai Khan. It was nothing like what he had seen in Europe. Kinsay's capital city was large but well-organized and clean. Wide roads and massive civil engineering projects like the Grand Canal were far beyond what he had seen back home. Everything was new and exciting, from the food to the people to the animals, such as orangutans and rhinos.

1. The _____ Road was a network of trade routes that connected major cities and trading posts.
   a. Reddit
   b. Silk
   c. Forest

2. Who intended to travel all the way to China and return the goods to Venice?
   a. Marco Polo's father and uncle
   b. Marco Polo
   c. Marco Polo mother and aunt

3. Marco Polo was a merchant and _____.
   a. artist
   b. explorer
   c. painter

4. Marco was born in 1254 in _____, Italy
   a. Vincent
   b. Vance
   c. Venice

5. Marco left for China for the first time when he was _____.
   a. seventeen years old
   b. eighteen years old.
   c. 21 years old

6. The Silk Road was named because silk ____ was China's main export.
   a. cloth
   b. curtains
   c. shoes

7. ____ was the ruler of all of China.
   a. Kubilla
   b. Kublai
   c. Kyle

8. How many year Marco Polo traveled to China?
   a. for four years.
   b. for 3 years.
   c. for 5 years.

* Reading Comprehension: Law Enforcement Dogs

Score: _____

Date: _____

Police dogs are dogs that assist cops in solving crimes. In recent years, they have grown to be an essential part of law enforcement. With their unique abilities and bravery, police dogs have saved many lives. They are often regarded as an important and irreplaceable part of many police departments because they are loyal, watchful, and protective of their police officer counterparts.

Today, police dogs are trained in specific areas. They could be considered experts in their field. Some of the particular police dog roles are as follows:

Tracking: Tracking police dogs use their keen sense of smell to locate criminal suspects or missing people. Tracking dogs are trained for years and can track down even the most elusive criminal. Without police tracking dogs, many suspects would be able to elude capture.

Substance Detectors: Like tracking dogs, these police dogs use their sense of smell to assist officers. Substance dogs are trained to detect a specific substance. Some dogs are trained to detect bombs or explosives. These brave dogs are trained not only to detect explosives but also to respond (very carefully!) and safely alert their officer partner to the explosive location. Other dogs may be drawn to illegal drugs. By quickly determining whether an illegal substance is nearby, these dogs save officers from searching through luggage, a car, or other areas by hand.

Public Order - These police dogs assist officers in keeping the peace. They may pursue a criminal suspect and hold them until an officer arrives, or they may guard an area (such as a jail or prison) to prevent suspects from fleeing.

Cadaver Dogs: Although it may sound disgusting, these police dogs are trained to locate dead bodies. This is a critical function in a police department, and these dogs perform admirably.

A police dog is not just any dog. Police dogs require very special and specialized training. There are numerous breeds of dogs that have been trained for police work. What breed they are often determined by the type of work they will do. German Shepherds and Belgian Malinois are two of the most popular breeds today, but other dogs such as Bloodhounds (good for tracking) and Beagles (good for drug detection) are also used. Police dogs, regardless of breed, are typically trained to do their job from the time they are puppies.

Typically, police dogs are regarded as heroes. They frequently go to live with their human partner police officer. They've known this person for years and have grown to consider them family, which works out well for both the officer and the dog.

1. Tracking police dogs use their _____ to locate criminal suspects or missing people.
   a. keen sense of training
   b. keen sense of taste
   c. keen sense of smell

2. Some substance dogs are trained to detect _____.
   a. runaway children
   b. bombs or explosives
   c. metal and iron

3. Police dogs are trained in ___ areas.
   a. many
   b. a few
   c. specific

4. Police dogs are dogs that assist cops in solving _____.
   a. littering
   b. homelessness
   c. crimes

5. Substance dogs are trained to detect a specific _____.
   a. substance
   b. person
   c. other police dogs

6. What type of police dog is trained pursue a criminal suspect and hold them until an officer arrives?
   a. Crime Fighting dog
   b. Tracking dog
   c. Public Order dog

7. These police dogs are trained to locate dead bodies
   a. Law and Order dogs
   b. Cadaver dogs
   c. Deadly Substance dogs

8. What are the two most popular police dogs used today?
   a. German Shepherds and Belgian Malinois
   b. Bloodhounds and German Shepherds
   c. Belgian Malinois and Rottweiler

* Health Reading
Comprehension: Food & Sports

First, read the entire passage. After that, go back and fill in the blanks. You can skip the blanks you're unsure about and finish them later.

dairy	muscles	cramping	sluggish	journal
nutrients	sports	fresh	faint	supplements
mitt	fortified	balance	shin	faster
protein	activity	energy	leafy	Cereals

You have to have equipment if you play sports, right? Would you be willing to play baseball without a _____?

Would you play soccer if you didn't have _____ guards? No, it does not. Would you consider participating in sports

if you didn't have the most important piece of equipment - a fully fueled and ready-to-go body? Unfortunately, many children do

exactly that. You must eat healthily and fuel up before your _____ by eating the right foods at the right times.

Everything revolves around timing. You can eat healthy, but if you overeat before exercising, you will feel _____

and may experience stomach upset or _____. On the other hand, if you don't eat anything before working out,

you may feel weak, _____, or tired. It is always a good idea to eat a healthy breakfast and best prepare for your

day. If you're going to eat a large healthy meal, make sure you eat it at least three to four hours before exercising. Eat a smaller,

more nutritious meal if you only have two hours before your game. It would help if you also ate after exercising to help your

_____ recover.

So, what are you going to eat? Carbohydrates are your body's primary source of _____, so eat foods high in

carbohydrates but low in fat. Carbohydrates will be converted into energy by your body. _____, breads,

vegetables, pasta, rice, and fruit are all good carbohydrate sources. Proteins and fats are best consumed after exercise to help

your muscles recover. Meat, _____ products, and nuts are examples of high _____ foods. Water

consumption is also essential. Unless you exercise vigorously for more than 60 minutes, water is preferable to

_____ drinks such as Gatorade.

The American College of Sports Medicine recommends drinking enough fluid to _____ your daily fluid losses

during exercise to stay healthy and hydrated. On days when the temperature and humidity are high, you'll probably need more.

Before your workout:

- Drink 2 to 3 cups (0.5 to 0.8 liters) of water.

- Drink approximately 2 to 3 cups (0.5 to 0.8 liters) of water after your workout for every pound (0.5 kilograms) of weight lost.

- During your workout, drink about 1 cup (0.25 liters) of water every 15 to 20 minutes.

The larger your body or, the warmer the weather, the more you may require.

Everyone is unique, and you should listen to your body when deciding which healthy foods to eat and when. Pay close attention to what feels suitable for you. Keep a food _____ for a few days to see how much you're eating and if you're getting all of the nutrients you need.

Calcium and iron are two essential _____ for children. Calcium aids in the formation of strong bones, while iron provides energy. Dairy products, such as milk, yogurt, and cheese, are high in calcium. Dark, green _____ vegetables and calcium-fortified products, such as orange juice, are also good sources.

Iron can be found in various foods, including meat, dried beans, and _____ cereals.

Remember that if you don't get enough iron, you'll get tired _____. Make sure that you are not on a diet. When you're a kid athlete, your body needs every opportunity to grow to its full potential. Talk to your parents or another trusted adult if anyone, such as a coach or teammate, suggests that you change your diet to gain or lose weight. Avoid any diet _____ or aids as well. These could be harmful to a developing body. Eating healthy is appropriate at any age. When you're a kid athlete, you're always on the go, and it can be challenging to find time to eat healthy. Keeping a cooler in the car with _____ fruit, water, and a sandwich on whole-grain bread is preferable to driving through a fast-food restaurant. Plan ahead of time, but it will be worthwhile.

Remember to look after your most important piece of equipment: your body. If you do, you will be able to perform at your best and, more importantly, feel at your best.

Multiplication Drill

Name: _____   Date: _____   Score: ___ /100

Calculate each product.

7	3	4	8	5	12	6	12	2	10
×9	×11	×12	×11	×11	×10	×4	×2	×2	×9

6	4	10	5	6	3	10	9	6	5
×8	×7	×4	×10	×12	×10	×6	×11	×2	×4

2	2	9	3	6	4	8	5	2	6
×9	×8	×9	×3	×7	×8	×8	×8	×11	×11

6	2	5	2	7	9	11	9	11	8
×3	×4	×12	×3	×7	×12	×10	×3	×11	×10

6	5	10	8	4	4	6	12	11	3
×6	×7	×2	×3	×11	×9	×9	×8	×12	×4

8	12	7	6	8	3	10	4	5	7
×7	×12	×11	×5	×9	×12	×7	×4	×3	×2

9	3	5	7	2	10	8	3	10	9
×5	×7	×5	×12	×5	×10	×5	×4	×12	×6

8	6	3	10	2	9	11	2	2	6
×8	×5	×9	×6	×12	×4	×11	×5	×9	×3

12	11	4	5	8	3	7	2	5	9
×9	×9	×5	×12	×6	×12	×2	×3	×5	×9

9	7	3	10	12	10	11	4	3	7
×5	×8	×11	×5	×7	×3	×12	×7	×3	×9

* English: Tenses

Verbs are classified into three tenses: past, present, and future. The term "past" refers to events that have already occurred (e.g., earlier in the day, yesterday, last week, three years ago). The present tense is used to describe what is happening right now or what is ongoing. The future tense refers to events that have yet to occur (e.g., later, tomorrow, next week, next year, three years from now).

borrowed	went	eat	play	go	giving
read	give	gave	will eat	yelled	seeing
will have	had	reading	will go	do	will borrow
playing	doing	yelling	did	will yell	will do
will give	fight	borrow	yell	will fight	will play
borrowing	played	fighting	read	have	will see
going	see	will read	fought	eating	ate
saw	having				

Simple Present (11)	Present Progressive (IS/ARE +) (11)	Past (11)	Future (11)

* English: Apostrophe

An apostrophe is a punctuation mark used to indicate where something has been removed. It can be used in contractions, to show possession, to replace a phrase, for the plural form of family names, for irregular plural possessives, and, on rare occasions, to provide clarity for a non-possessive plural. Avoid common apostrophe mistakes, such as using 'it's' for the possessive 'its,' which should be 'its.' Omitting the apostrophe, putting it in the wrong place for a possessive plural, and using 'of' when you mean to contract a word with 'have' are other common errors.

Apostrophes, like any other aspect of language, are prone to errors. The omission of the apostrophe is one of the most common.

Here are some examples:

'Let's go to McDonalds.' Correct: 'McDonald's'
'Whos responsible for the bill?' Correct: 'Who's'
'Its about five o'clock.' Correct: 'It's.' We are saying 'it is' here, so we need the apostrophe.

1. Where should the apostrophe go in didnt?
   a. didn't
   b. did'nt

2. How do you make the contraction for was not?
   a. was'nt
   b. wasn't

3. How do you make Jimmy possessive?
   a. Jimmy's
   b. Jimmys

4. Where should the apostrophe go in shouldnt?
   a. should'nt
   b. shouldn't

5. How do you make the contraction for she would?
   a. she'd
   b. sh'ed

6. What is the correct use of the apostrophe?
   a. brother's toys
   b. brother's toys

7. Which of the following is the correct way to show possession with a plural noun ending in 's'?
   a. Add an apostrophe at the end.
   b. No apostrophe is required.

8. How would you express the plural possessive of the word 'child'?
   a. Child's
   b. Children's

9. What is the proper way to contract the possessive form of 'it'?
   a. Its
   b. It's

10. The _____ awfully good today.
    a. weather
    b. weather's

11. Adam believes _____ going to snow later.
    a. it's
    b. its

12. The dog was wagging _____ tail excitedly.
    a. its
    b. it's

13. Where did you leave _____ book?
    a. your
    b. you're

14. _____ going to Ms. Katy's room.
    a. We're
    b. We're

15. Bobby always kicks _____ dolls around.
    a. Kim and Sandy's
    b. Jennifer and Katie

16. _____ not allowed to listen to music while they read.
    a. They're
    b. Their're

* ELA: Informational Text

An informational text is a nonfiction piece of writing that aims to educate or inform the reader about a specific topic. An informational text, unlike fiction or some other types of nonfiction texts, does not contain any characters. It presents information in a way that allows the reader to learn more about something of interest to them.

Informational text is a type of nonfiction that is intended to convey factual information about a specific topic. The purpose of informational text is to deliver information about a topic, and it is distinguished by its formatting, which includes organization, written cues (visual variations in text), and visuals/graphics.

Literary nonfiction, expository writing, persuasive/argumentative writing, and procedural writing are the four basic types of informational text. Examples of informational text can be found in a variety of formats both online and in print.

Select the best answer for each question.

1. Identify the main idea: "You wouldn't use a nail file to peel carrots. You can't tune an engine with a cheese grater, either. So why would you buy a wrench to do the job of a screwdriver?"
   a. Always use the right tool.
   b. Wrench and screwdrivers are basically the same.
   c. Use nail file for your fingernails.

2. Autobiographies are written in which point of view?
   a. second
   b. third
   c. first

3. Differentiate between a plot and a theme.
   a. A plot is the ending in a story, a theme conveys the message in first person
   b. A theme is a collection of the main idea, while a plot conveys the point of the ending
   c. A plot is more of what happens in a story, whereas a theme conveys the message of the story

4. Which is not an article in a reference book?
   a. thesaurus entry for the word army
   b. encyclopedia article on World War II
   c. a review of a novel

5. When creating summaries, it's important to _____.
   a. tell the ending of the story
   b. Write down the main points in your own words
   c. Use the first person exact words

6. Which type of literary nonfiction is not meant to be published or shared?
   a. biography
   b. diary
   c. memoir

7. Which of the following should you do as you read an informational text?
   a. Take notes
   b. find clue words and text
   c. read as quickly as possible

8. What makes a speech different from an article?
   a. speeches are meant to be spoken aloud to an audience
   b. speeches do not inform about a topic
   c. articles can persuade a reader

9. Which type of literary nonfiction is a short piece on a single topic?
   a. essay
   b. letter
   c. memoir

10. Procedural writing example:
    a. letter to the editor, blog entry
    b. textbook, travel brochure
    c. cookbooks, how-to articles, instruction manuals

* English: Nouns, Verbs, Adjectives, Adverbs

A noun is defined as a person, place, thing, or idea that has been used for thousands of years in all spoken languages.

An action verb is a word that shows action. 'What did they do in the sentence?' is one way to find the action verb. Action verbs are necessary for descriptive and informative writing.

Adjectives are descriptive words for nouns. We use them to provide our audience with a more complete and detailed picture of the noun we are describing. What words would you use to describe yourself? Would you describe yourself as intelligent or amusing? Is your room cluttered or neat? When describing something, adjectives are used.

An adverb is a word that modifies another word, such as a verb, adjective, or adverb. Adverbs improve the precision and interest of writing. Adverbs answer these questions:

- When?
- Where?
- In what manner?
- To what extent?

1. Which of the following is NOT a noun?
   a. place
   b. person
   c. action

2. A verb is a(n) _____.
   a. action
   b. word that describes a noun
   c. person, place, thing, or idea

3. True or False: An adjective describes a verb.
   a. True
   b. False

4. Adverbs describe or modify _____.
   a. adverbs
   b. adjectives
   c. verbs

5. What is the adverb in the sentence? Peter neatly wrote a shopping list.
   a. Peter
   b. wrote
   c. neatly

6. Which sentence shows the proper use of an adverb?
   a. Jim quick walked.
   b. Jim walked quickly.
   c. Jim walked quick

7. Which of the following words is a common noun identifying a person?
   a. Dr. Jones
   b. doctor
   c. Mr. Jones

8. Which of the following nouns is a proper noun?
   a. Cat
   b. Central Park
   c. Fireman

9. Which sentence part contains an action verb?
   a. baseball or soccer
   b. eat an ice cream cone
   c. to the top of the hill and back

10. Adjectives are words that describe what?
    a. nouns
    b. other adjectives
    c. verbs

11. Which adjective would best describe a cat?
    a. sharp
    b. furry
    c. cold

12. Which sentence gives the clearest picture using adjectives?
    a. The tall, fast lady runs.
    b. The lady runs fast.
    c. The sleek, slender, funny little lady runs.

Science: Coral Reefs

One of the most important marine __biomes__ is the coral reef.

Coral reefs are home to approximately __25%__ of all known marine species, despite being a relatively small biome.

Coral reefs may appear to be made of __rocks__ at first glance, but they are actually __living__ organisms.

When polyps die, they __harden__ and new polyps grow on top of them, causing the reef to expand.

Because polyps must eat to __survive__, you can think of the coral reef as eating as well.

They eat plankton and __algae__, which are small animals.

__Photosynthesis__ is how algae get their food from the sun.

To form, coral reefs require warm, __shallow__ water.

Southeast Asia and the region around __Australia__ are home to a sizable portion of the world's coral reefs.

The __Great__ Barrier Reef is 2,600 miles long.

__Fringe__ reefs are reefs that grow close to the shore.

__Barrier__ reef - Barrier reefs grow away from the shoreline, sometimes for several miles.

An __atoll__ is a coral ring that surrounds a lagoon of water. It begins as a fringe reef surrounding a volcanic island.

Some atolls are large enough to support human __habitation__.

* Science: Ecosystem

First, read the entire passage. After that, go back and fill in the blanks. You can skip the blanks you're unsure about and finish them later.

sunlight	grass	another	chain	decaying
running	photosynthesis	living	herbivores	zebra

To survive, every __living__ plant and animal requires energy. Plants get their energy from the soil, water, and the sun. Plants and other animals provide energy to animals. Plants and animals in an ecosystem rely on one __another__ to survive. Scientists may use a food chain or a food web to describe this dependence.

A food chain describes how various organisms eat one another, beginning with a plant and ending with an animal.

For example, the food chain for a lion could be written as follows: grass ---> zebra ---> lion
The lion eats the __zebra__, which consumes the __grass__.

The grasshopper consumes grass, the frog consumes the grasshopper, the snake consumes the frog, and the eagle consumes the snake. Each link in the food __chain__ has a name to help describe it. The terms are determined mainly by what the organism eats and how it contributes to the ecosystem's energy.

Producers - Plants are creators. This is because they generate energy for the ecosystem. They do this because __photosynthesis__ absorbs energy from the sun. They require water and nutrients from the soil as well, but plants are the only source of new energy.

Consumers - Consumers include animals. This is because they do not generate energy; instead, they consume it. Primary consumers, also known as __herbivores__, are animals that eat plants. Secondary consumers or carnivores are animals that eat other animals. A carnivore is referred to as a tertiary consumer when it consumes another carnivore. Some animals perform both functions, eating both plants and animals. They are known as omnivores.

Decomposers are organisms that consume __decaying__ matter (like dead plants and animals). They aid in the reintroduction of nutrients into the soil for plant consumption. Worms, bacteria, and fungi are examples of decomposers.

As previously stated, all energy produced in the food chain is produced by producers or plants, who convert __sunlight__ into energy through photosynthesis. The rest of the food chain merely consumes energy. As a result, as you move up the food chain, less and less energy is available. As a result, as you move up the food chain, there are fewer and fewer organisms. In the preceding example, there is more grass than zebras and more zebras than lions. The zebras and lions expend energy by __running__, hunting, and breathing.

* English: Personal Pronouns

Personal pronouns are words that are used to replace the subject or object of a sentence to make it easier for readers to understand.

To give a brief, personal pronouns are:

1. Replace nouns and other pronouns to make sentences easier to read and understand.

2. A sentence's subject or object can be either. For example, 'I' is the first-person subject pronoun, whereas 'me' is the first-person object pronoun.

3. It is possible to use the singular or plural form.

4. They must agree on gender and number with the words they are substituting.

1. Which of the following sentences has a plural subject pronoun and a plural object pronoun?
- a. She wants to live as long as she can, as long as she have someone by her side.
- b. While Tom believe everything will be fine, many don't agree with him.
- c. Whether we lived or died, it didn't matter to us either way.

2. Which of the following words would make the following sentence grammatically correct? '6th graders should check with their teachers before you leave the classroom.'
- a. Replace 'their' with 'they'
- b. Replace 'you' with 'they'
- c. Replace '6th graders' with 'they'

3. The pronoun 'my' is a . . .
- a. 1st person possessive pronoun
- b. 3rd person nominative pronoun
- c. 2nd person possessive pronoun

4. Which of the following correctly identifies the subjective and objective pronouns in the sentence here? 'Run away from the dinosaurs with the giant feet?' she asked. 'You don't have to tell me twice.'
- a. she - subject pronoun; you - subject pronoun; me - object pronoun
- b. she - object pronoun; you - object pronoun; me - object pronoun
- c. she - object pronoun; you - subject pronoun; me - object pronoun

5. The pronoun 'your' is a . . .
- a. 2nd person possessive pronoun
- b. 1st person possessive pronoun
- c. 2nd person objective pronoun

6. Which pronouns are found in the following sentence? 'I kept telling her that we would go back for John, but I knew we had left him behind. '
- a. I, we, knew, we, him
- b. I, her, we, I, we, him
- c. I, we, I, we, him

7. Kevin likes playing basketball. _____ is a very good player.
- a. Him
- b. He
- c. Their

8. The pronoun 'its' is a . . .
- a. 3rd person possessive pronoun
- b. 2nd person possessive pronoun
- c. 3rd person objective pronoun

9. The pronoun 'their' is a . . .
- a. 2nd person possessive pronoun
- b. 3rd person objective pronoun
- c. 3rd person possessive pronoun

10. Kimmy is a very good cook. _____ can cook any kind of food.
- a. She
- b. Hey
- c. Their

Reading Comprehension:
Social Media Safety

1. In the last 20 years, socializing has evolved dramatically. __Interactions__ between people are referred to as socializing.
2. It now frequently refers to accessing the Internet via social media or websites that allow you to __connect__ and interact with other people.
3. Ascertain that your computer is outfitted with up-to-date computer __security__ software.
4. This software detects and removes __viruses__ that are harmful to your computer.
5. When you use your computer, these viruses can sometimes hack into it and __steal__ your information, such as __logins__ .
6. Create strong __passwords__ for all of your social media accounts.
7. These can be as loose or as __restrictive__ as you want them to be.
8. This enables your computer to block __pop-ups__ and warn you when you are about to visit a potentially harmful website.
9. - Don't __post__ anything you wouldn't want broadcast to the entire world.
10. __Personal__ information about one's identity should not be posted or shared on social media.
11. This information can be used to recreate your __identity__ and should never be made public.
12. Make use of the __privacy__ settings on the social media website.
13. Be cautious about what you post on any social media __platform__ .
14. Posting something __negative__ about someone hurts their character and opens the door for them, or someone else, to do the same to you.
15. If you are not in a good mood or are upset, think twice.
16. What you post could be __harmful__ to you or someone else.
17. If you are in a bad social media __relationship__ and are being harassed or bullied, you can report it to the social media company.
18. They all have __policies__ in place to deal with people who __abuse__ their websites.
19. Make a note of these __incidents__ and report them to the company. You may also save the life of another person.

* Art: Mary Cassatt

First, read the entire passage. After that, go back and fill in the blanks. You can skip the blanks you're unsure about and finish them later.

influenced	private	Fine	museums	techniques
pastels	Pittsburgh	Japanese	childhood	enrolled

Mary Cassatt was born on May 22, 1844, into a prosperous family near Pittsburgh , Pennsylvania. She spent a significant portion of her childhood in France and Germany, where she learned French and German. She developed an interest in art while in Europe and decided that she wanted to be a professional artist early on.

Despite her parents' reservations about Mary pursuing a career as an artist, she enrolled in the Pennsylvania Academy of Fine Arts in 1860. Mary studied art at the academy for several years but became dissatisfied with the instruction and limitations on female students. Mary moved to Paris in 1866 and began taking private lessons from art instructor Jean-Leon Gerome. She also studied paintings in museums such as the Louvre on her own. One of her paintings (A Mandolin Player) was accepted for exhibition at the prestigious Paris Salon in 1868. Cassatt continued to paint with some success over the next few years.

By 1877, Mary Cassatt had grown dissatisfied with Paris's traditional art scene. Fortunately, Mary became close friends with Impressionist painter Edgar Degas around this time. She began to experiment with new painting techniques and discovered a whole new world of art in Impressionism. She began to exhibit her paintings alongside the Impressionists and gained further acclaim in the art world.

Early on, Cassatt's artistic style was influenced by European masters, and later, by the Impressionist art movement (especially Edgar Degas). Mary also studied Japanese art, which is evident in many of her paintings. Mary wanted to use her art to express light and color. She frequently used pastels . The majority of her paintings depict people. She primarily painted her family for many years. Later, scenes depicting a mother and child together became a major theme in her paintings.

Mary Cassatt is widely regarded as one of America's greatest artists. She rose to prominence in the art world at a time when it was extremely difficult for women to do so. Many of her paintings are currently on display at museums such as the National Gallery of Art, The Metropolitan Museum of Art, and the National Portrait Gallery.

* Music: History of the Violin

First, read the entire passage. After that, go back and fill in the blanks. You can skip the blanks you're unsure about and finish them later.

strings	France	soundhole	bowed	ages
introduced	Italy	Baroque	existence	existence

Stringed instruments that use a bow to produce sound, such as the violin, are referred to as __bowed__ stringed instruments. The ancestors of the violin are said to be the Arabian rabab and the rebec, which came from the Orient in the middle __ages__ and were popular in Spain and __France__ in the fifteenth century. A bowed stringed instrument known as a fiddle first appeared in Europe near the end of the Middle Ages.

In terms of completeness, the violin is in a class by itself when compared to its forefathers. Furthermore, it did not evolve gradually over time but instead appeared in its current form abruptly around 1550. However, none of these early violins are still in __existence__ today. The violin's history is inferred from paintings from this era that depicts violins.

The two earliest recorded violin makers are from northern __Italy__: Andre Amati of Cremona and Gasparo di Bertolotti of Salone (Gasparo di Salon). The history of the violin emerges from the fog of legend to hard fact thanks to these two violin makers. These two's violins are still in use today. The oldest violin still in __existence__ today is one built around 1565 by Andre Amati.

Though the violin was __introduced__ to the world in the middle of the sixteenth century, a similar-looking instrument called the viol was made around the fourteenth century.

The viol flourished in the sixteenth and seventeenth centuries, and the violin and viol coexisted during the __Baroque__ period.

The viol family's instruments did not have the f-shaped __soundhole__ of the violin, but rather a C-shaped soundhole or a more decorative shape. The viol differs from the violin in that it has six, seven, or more __strings__ tuned in fourths (as opposed to the violin's four strings tuned in fifths), a fretted fingerboard, and a relatively thick body due to the sloping shoulder shape at the neck-body joint. There are several sizes, but the Viola da Gamba, which has a lower register similar to the cello, is the most well-known.

* Geography: Himalayas

The Himalayas are an Asian mountain range. The Himalayan region includes Nepal, Tibet, Bhutan, India, Afghanistan, and Pakistan. The Himalayas are home to the majority of the world's _tallest_ mountains.

I'm almost sure you've heard of _Mount_ Everest, the world's tallest mountain. Climbers train for years to scale this massive chunk of rock and ice. Because Everest is so high, most climbers require _oxygen_, which is a pure component of the air we breathe, to reach the summit, and many climbers must abandon their efforts before reaching the summit.

Plate tectonics created the Himalayas, which may sound like a technical term, but it's quite simple. Large swaths of land make up the earth's _surface_. Plate tectonics is basically what happens when the pieces move slightly and collide with each other. When these plates collide, one piece of land is forced beneath the other, raising the piece on top and eventually forming _mountains_. Everest grew to a height of 29,000 feet as a result of this process!

The shifting that formed the Himalayas began during the _Jurassic_ period; I wonder what the dinosaurs thought of the earth moving beneath their feet? But, just like us, they probably couldn't feel anything because plate tectonics is invisible to anyone living on the earth's surface - that is, until an _earthquake_ occurs, which is an extreme example of how plate tectonics work.

The name Himalayas means "home of snow," but most of the Himalayas are lower than the parts always covered in snow. The Himalayas are home to forests and _grasslands_ as well as ice. As you descend the mountains, the temperatures rise, and the snow melts. The Himalayas are the source (beginning point) of many important rivers in Asia, including the Ganges and the Yangtze. Many different kinds of animals and plants live in the forests and grasslands.

It's challenging to get past the image of bare mountains, but some areas of the Himalayas have fertile soil. The majority of farmable land in Nepal is in the foothills or lower hilly parts of the mountains. The majority of Nepal's rice is grown there. Apple, cherry, and grape orchards can be found in the Vale of the Kashmir region. _Sheep_, goats, and yaks are also raised. When the weather is warm, the animals graze higher in the mountains, but they move to lower pastures like snowfalls.

Have you ever heard of a Yeti? The Yeti, also known as the _Abominable_ Snowman, is a mythical creature that roams the Himalayas and resembles a giant hairy man. It is said to have shaggy, white fur and sharp teeth ready to devour anyone who comes into contact with it! According to monks, there are the remains of a Yeti hand in a Buddhist monastery in Pangboche, Nepal. Scientists believe they have proof that the Yeti is a rare type of polar bear, but others are skeptical. What are your thoughts? Is the Yeti a bear or a previously unknown monster?

* Geography: The North Pole

First, read the entire passage. After that, go back and fill in the blanks. You can skip the blanks you're unsure about and finish them later.

historians	cold	frozen	solar	survive
Frederick	Arctic	bears	axis	fish

What is the world's most northern location? You may be familiar with it as the location of Santa's workshop, but let's take a look at the North Pole's history, environment, and wildlife. It is situated in the middle of the __Arctic__ Ocean, which is almost entirely __frozen__ all year. The only direction you could travel if you stood precisely on the North Pole is south!

For hundreds of years, explorers have attempted to reach the North Pole. Many exploration trips ended in disaster or with the explorers turning around and returning home due to inclement weather. __Frederick__ Cook was an American explorer who claimed to have discovered the North Pole for the first time in 1908. A year later, another American explorer, Robert Peary, made the same claim. Scientists and __historians__ have not been able to back up these claims. There are currently numerous expeditions to the North Pole, many traveling by airplane, boat, or submarine.

We all know the North Pole is __cold__, but compared to the South Pole, the weather is like summer. That is if you consider average winter temperatures of -22 degrees Fahrenheit to be comparable to summer temperatures! Summer temperatures hover around 32 degrees Fahrenheit on average. Pack your shorts and flip-flops for a trip to the North Pole!

There aren't many animals that can __survive__ in this environment because it's so cold all year. Many people believe that polar __bears__ live in the North Pole, but they do not travel that far north. Several bird species, including the Arctic snow bunting and the Arctic tern, travel to the North Pole. Every year, the tern travels to and from the South and North Poles!

Sealife is also scarce. Scientists discovered shrimp and __fish__, including Arctic cod, in the Arctic Ocean near the North Pole. Many sea animals, however, do not travel far enough north to reach the North Pole.

At the North Pole, day and night are very different. Because the Earth's __axis__ is tilted and the North Pole is at the top of the world, there is only one sunrise and one sunset each year. In the winter, there is constant darkness, whereas, in the summer, there is daylight all day and night!

An aurora is a unique event that occurs in polar areas, both north and south. These are brilliant colorful flashes of light in the night sky that are commonly referred to as polar lights. Auroras are caused by __solar__ winds and electromagnetic activity in the atmosphere.

* Reading Comprehension:
Marco Polo

Marco Polo was a merchant and explorer who spent much of his life traveling throughout the Far East and China. For many years, his stories were the foundation of what much of Europe knew about Ancient China. He lived between 1254 and 1324.

Marco was born in 1254 in Venice, Italy. Marco's father was a merchant in Venice, a prosperous trading city.

The Silk Road was a network of trade routes that connected major cities and trading posts from Eastern Europe to Northern China. The Silk Road was named because silk cloth was China's main export. Few people completed the entire route. Trading was mostly done between cities or small sections of the route, and goods would slowly make their way from one end to the other, changing hands several times along the way. Marco Polo's father and uncle desired to try something new. They intended to travel all the way to China and return the goods to Venice. They believed that by doing so, they would be able to make a fortune. It took them nine years, but they eventually returned home.

Marco left for China for the first time when he was 17 years old. He accompanied his father and uncle on the trip. During their first trip to China, his father and uncle met the Mongol Emperor Kublai Khan and promised him they would return. At the time, Kublai was the ruler of all of China.

Marco Polo traveled to China for three years. Along the way, he visited many great cities and sites, including the holy city of Jerusalem, the Hindu Kush mountains, Persia, and the Gobi Desert. He met a wide range of people and had numerous adventures.

Marco spent many years in China, where he learned the language. As a messenger and spy for Kublai Khan, he traveled throughout China. He even went as far south as Myanmar and Vietnam are today. He learned about different cultures, foods, cities, and people during these visits. He saw places and things that no European had ever seen before.

Marco was captivated by the wealth and luxury of Chinese cities and the court of Kublai Khan. It was nothing like what he had seen in Europe. Kinsay's capital city was large but well-organized and clean. Wide roads and massive civil engineering projects like the Grand Canal were far beyond what he had seen back home. Everything was new and exciting, from the food to the people to the animals, such as orangutans and rhinos.

1. The _____ Road was a network of trade routes that connected major cities and trading posts.
   a. Reddit
   b. Silk
   c. Forest

2. Who intended to travel all the way to China and return the goods to Venice?
   a. Marco Polo's father and uncle
   b. Marco Polo
   c. Marco Polo mother and aunt

3. Marco Polo was a merchant and _____.
   a. artist
   b. explorer
   c. painter

4. Marco was born in 1254 in _____, Italy
   a. Vincent
   b. Vance
   c. Venice

5. Marco left for China for the first time when he was _____.
   a. seventeen years old
   b. eighteen years old.
   c. 21 years old

6. The Silk Road was named because silk _____ was China's main export.
   a. cloth
   b. curtains
   c. shoes

7. _____ was the ruler of all of China.
   a. Kubilla
   b. Kublai
   c. Kyle

8. How many year Marco Polo traveled to China?
   a. for four years.
   b. for 3 years.
   c. for 5 years.

* Reading Comprehension: Law Enforcement Dogs

Police dogs are dogs that assist cops in solving crimes. In recent years, they have grown to be an essential part of law enforcement. With their unique abilities and bravery, police dogs have saved many lives. They are often regarded as an important and irreplaceable part of many police departments because they are loyal, watchful, and protective of their police officer counterparts.

Today, police dogs are trained in specific areas. They could be considered experts in their field. Some of the particular police dog roles are as follows:

Tracking: Tracking police dogs use their keen sense of smell to locate criminal suspects or missing people. Tracking dogs are trained for years and can track down even the most elusive criminal. Without police tracking dogs, many suspects would be able to elude capture.

Substance Detectors: Like tracking dogs, these police dogs use their sense of smell to assist officers. Substance dogs are trained to detect a specific substance. Some dogs are trained to detect bombs or explosives. These brave dogs are trained not only to detect explosives but also to respond (very carefully!) and safely alert their officer partner to the explosive location. Other dogs may be drawn to illegal drugs. By quickly determining whether an illegal substance is nearby, these dogs save officers from searching through luggage, a car, or other areas by hand.

Public Order - These police dogs assist officers in keeping the peace. They may pursue a criminal suspect and hold them until an officer arrives, or they may guard an area (such as a jail or prison) to prevent suspects from fleeing.

Cadaver Dogs: Although it may sound disgusting, these police dogs are trained to locate dead bodies. This is a critical function in a police department, and these dogs perform admirably.

A police dog is not just any dog. Police dogs require very special and specialized training. There are numerous breeds of dogs that have been trained for police work. What breed they are often determined by the type of work they will do. German Shepherds and Belgian Malinois are two of the most popular breeds today, but other dogs such as Bloodhounds (good for tracking) and Beagles (good for drug detection) are also used. Police dogs, regardless of breed, are typically trained to do their job from the time they are puppies.

Typically, police dogs are regarded as heroes. They frequently go to live with their human partner police officer. They've known this person for years and have grown to consider them family, which works out well for both the officer and the dog.

1. Tracking police dogs use their _____ to locate criminal suspects or missing people.
   a. keen sense of training
   b. keen sense of taste
   c. keen sense of smell

2. Some substance dogs are trained to detect _____.
   a. runaway children
   b. bombs or explosives
   c. metal and iron

3. Police dogs are trained in ___ areas.
   a. many
   b. a few
   c. specific

4. Police dogs are dogs that assist cops in solving _____.
   a. littering
   b. homelessness
   c. crimes

5. Substance dogs are trained to detect a specific ____.
   a. substance
   b. person
   c. other police dogs

6. What type of police dog is trained pursue a criminal suspect and hold them until an officer arrives?
   a. Crime Fighting dog
   b. Tracking dog
   c. Public Order dog

7. These police dogs are trained to locate dead bodies
   a. Law and Order dogs
   b. Cadaver dogs
   c. Deadly Substance dogs

8. What are the two most popular police dogs used today?
   a. German Shepherds and Belgian Malinois
   b. Bloodhounds and German Shepherds
   c. Belgian Malinois and Rottweiler

* Health Reading
Comprehension: Food & Sports

You have to have equipment if you play sports, right? Would you be willing to play baseball without a _mitt_ ?

Would you play soccer if you didn't have _shin_ guards?

You must eat healthily and fuel up before your _activity_ by eating the right foods at the right times.

You can eat healthy, but if you overeat before exercising, you will feel _sluggish_ and may experience stomach upset or _cramping_ .

On the other hand, if you don't eat anything before working out, you may feel weak, _faint_ , or tired.

It would help if you also ate after exercising to help your _muscles_ recover.

So, what are you going to eat? Carbohydrates are your body's primary source of _energy_ , so eat foods high in carbohydrates but low in fat.

Cereals , breads, vegetables, pasta, rice, and fruit are all good carbohydrate sources.

Meat, _dairy_ products, and nuts are examples of high _protein_ foods.

Water consumption is also essential. Unless you exercise vigorously for more than 60 minutes, water is preferable to _sports_ drinks such as Gatorade.

The American College of Sports Medicine recommends drinking enough fluid to _balance_ your daily fluid losses during exercise to stay healthy and hydrated.

Keep a food _journal_ for a few days to see how much you're eating and if you're getting all of the nutrients you need.

Calcium and iron are two essential _nutrients_ for children. Calcium aids in the formation of strong bones, while iron provides energy.

Dairy products, such as milk, yogurt, and cheese, are high in calcium. Dark, green _leafy_ vegetables and calcium-fortified products, such as orange juice, are also good sources.

Iron can be found in various foods, including meat, dried beans, and _fortified_ cereals.

Remember that if you don't get enough iron, you'll get tired _faster_ .

Avoid any diet _supplements_ or aids as well. These could be harmful to a developing body.

Keeping a cooler in the car with _fresh_ fruit, water, and a sandwich on whole-grain bread is preferable to driving through a fast-food restaurant.

ANSWERS

7	3	4	8	5	12	6	12	2	10
×9	×11	×12	×11	×11	×10	×4	×2	×2	×9
63	33	48	88	55	120	24	24	4	90

6	4	10	5	6	3	10	9	6	5
×8	×7	×4	×10	×12	×10	×6	×11	×2	×4
48	28	40	50	72	30	60	99	12	20

2	2	9	3	6	4	8	5	2	6
×9	×8	×9	×3	×7	×8	×8	×8	×11	×11
18	16	81	9	42	32	64	40	22	66

6	2	5	2	7	9	11	9	11	8
×3	×4	×12	×3	×7	×12	×10	×3	×11	×10
18	8	60	6	49	108	110	27	121	80

6	5	10	8	4	4	6	12	11	3
×6	×7	×2	×3	×11	×9	×9	×8	×12	×4
36	35	20	24	44	36	54	96	132	12

8	12	7	6	8	3	10	4	5	7
×7	×12	×11	×5	×9	×12	×7	×4	×3	×2
56	144	77	30	72	36	70	16	15	14

9	3	5	7	2	10	8	3	10	9
×5	×7	×5	×12	×5	×10	×5	×4	×12	×6
45	21	25	84	10	100	40	12	120	54

8	6	3	10	2	9	11	2	2	6
×8	×5	×9	×6	×12	×4	×11	×5	×9	×3
64	30	27	60	24	36	121	10	18	18

12	11	4	5	8	3	7	2	5	9
×9	×9	×5	×12	×6	×12	×2	×3	×5	×9
108	99	20	60	48	36	14	6	25	81

9	7	3	10	12	10	11	4	3	7
×5	×8	×11	×5	×7	×3	×12	×7	×3	×9
45	56	33	50	84	30	132	28	9	63

* English: Tenses

Verbs are classified into three tenses: past, present, and future. The term "past" refers to events that have already occurred (e.g., earlier in the day, yesterday, last week, three years ago). The present tense is used to describe what is happening right now or what is ongoing. The future tense refers to events that have yet to occur (e.g., later, tomorrow, next week, next year, three years from now).

borrowed	went	eat	play	go	giving
read	give	gave	will eat	yelled	seeing
will have	had	reading	will go	do	will borrow
playing	doing	yelling	did	will yell	will do
will give	fight	borrow	yell	will fight	will play
borrowing	played	fighting	read	have	will see
going	see	will read	fought	eating	ate
saw	having				

Simple Present (11)	Present Progressive (IS/ARE +) (11)	Past (11)	Future (11)
play	playing	played	will play
go	going	went	will go
read	reading	read	will read
borrow	borrowing	borrowed	will borrow
eat	eating	ate	will eat
have	having	had	will have
see	seeing	saw	will see
fight	fighting	fought	will fight
do	doing	did	will do
give	giving	gave	will give
yell	yelling	yelled	will yell

Acronym

Name: _____

Date: _____

A common way to make an acronym is to use the first letter of each word in a phrase to make a word that can be spoken. This is a great way to make a longer, more complicated phrase easier to say and shorter.

Carefully choose the acronym for each word or phrase.

1. Also Known As
   a. AKA
   b. KAA

2. Central Standard Time
   a. CST
   b. TCS

3. Doing Business As
   a. DBA
   b. ASDOING

4. Do Not Disturb
   a. NOTDN
   b. DND

5. Electronic Data Systems
   a. SDE
   b. EDS

6. End of Day
   a. EOD
   b. ENDDAY

7. Eastern Standard Time
   a. EST
   b. TSE

8. Estimated Time of Arrival
   a. ET
   b. ETA

9. Human Resources
   a. HRS
   b. HR

10. Masters of Business Administration
    a. MOBA
    b. MBA

11. MST - Mountain Standard Time
    a. MST
    b. MSTS

12. Overtime
    a. OTIME
    b. OT

13. Point Of Service
    a. POS
    b. POOS

14. Pacific Standard Time
    a. PST
    b. PSTE

15. Anti-lock Braking System
    a. LOCKBS
    b. ABS

16. Attention Deficit Disorder
    a. ADD
    b. ATTDD

17. Attention Deficit Hyperactivity Disorder
    a. ADHP
    b. ADHD

18. Acquired Immune Deficiency Syndrome
    a. ACQIMDEF
    b. AIDS

19. Centers for Disease Control and Prevention
    a. CDC
    b. CDCP

20. Dead On Arrival
    a. DONA
    b. DOA

21. Date Of Birth
    a. DOB
    b. DOFB

22. Do It Yourself
    a. DIY
    b. DIYO

23. Frequently Asked Questions
    a. FAQA
    b. FAQ

24. Graphics Interchange Format
    a. GIF
    b. GIFF

25. Human Immunodeficiency Virus
    a. HIV
    b. HIMMV

26. Medical Doctor
    a. MD
    b. MED

27. Over The Counter
    a. OTC
    b. OTHEC

28. Pay Per View
    a. PPV
    b. PAYPPV

29. Sound Navigation And Ranging
    a. SONAR
    b. SONAVR

30. Sports Utility Vehicle
    a. SPOUV
    b. SUV

The History of the Calendar

Is there a calendar in your family's home? Every day, the majority of households use a calendar. Calendars help us stay organized. Using a calendar, you can keep track of the passing of time and plan ahead. The ancients based their calendars on the most apparent regular events they were aware of—the Sun, Moon, and stars changing positions. These calendars assisted them in determining when to plant and harvest their crops. Different groups of people developed other calendars over time based on their own needs and beliefs.

The Gregorian calendar is used by people all over the world. In 1752, the world switched to the Gregorian calendar. Otherwise, different calendars were used by people all over the world.

Julius Caesar first introduced the 12 months of the calendar as we know them today on January 1st, 45 BC.

The previous Roman calendar had the year begin in March and end in December. Romulus, Rome's legendary first king, had used it since 753 BC. Because it only accounted for 304 days in a year, this calendar was later modified.

To account for the missing days, Rome's second king, Numa Pompilius, added two months at the end of the calendar, Januarius and Februarius. He also put in place an intercalary month that fell after Februarius in some years. These years were nicknamed "leap years." In addition, he deleted one day from each month with 30 days, making them 29 days instead.

This resulted in 355 days in a regular year and 377 days in a leap year. The leap years were declared at the king's discretion. Despite its instability, the calendar was in use for 700 years.

However, it became highly perplexing because the seasons and calendars did not correspond. It wreaked havoc on the farmers.

So, in 45 BC, Julius Caesar, with the help of his astronomers, decided to change the calendar and make it more stable. The seasons finally had a chance to catch up.

Since 1752, when the Gregorian calendar was adopted worldwide to synchronize it with the English and American colonies, the same calendar had been in use. Since Caesar's time, the world and its boundaries have expanded dramatically! The Gregorian calendar corrected the Julian calendar error of calculating one revolution of the earth around the sun to account for 365.2422 days.

That's all there is to it! Julius Caesar was the first to institute the 12-month calendar we have today!

Unscramble the calendar words.

Tuesday	Saturday	November	February	Monday	March
Friday	weekend	May	Wednesday	Sunday	January
weekday	October	June	September	December	August
April	Thursday	July			

1. rauanjy   _ a _ _ _ _ y

2. uraeybfr   _ e _ _ u _ _ _

3. macrh   _ _ _ _ h

4. iralp   _ p _ _ _

5. yma   _ a _

6. nuej   J _ _ _

7. luyj   J _ _ _

8. suagut   A _ _ u _ _

9. ebpmeetrs   _ e _ _ _ m _ _ _

10. btcreoo   _ c _ _ _ e _

11. vmbeneor   _ o _ _ _ b _ _

12. eedcrmbe   D e _ _ _ _ _ _

13. dmnyoa   _ o _ _ a _

14. saetudy   _ _ _ _ d a _

15. deeawysnd   W _ d _ _ _ _ _ _

16. shtayudr   _ h _ r _ _ _ _

17. rdayfi   _ _ _ _ a y

18. yuartdas   _ _ _ _ _ d _ y

19. ydsaun   S _ _ _ a _

20. eenekwd   _ _ _ _ e n _

21. kaewedy   _ _ _ _ d a _

This, That, These, and Those

Score: _____

Date: _____

This, that, these and those are demonstratives. We use this, that, these, and those to point to people and things. This and that are singular. These and those are plural.

1. _____ orange I'm eating is delicious.
    a. This
    b. These
    c. Those
    d. That

2. It is better than _____ apples from last week.
    a. that
    b. those
    c. these
    d. this

3. Let's exchange _____ bread for these crackers.
    a. those
    b. this
    c. these
    d. that

4. Let's try some of _____ freeze-dried steak.
    a. this
    b. this here
    c. them
    d. those there

5. Is _____ water boiling yet?
    a. these here
    b. that
    c. that there
    d. this here

6. _____ granola bars are tasty too.
    a. These
    b. This here
    c. Them
    d. These here

7. _____ mountains don't look that far away.
    a. This
    b. Those
    c. These
    d. That

8. I like _____ pictures better than those.
    a. this
    b. that
    c. those
    d. these

9. _____ car at the far end of the lot is mine.
    a. That
    b. This
    c. These
    d. Those

10. I like the feel of _____ fabric.
    a. those
    b. this here
    c. that there
    d. this

11. In _____ early days, space travel was a dream.
    a. that
    b. them
    c. those
    d. this

12. _____ days, we believe humans will go to Mars.
    a. These
    b. This
    c. Those
    d. That

Littering

First, read the entire passage. After that, go back and fill in the blanks. You can skip the blanks you're unsure about and finish them later.

butts	jail	negative	neighborhood	amount
suspension	recreational	streets	fine	community

The annual cost of cleaning up litter in the nation's _____, parks, and coastal areas is estimated to be in the millions of dollars. The cleanup of trash has a direct expense, but it also has a _____ impact on the surrounding environment, the value of property, and other economic activity. Food packaging, bottles, cans, plastic bags, and paper are the most common sources of litter. Did you know cigarette _____ remain the most littered item in the U.S. and across the globe? One of the many strategies that states can use to reduce the amount of litter in their communities is to enact and strictly adhere to laws that carry criminal penalties for the behavior. The penalties for littering vary significantly from state to state, depending on the _____, nature, and location of the litter. The seriousness of the offense is determined by the weight or volume of litter in 10 states, for example. For instance, several states penalize people for disposing of large goods like furniture or major appliances in public places. Legislation addressing trash on public roadways, along the beaches, and in _____ areas has been passed in several states due to these concerns.

In situations that are considered to be relatively small, the courts will typically impose a fine. They may also compel the defendant to perform _____ service, such as picking up garbage. In Massachusetts, for instance, the minimum _____ is $25, whereas, in the state of Maryland, the maximum penalty is $30,000. When a crime is more serious, the offender may be sentenced to up to six years in _____, depending on the state. In addition, the laws in the states of Maryland, Massachusetts, and Louisiana all include provisions that allow the _____ of a driver's license for those who violate the laws. In almost every state, a person's sentence worsens with each subsequent conviction.

It doesn't matter if someone throws trash out on purpose or accidentally; either way, they're contributing to pollution by doing so. Our city's parks, sidewalks, roads, and private property and parks are all impacted by litter. Research has shown that litter leads to the accumulation of even more garbage. A clean _____, on the other hand, lowers the incidence of littering and enhances both the local living standards and the quality of life.

Capitalization Rules Refresher

Score: _____

Date: _____

1. What are the most common pronouns?

2. What is a proper noun?

3. Do common nouns name specific persons, places, things, or ideas?

4. Always capitalize the first letter in the first word of a sentence?

5. Always capitalize the first letter in the first word in a quotation?

6. Always capitalize the first letter in the first word of a greeting or closing?

7. Always capitalize the first letter in the first and last name of a person?

8. Never capitalize the pronoun "I"?

9. Always capitalize the first letter in the names of: streets, roads, cities, and states?

10. Always capitalize the first letter in each part of the name of a specific building or monument: Statue of Liberty, Empire State Building, Pensacola Chamber of Commerce . . .?

11. Always capitalize the titles of: video games, stories, movies, and TV shows

12. Always capitalize the days of the weeks?

13. The names of months should not be capitalized?

14. Always capitalize major holidays except christmas and thanksgiving?

Lumberjack Paul Bunyan

First, read the entire passage. After that, go back and fill in the blanks. You can skip the blanks you're unsure about and finish them later.

chunks	household	journalist	national	carved
hands	complicated	Blue	nicknamed	Bangor

According to legend, it took five massive storks to deliver the infant (already enormous) Paul Bunyan to his parents in _____, Maine. As he grew older, a single drag of the mighty lumberjack's massive ax _____ out the Grand Canyon, while the giant footprints of his trusty companion, Babe the _____ Ox, filled with water and became Minnesota's 10,000 lakes. There is no way to know for sure, but was Paul Bunyan really a real person? As it turns out, there's more to this iconic figure's past than meets the eye.

Scholars believe that Bunyan was based on a real lumberjack: Fabian Fournier, a French-Canadian who moved south after the Civil War and became the foreman of a logging crew in Michigan after the war. Fournier was _____ "Saginaw Joe" because he was six feet tall (at a time when the ordinary person was barely five feet) and had huge _____. This man was known to have two full sets of teeth and was known to chew off _____ of rail in his spare time while also indulging in a bit of drinking and a little brawling. Fournier was killed on a November night in 1875 in the notoriously rowdy lumber town of Bay City, Michigan. People told stories about Saginaw Joe's _____ life in logging camps in Michigan, Minnesota, Wisconsin, and other places after his death and the dramatic trial of his alleged killer (who was acquitted).

"Round River," the first Paul Bunyan story, was published in 1906 by _____ James MacGillivray for a local newspaper in Oscoda, Michigan. MacGillivray and a poet collaborated on a Bunyan-themed poem for American Lumberman magazine in 1912, giving Paul Bunyan his first _____ exposure. Two years later, the first illustrations of the larger-than-life lumberjack appeared in an ad campaign for Minnesota's Red River Lumber Company. His prominent appearance as Red River's mascot and pamphlets rolling tales of his adventures would help turn Paul Bunyan into a _____ name and an enduring American icon.

Commonly misspelled words that sound alike but are spelled differently

Score: _____

Date: _____

Carefully circle the correct spelling combinations of words.

	A	B	C	D
1.	Sun/Sn	Son/Son	Sun/Son	Son/Sn
2.	Hare/Hiar	Harre/Hair	Hare/Hair	Harre/Hiar
3.	Cache/Cassh	Cache/Cash	Cache/Casch	Cacha/Cash
4.	Cytte/Sight	Cite/Sight	Cyte/Sight	Citte/Sight
5.	Worrn/Warn	Wurn/Warn	Wurrn/Warn	Worn/Warn
6.	Minerr/Minor	Miner/Minur	Miner/Minor	Minerr/Minur
7.	Wratch/Retch	Wretch/Retch	Wrretch/Retch	Wrratch/Retch
8.	Floor/Flower	Flloor/Flower	Flour/Flower	Fllour/Flower
9.	Whille/Wile	While/Wile	Whylle/Wile	Whyle/Wile
10.	Calous/Callus	Caloos/Callus	Callous/Callus	Calloos/Callus
11.	Build/Biled	Build/Billed	Boild/Billed	Boild/Biled
12.	Marrten/Martin	Marten/Martin	Marten/Martyn	Marrten/Martyn
13.	Humerrus/Humorous	Humerus/Humorous	Humerrus/Humoroos	Humerus/Humoroos
14.	Housse/Hoes	Hose/Hoes	House/Hoes	Hosse/Hoes
15.	Mei Be/Maybe	Mai Be/Maybe	May Be/Maybe	Mey Be/Maybe
16.	Matal/Metle/Meddle	Metal/Mettle/Meddle	Matal/Mettle/Meddle	Metal/Metle/Meddle
17.	Halve/Have	Hallva/Have	Hallve/Have	Halva/Have
18.	Wee/We	Wea/We	We/We	Wa/We
19.	Taper/Tapir	Taperr/Tapyr	Taperr/Tapir	Taper/Tapyr
20.	Timberr/Timbre	Tymber/Timbre	Tymberr/Timbre	Timber/Timbre
21.	Minse/Mintts	Mince/Mintts	Minse/Mints	Mince/Mints
22.	Eies/Ayes	Eyesc/Ayes	Eyes/Ayes	Eyess/Ayes
23.	Guesced/Guest	Guessed/Guest	Guesed/Guest	Gueced/Guest
24.	Yore/Your/You'Re	Yore/Yoor/You'Re	Yorre/Your/You'Re	Yorre/Yoor/You'Re
25.	Oarr/Or/Ora	Oarr/Or/Ore	Oar/Or/Ore	Oar/Or/Ora
26.	Bate/Biat	Bate/Bait	Batte/Biat	Batte/Bait
27.	Tax/Tacks	Tax/Taks	Tax/Tacksc	Tax/Tackss

28.	Bald/Ballad/Bawled	Bald/Baled/Bawled	Bald/Balled/Bawled	Bald/Balad/Bawled
29.	Ewe/Yuo/Yew	Ewe/Yoo/Yew	Ewe/You/Yew	Ewe/Yoo/Yw
30.	Eei/I/Aye	Eie/I/Ae	Eye/I/Aye	Eie/I/Aye
31.	Hoes/Hose	Hoess/Hose	Hoess/House	Hoes/House
32.	Tou/Two/To	Tu/Two/To	To/Two/To	Too/Two/To
33.	Ceres/Series	Cerres/Series	Ceres/Sereis	Cerres/Sereis
34.	Hansom/Handsome	Hansum/Handsome	Hanscom/Handsome	Hanssom/Handsome
35.	Residance/Residents	Residence/Residents	Ressidence/Residents	Ressidance/Residents
36.	Surrf/Serf	Surf/Serf	Surrph/Serf	Surph/Serf
37.	Siall/Sale	Saill/Sale	Sail/Sale	Sial/Sale
38.	Therre's/Thiers	There's/Thiers	There's/Theirs	Therre's/Theirs
39.	Roed/Rode	Roed/Rude	Rued/Rude	Roed/Rue
40.	Aid/Aie	Ayd/Aide	Ayd/Aie	Aid/Aide
41.	Taem/Teem	Taem/Tem	Team/Tem	Team/Teem
42.	Ilusion/Allusion	Ilution/Allusion	Illution/Allusion	Illusion/Allusion
43.	Hi/Hih	Hy/High	Hi/High	Hy/Hih
44.	Barred/Bard	Bared/Bard	Barad/Bard	Barrad/Bard
45.	Mewll/Mule	Mewl/Mule	Mewll/Mole	Mewl/Mole
46.	Rowss/Rose	Rows/Rose	Rowss/Rouse	Rows/Rouse
47.	Chep/Cheap	Cheep/Chaep	Cheep/Cheap	Chep/Chaep
48.	Bah/Ba	Beh/Ba	Bah/Baa	Beh/Baa
49.	Gofer/Gopher	Gopher/Gopher	Gophfer/Gopher	Goffer/Gopher
50.	Don/Doe	Dun/Doe	Dun/Done	Don/Done
51.	Ryte/Write/Right	Ritte/Write/Right	Rytte/Write/Right	Rite/Write/Right
52.	Mite/Might	Mitte/Might	Myte/Might	Mytte/Might
53.	Latter/Ladder	Later/Ladder	Latar/Ladder	Lattar/Ladder
54.	Gorred/Goord	Gored/Gourd	Gored/Goord	Gorred/Gourd
55.	Ball/Belle	Bell/Belle	Bal/Belle	Bel/Belle
56.	Ruscell/Rustle	Russell/Rustle	Rusell/Rustle	Rucell/Rustle
57.	Tuat/Taught	Tautt/Taught	Tuatt/Taught	Taut/Taught
58.	Cozen/Cousin	Cozen/Coosin	Cozen/Coossin	Cozen/Coussin
59.	Morn/Mourn	Morrn/Moorn	Morrn/Mourn	Morn/Moorn
60.	Stare/Stiar	Stare/Stair	Sttare/Stiar	Sttare/Stair
61.	Wrrap/Rap	Wrrep/Rap	Wrap/Rap	Wrep/Rap

62.	Centts/Ssents	Centts/Scents	Cents/Scents	Cents/Ssents
63.	Basste/Based	Baste/Baced	Baste/Based	Bascte/Based
64.	Foorr/Fore/For	Foor/Fore/For	Fourr/Fore/For	Four/Fore/For
65.	Knikers/Nickers	Knickerrs/Nickers	Knikerrs/Nickers	Knickers/Nickers
66.	Marre/Mayor	Mare/Mayor	Mare/Meyor	Marre/Meyor
67.	Surrje/Serge	Surje/Serge	Surrge/Serge	Surge/Serge
68.	Steal/Steel	Steal/Stel	Stael/Steel	Stael/Stel
69.	Haerrt/Hart	Heart/Hart	Hearrt/Hart	Haert/Hart
70.	Holed/Hold	Huled/Hold	Holled/Hold	Hulled/Hold
71.	Way/Wiegh/Whey	Wai/Wiegh/Whey	Wai/Weigh/Whey	Way/Weigh/Whey
72.	Diieng/Dying	Dyieng/Dying	Dieing/Dying	Dyeing/Dying
73.	Holay/Holy/Wholly	Holay/Holy/Wholy	Holey/Holy/Wholy	Holey/Holy/Wholly
74.	Sworrd/Soared	Swurrd/Soared	Swurd/Soared	Sword/Soared
75.	Cane/Cyan	Cane/Cian	Cane/Cayn	Cane/Cain
76.	Arreil/Aerial	Ariel/Aerial	Arriel/Aerial	Areil/Aerial
77.	Brut/Brute	Brrot/Brute	Brot/Brute	Brrut/Brute
78.	Frrays/Phrase	Frays/Phrase	Frreys/Phrase	Freys/Phrase
79.	Throne/Thrown	Thrrune/Thrown	Thrune/Thrown	Thrrone/Thrown
80.	Ha'd/Hed	He'd/Heed	He'd/Hed	He'd/Head
81.	Waerr/Where/Ware	Wear/Where/Ware	Wearr/Where/Ware	Waer/Where/Ware
82.	Brraed/Bred	Bread/Bred	Braed/Bred	Brread/Bred
83.	We've/Waeve	We've/Weave	Wa've/Weave	Wa've/Waeve
84.	Hew/Hoe/Huh	Hew/Hue/Hugh	Hew/Hoe/Hugh	Hew/Hoe/Hogh
85.	Nikerrs/Knickers	Nickerrs/Knickers	Nikers/Knickers	Nickers/Knickers
86.	Call/Sell	Cell/Sell	Cal/Sell	Cel/Sell
87.	Isle/I'l/Aisle	Isle/I'll/Aisle	Isle/I'll/Aysle	Isle/I'l/Aysle
88.	Brruice/Brews	Bruise/Brews	Brruise/Brews	Bruice/Brews
89.	Except/Accept	Exsept/Accept	Exsept/Acept	Except/Acept

Grammar: Homophones vs Homographs vs. Homonyms

How do you know which 'there,' 'their,' or 'they're' to use when you're writing? Isn't it a difficult one? These words sound similar but have completely different meanings.

Words with the same sound but different meanings are referred to as **homophones**. Homophones can be spelled differently or the same way. Rose (the flower), rose (the past tense of 'rise,' and rows (a line of items or people) are all homophones.

Homographs are two or more words that have the same spelling but different meanings and it **doesn't have to sound the same**. Because homographs are words with multiple meanings, how can you tell which one is being used? Readers can determine which form of a homograph is being used by looking for context clues, or words surrounding it that provide information about the definition. Take a look at these homograph examples.

A **bat** is either a piece of sporting equipment or an animal.
Bass is either a type of fish or a musical genre.
A **pen** is a writing instrument or a small enclosure in which animals are kept.
Lean is a word that means to be thin or to rest against something.
A **skip** is a fictitious jump or missing out on something.

Homonyms are words that have the same spelling or pronunciation but different meanings. These words can be perplexing at times, especially for students learning to spell them. For example, right means moral, the opposite of left, and a personal freedom. Homonyms can refer to both homophones and homographs. Both a homograph and a homophone are included in the definition of a homonym. For example, the words 'bear,' 'tear,' and 'lead' are all homographs, but they also meet the criteria for homonyms. They simply have to have the same look or sound. Similarly, while the words 'sell,' 'cell,' 'by,' and 'buy' are all homophones, they are also homonyms.

1. 'there,' 'their,' or 'they're' are examples of _____.
   a. Homophones
   b. Homographs

2. _____ are words that have the same spelling or pronunciation but different meanings.
   a. Homonyms
   b. Hemograms

3. Choose the correct homophone for this sentence: Please don't drop and _____that bottle of hand sanitizer!
   a. brake
   b. break

4. Homographs are two or more words that have the same spelling but different _____.
   a. ending sounds
   b. meanings

5. Current (A flow of water / Up to date) is both homograph and homophone.
   a. True
   b. False

6. To, two and too are _____.
   a. Homagraphs
   b. Homonyms

7. The candle filled the _____ with a delicious scent.
   a. heir
   b. air

8. Kim drove _____ the tunnel.
   a. threw
   b. through

9. John wants to go to _____ house for dinner, but they don't like her, so _____ going to say no.
   a. their, they're
   b. there, they're

10. We won a $95,000 _____!
   a. cheque
   b. check

11. For example, a pencil is not really made with _____.
   a. led
   b. lead

12. Choose the correct homophone for this sentence: Timmy was standing _____ in line.
   a. fourth
   b. forth

13. Homophones are two words that sound the same but have a different meanings.
   a. True
   b. False

14. The word ring in the following two sentences is considered what? She wore a ruby ring. | We heard the doorbell ring.
   a. hologram
   b. homograph

15. A Homograph is a word that has more than one meaning and doesn't have to sound the same.
   a. True
   b. False

16. Homophones occur when there are multiple ways to spell the same sound.
   a. True
   b. False

17. Select the correct homophone: I have very little (patience/patients) when students do not follow directions.
   a. patients
   b. patience

18. The correct homophone (s) are used in the sentence: Personally, I hate the smell of read meet.
   a. True
   b. False

19. The correct homophone(s) is used in the sentence: We saw a herd of cattle in the farmer's field.
   a. True
   b. False

20. What is NOT an example of a homograph?
   a. or, oar
   b. live, live

* Grammar Overview: Nouns, Verbs, Adjectives

A noun is a word that describes someone, a place, something, or an idea. Names, locations, physical objects, or objects and concepts that do not exist in the physical world, such as a dream or a theory, are examples of nouns. A noun is a single word, such as sister, home, desk, wedding, hope, pizza, or squirrel.

There are numerous ways to use nouns in language, and these various types of nouns are classified. In general, there are ten distinct types of nouns that are used in specific and unique contexts, but let's look at eight of them today.

Common Noun	a non-specific person, place, or thing	baby, mom
Compound Nouns	made up of two nouns	bus driver, sunflower
Collective Noun	group of individuals	team, family
Proper Noun	A specific person, place, or thing	Dr. Morgan, Amazon
Concrete Noun	identified through one of the five senses	air, chirps
Plural Noun	Multiple people, places, or things	bottles, pencils
Singular Noun	One person, place, or thing	chair, desk
Abstract Noun	things that don't exist as physical objects	fear, love

Common Noun: A generic name for a person, place, or thing in a class or group is a common noun. In contrast to proper nouns, common nouns are not capitalized unless they begin a sentence or appear in a title. All nouns fall into one of two categories: common or proper. Proper nouns are distinct from common nouns in that they name something specific. Nouns in common use do not. Unnecessary capitalization of common nouns is a common spelling error. Some words, such as president, seem to beg for a capital letter because we instinctively want to emphasize their significance. However, if it does not name something or someone specific, even this lofty title is a common noun (in this case, a specific president).

Compound Noun: Every compound noun is made up of two or more words that are combined to form a noun. These distinct words do not have to be nouns in and of themselves; all they need to do is communicate a specific person, place, idea, or thing. A compound noun can be a common noun (for example, fish sticks), a proper noun (for example, Pizza Hut), or an abstract noun (lovesickness). They can be hyphenated or not, and they can have a space between words—especially if one of the words has more than one syllable, as in living room. You'll start noticing compound nouns everywhere once you've learned to recognize them. Fire-flies? Compound noun. Sub sandwich? Compound noun. Software developer, mother-in-law, underworld, toothache, garlic knot? They are all compound nouns.

Collective Noun: A collective noun is a word or phrase that refers to a group of people or things as if they were a single entity. There are some exceptions to the rule that collective nouns are treated as singular. Collective nouns such as team, family, class, group, and host use a singular verb when the entity acts as a whole and a plural verb when the individuals who make up the entity act individually.

Collective nouns refer to more than one person or thing in a category. A pride cannot have just one lion, and a single flower does not make a bouquet. As a result, a collective noun always refers to a plurality of some kind.

Example: The group is working on a mural. (Because the mural is painted collectively by the group, the verb is singular.)

Example: The group cannot agree on how to paint the mural. (Because the group members disagree with one another, the verb is plural.)

Proper Noun: A proper noun is a name that is specific (as opposed to generic) to a specific person, place, or thing. In English, proper nouns are always capitalized, regardless of where they appear in a sentence. That is, whether it appears at the beginning, middle, or end of a sentence, it is always written with the first letter in capital letters. In a sentence, a proper noun is used to name a person, place, or organization, such as Jim, Molly, India, Germany, Amazon, Microsoft, and so on.

Concrete Noun: A concrete noun is one that can be identified using at least one of the five senses (taste, touch, sight, hearing, or smell). Objects and substances that we cannot perceive (see, hear, taste, touch, or smell) with our sense organs are NOT concrete nouns. The majority of nouns become concrete nouns because we can feel them (for example, all animals and people) with our sense organs. Concrete nouns can be common nouns, countable nouns, proper nouns, uncountable nouns, collective nouns, and so on. All nouns are classified into two types: concrete nouns and abstract nouns.

Abstract Nouns: An abstract noun is one that cannot be perceived through any of the five senses (i.e., taste, touch, sight, hearing, smelling). In other words, an abstract noun is a noun that exists only in our minds and cannot be recognized by our senses.

Concrete nouns are tangible, whereas abstract nouns are intangible.

Concrete nouns can be experienced with the five senses, whereas abstract nouns cannot.

Singular Noun: Singular nouns are used in sentences to refer to a single person, place, thing, or idea. Singular nouns include things like boy, girl, teacher, boat, goat, hand, and so on.

Plural noun: There are numerous plural noun rules, and because nouns are used so frequently in writing! The correct spelling of plurals is usually determined by what letter the singular noun ends in. Take a look at some examples.

Add s to the end of regular nouns to make them plural.

cat – cats

house – houses

If the singular noun ends in s, ss, sh, ch, x, or z, add es to make it plural.

bus – buses

lunch – lunches

Singular nouns ending in -s or -z may require you to double the -s or -z before adding the -es for pluralization in some cases.

quiz – quizzes

gas –gasses

If the noun ends in f or fe, the f is frequently changed to ve before adding the -s to form the plural form.

calf–calves

wife – wives

Exceptions:

roof – roofs

chef – chefs

When some nouns are pluralized, they do not change at all.

sheep – sheep

species – species

There are additional rules that we did not cover here. Please spend some time studying the following:

If the final letter of a singular noun is -y and the letter preceding the -y is a consonant, the noun ends in -y. puppy – puppies

If the singular noun ends in -y and the letter preceding the -y is a vowel, add an -s. boy – boys

If the singular noun ends in -o, make it plural by adding -es. potato – potatoes Exception: photo – photos

If a singular noun ends in -us, the plural ending is usually -i. cactus – cacti

When a singular noun ends in -is, the plural ending is -es. ellipsis – ellipses

If a singular noun ends in -on, the plural noun ends in -a. criterion – criteria

Verbs

In theory, verbs are easy to understand. A verb is a word that describes an action, an occurrence, or a state of being. Of course, there are many different types of verbs, but remember that a verb should indicate that something is happening because an action is taking place in some way. When first learning about verbs, many students simply refer to them as 'doing words,' because they always indicate that something has been done, is being done, or will be done in the future (depending on the tense that you are writing in).

Verbs, like nouns, are the main part of a sentence or phrase, telling a story about what is going on. In fact, full thoughts cannot be conveyed without a verb, and even the simplest sentences, such as (Kim sings.) Actually, a verb can be a sentence in and of itself, with the subject, in most cases you, implied, as in Sing! and Drive!

The location of the verb in relation to the subject is one clue that can help you identify it. Verbs are almost always followed by a noun or pronoun. The subject is made up of these nouns and pronouns.

1. Jim **eats** his dinner quickly.
2. We **went** to the bank.

Adjectives

Adjectives are descriptive words for nouns. A noun is defined as a person, place, thing, or idea. We want to be as descriptive as possible when we speak or write. Being descriptive allows the reader or listener to understand better what you are attempting to describe. You want your audience to have the best possible understanding of what you're describing.

What image comes to mind when I say, "I saw a cat?" You might see a spotted cat, a small orange cat, or a shaggy gray cat, depending on your experience. I didn't give you enough adjectives to paint a complete picture.

Do you have a better mental image if I say, "I saw a big, wet, sad, shaggy, orange and white cat"? Of course, you do because I used adjectives to clarify things.

* Grammar: Nouns, Verbs, Adjectives

DIRECTIONS: SORT the words (below) by their corresponding *part-of-speech*.

color	chickens	kittens	banjo	library	goldfish
grieving	adorable	cough	stand	nasty	powerful
dance	build	cry	break	easy	circle
coach	aggressive	careful	eat	adventurous	think
mysterious	face	sticks	drink	guitar	busy
calm	window	worm	coast	draw	polka dot
eager	handsome	explain			

Nouns (13)	Verbs (13)	Adjectives (13)

* Grammar: Compound Nouns

A compound noun is one that is composed of two or more words. Each word contributes to the meaning of the noun.

Compound nouns can be written three ways:

A single word	Two words	Hyphenated
haircut	rain forest	self-esteem

Instructions: Match the compound noun pairs correctly.

1	☐	Fund	crow		A
2	☐	News	dresser		B
3	☐	Sun	glasses		C
4	☐	Child	paper		D
5	☐	Door	attack		E
6	☐	heart	hood		F
7	☐	tooth	plane		G
8	☐	apple	cut		H
9	☐	full	ring		I
10	☐	hair	paste		J
11	☐	air	sauce		K
12	☐	ear	book		L
13	☐	scare	moon		M
14	☐	post	way		N
15	☐	hair	raiser		O
16	☐	note	office		P

* Grammar: Collective Noun

A collective noun is a noun that refers to a group of people, animals, or things. They are described as a single entity. Collective nouns are distinct from singular nouns in that singular nouns describe only one person or object.

Many collective nouns are common nouns, but when they are the name of a company or other organization with more than one person, such as Microsoft, they can also be proper nouns.

Find the collective noun in each sentence.

1. Our class visited the natural history museum on a field trip.

2. The bison herd stampeded across the prairie, leaving a massive dust cloud in its wake.

3. We eagerly awaited the verdict of the jury.

4. This year's basketball team features three players who stand taller than six feet.

5. At Waterloo, Napoleon's army was finally defeated.

6. The plans for a new park have been approved by the town council.

7. He comes from a large family, as the oldest of eleven children.

8. The rock group has been on tour for several months.

9. When Elvis appeared on stage, the entire audience erupted in applause.

10. The San Francisco crowd were their usual individualistic selves.

11. The crew of sailors boarded the ships.

12. A mob destroyed the company's new office.

13. The fleet of ships was waiting at the port.

14. It was difficult for the committee to come to a decision.

* Grammar: Concrete & Abstract Noun

Score: _____

Date: _____

In the English language, both concrete and abstract nouns are essential parts of speech. The primary distinction between concrete and abstract nouns is that concrete nouns refer to people, places, or things that take up physical space, whereas abstract nouns refer to intangible ideas that cannot be physically interacted with.

Words like "luck," "disgust," and "empathy" are examples of abstract nouns. While it is possible to see someone being empathetic, empathy is not a visible or tangible entity. The majority of feelings, emotions, and philosophies can be classified as abstract nouns.

1. FIND THE ABSTRACT NOUN
   a. KIND
   b. BOOK

2. FIND THE ABTRACT NOUN: THE KING WAS KNOWN FOR HIS JUSTICE
   a. JUSTICE
   b. KING

3. WHICH NOUN BELOW IS AN ABSTRACT NOUN?
   a. TRAIN
   b. LOVE

4. WHAT IS A CONCRETE NOUN?
   a. A NOUN THAT YOU CAN EXPERIENCE WITH AT LEAST 1 OF YOUR 5 SENSES.
   b. A NOUN THAT YOU CAN'T EXPERIENCE WITH AT LEAST 1 OF YOUR 5 SENSES.

5. WHICH WORD BELOW IS NOT A CONCRETE NOUN?
   a. HAMBURGER
   b. ANGER

2. FIND THE CONCRETE NOUNS
   a. WINDOW
   b. LOVE

4. WHAT ARE THE 5 CONCRETE NOUNS
   a. TASTE, SMELL, WALKING, EYEING, TOUCHING
   b. SMELL,TASTE, SIGHT, HEARING,TOUCH

6. IS THE FOLLOWING NOUN CONCRETE OR ABSTRACT? CUPCAKES
   a. ABSTRACT
   b. CONCRETE

8. WHICH WORD BELOW IS AN ABSTRACT NOUN?
   a. BRAVERY
   b. FRIEND

10. IS THE WORD THOUGHTFULNESS A CONCRETE OR ABSTRACT NOUN?
   a. ABSTRACT
   b. CONCRETE

* Science: Vertebrates

To begin, all animals are classified as either vertebrates or invertebrates. Invertebrates lack a backbone, whereas vertebrates do. Scientists can't stop there, because each group contains thousands of different animals! As a result, scientists divide vertebrates and invertebrates into increasingly smaller groups. Let's talk about vertebrates and some of their classifications.

Vertebrates range in size from a frog to a blue whale. Because there are at least 59,000 different types of vertebrates on the planet, they are further classified into five major groups: mammals, birds, fish, amphibians, and reptiles. Remember that animals are classified into these groups based on what they have in common. Why is an elephant classified as a mammal while a crocodile is classified as a reptile? Let's go over some of the characteristics of each vertebrate group.

Warm-blooded animals are mammals. This means that their bodies maintain their temperature, which is usually higher than the temperature of the surrounding air. They also have hair or fur; they have lungs to breathe air; that they feed milk to their babies; and that most give birth to live young, rather than laying eggs, as a dog does.

- Birds have feathers, two wings (though not all birds, such as the ostrich and penguin, can fly), are warm-blooded, and lay eggs.
- Fish have fins or scales, live in water, and breathe oxygen through gills.
- Like salamanders and frogs, Amphibians have smooth, moist skin (amphibians must keep their skin wet); lay eggs in water; most breathe through their skin and lungs.
- Reptiles have scales (imagine a scaly lizard), are cold-blooded (their body temperature changes as the temperature around them changes), breathe air. Most reptiles, including the crocodile and snake, lay hard-shelled eggs on land.

Vertebrates play several vital roles in an ecosystem. Many predator species are large vertebrates in ecosystems. Lions, eagles, and sharks are examples of predatory vertebrates. Many prey species in ecosystems are also vertebrates. Mice, rabbits, and frogs are examples of these animals. Many vertebrates serve as scavengers in ecosystems. They are significant because they remove dead animals from the environment. Turkey vultures and hyenas, for example, are both vertebrate scavengers. Furthermore, many vertebrates serve as pollinators in ecosystems. Bats and monkeys, for example, may aid in pollen spread by visiting various trees and plants.

Humans value vertebrates for a variety of reasons. Vertebrates are domesticated animals used by humans. These animals are capable of producing milk, food, and clothing. They can also help with work. Agricultural animals are usually vertebrates. Humans also hunt a variety of wild vertebrate animals for food.

1. Vertebrates range in _____ from a frog to a blue whale.
   a. age
   b. size

2. Fish have fins or scales, live in water, and breathe ___ through gills.
   a. oxygen
   b. water

3. Invertebrates lack a _____, whereas vertebrates _____.
   a. skin, whereas vertebrates do
   b. backbone, whereas vertebrates do

4. Warm-blooded animals are _____.
   a. mammals
   b. producers

5. Some vertebrates serve as _____, they remove dead animals from the environment.
   a. scavengers
   b. invertebrates

6. Lions, eagles, and sharks are examples of _____ vertebrates.
   a. ecofriendly
   b. predatory

7. _____ animals are capable of producing milk, food, and clothing.
   a. Non-producing
   b. Domesticated

8. Many vertebrates serve as _____ in ecosystems, they may aid in pollen spread by visiting various trees and plants.
   a. water lilies
   b. pollinators

* Science: Invertebrates

Invertebrates can be found almost anywhere. Invertebrates account for at least 95% of all animals on the planet! Do you know what one thing they all have in common? Invertebrates lack a backbone.

Your body is supported by a backbone, which protects your organs and connects your other bones. As a result, you are a vertebrate. On the other hand, invertebrates lack the support of bones, so their bodies are often simpler, softer, and smaller. They are also cold-blooded, which means their body temperature fluctuates in response to changes in the air or water around them.

Invertebrates can be found flying, swimming, crawling, or floating and provide essential services to the environment and humans. Nobody knows how many different types of invertebrates there are, but there are millions!

Just because an invertebrate lacks a spinal column does not mean it does not need to eat. Invertebrates, like all other forms of animal life, must obtain nutrients from their surroundings. Invertebrates have evolved two types of digestion to accomplish this. The use of intracellular digestion is common in the most simple organisms. The food is absorbed into the cell and broken down in the cytoplasm at this point. Extracellular digestion, in which cells break down food through the secretion of enzymes and other techniques, is used by more advanced invertebrates. All vertebrates use extracellular digestion.

Still, all animals, invertebrates or not, need a way to get rid of waste. Most invertebrates, especially the simplest ones, use the process of diffusion to eliminate waste. This is merely the opposite of intracellular digestion. However, more advanced invertebrates have more advanced waste disposal mechanisms. Similar to our kidneys, specialized glands in these animals filter and excrete waste. But there is a happy medium. Even though some invertebrates do not have complete digestive tracts like vertebrates, they do not simply flush out waste through diffusion. Instead, the mouth doubles as an exit.

Scientists have classified invertebrates into numerous groups based on what the animals have in common. Arthropods have segmented bodies, which means that they are divided into sections. Consider an ant!

Arthropods are the most numerous group of invertebrates. They can live on land, as spiders and insects do, or in water, as crayfish and crabs do. Because insects are the most numerous group of arthropods, many of them fly, including mosquitoes, bees, locusts, and ladybugs.

They also have jointed legs or limbs to help them walk, similar to how you have knees for your legs and elbows for your arms. The majority of arthropods have an exoskeleton, tough outer skin, or shell that protects their body. Have you ever wondered why when you squish a bug, it makes that crunching sound? That's right; it's the exoskeleton!

Mollusks are the second most numerous group of invertebrates. They have soft bodies and can be found on land or in water. Shells protect the soft bodies of many mollusks, including snails, oysters, clams, and scallops. However, not all, such as octopus, squid, and cuttlefish, have a shell.

1. Invertebrates lack a _____.
   a. backbone
   b. tailbone

2. Invertebrates are also ____.
   a. cold-blooded
   b. warm-blooded

3. _____ can live on land, as spiders and insects do, or in water, as crayfish and crabs do.
   a. Vertebrates
   b. Arthropods

4. All animals, invertebrates or not, need a way to get rid of ____.
   a. their skin
   b. waste

5. _____ have soft bodies and can be found on land or in water.
   a. Arthropods
   b. Mollusks

6. Just because an invertebrate lacks a _____ column does not mean it does not need to eat.
   a. spinal
   b. tissues

7. Your body is supported by a backbone, which protects your ____ and connects your other bones.
   a. organs
   b. muscles

8. Invertebrates lack the support of bones, so their bodies are often simpler, ___, and smaller.
   a. softer and bigger
   b. softer and smaller

* Science: Organelles

Do you and your dog have a similar appearance? We are all aware that people and dogs appear to be very different on the outside. However, there are some similarities on the inside. Cells make up all animals, including humans and dogs.

All animal cells appear to be the same. They have a cell membrane that contains cytoplasm, which is a gooey fluid. Organelles float in the cytoplasm. Organelles function as tiny machines that meet the needs of the cell. The term organelle refers to a "miniature organ." This lesson will teach you about the various organelles found in animal cells and what they do.

The nucleus of the cell is the cell's brain. It is in charge of many of the cell's functions. The nucleus is where DNA, the genetic instructions for building your body, is stored. DNA contains vital information! Your nucleus has its membrane to protect this essential information, similar to the membrane that surrounds the entire cell.

Your cells require energy. Energy is produced by mitochondria, which are oval-shaped organelles. Mitochondria convert the nutrients that enter the cell into ATP. Your cells use ATP for energy. Because they are the cell's powerhouses, you might think of these organelles as the mighty mitochondria.

The nutrients must be digested before they can be converted into energy by the mitochondria. Digestion is carried out by a group of organelles known as lysosomes. Digestive enzymes are found in lysosomes. Enzymes can sometimes be released into the cell. Because the enzymes kill the cell, lysosomes are known as "suicide bags."

Use Google or your preferred source to help match each term with a definition.

1	☐	nucleus	responsible for chromosome segregation	A
2	☐	lysosomes	degradation of proteins and cellular waste	B
3	☐	Golgi Apparatus	protein synthesis	C
4	☐	Mitochondria	lipid synthesis	D
5	☐	SER	site of photosynthesis	E
6	☐	RER	stores water in plant cells	F
7	☐	Microtubules	prevents excessive uptake of water, protects the cell (in plants)	G
8	☐	ribosomes	degradation of H2O2	H
9	☐	peroxysomes	powerhouse of the cell	I
10	☐	cell wall	modification of proteins; "post-office" of the cell	J
11	☐	chloroplast	protein synthesis + modifications	K
12	☐	central vacuole	where DNA is stored	L

* Science: Water Cycle

On stormy days, water falls to the earth. The ground absorbs it. The movement of water is a component of the water cycle. The water cycle is critical to all living things on the planet!

Other cycles exist in your life. Your daily routine is a cycle that begins with you waking up. You attend classes. You take the bus back home. You leave for soccer practice. You eat your dinner. You retire to your bed. These occurrences are part of a cycle. Every weekday, this cycle is repeated. The water cycle is also a series of repeated events that occur repeatedly.

The water cycle is comprised of repeated events such as evaporation, condensation, precipitation, and collection. These occurrences occur regularly.

- Evaporation occurs when water is heated and turns into a gas.
- Condensation occurs when a gas of water cools and condenses back into a liquid.
- Precipitation occurs when water returns to the earth.
- Water is collected when stored in bodies of water such as lakes, rivers, oceans, soil, and rocks.

Observing the water cycle is a good way to see how water moves around the Earth and atmosphere on a daily basis. It is a complicated system with numerous processes. Liquid water evaporates into water vapor, condenses into clouds, and falls back to earth as rain and snow. Water in various phases circulates through the atmosphere (transportation). Runoff is the movement of liquid water across land, into the ground (infiltration and percolation), and through the ground (groundwater). Groundwater moves into plants (plant uptake) and evaporates into the atmosphere from plants (transpiration). Solid ice and snow can spontaneously decompose into gas (sublimation). When water vapor solidifies, the opposite can occur (deposition).

Use the word bank to unscramble the words below.

molecule	pollutant	evaporation	radiation	groundwater	oceans
infiltration	nitrogen	deposition	environment	collection	sublimation
transpiration	hydrogen	condensation	organism	precipitation	oxygen
meltwater	movement	vapor	droplet	iceberg	weather
rainwater	glacier				

1. NMSALIITBOU   s u _ l _ _ _ _ _ _

2. IARTASRPONTIN   _ r _ _ _ _ _ _ _ _ i _ n

3. OMLLECUE   _ o _ e _ _ _ _

4. NEIRAVOTAOP   _ v _ _ _ _ a _ i _ _

5. ALEIGCR   _ l _ _ _ _ r

6. TONOINSNCEDA   c _ _ _ _ n s _ _ _ _ _

7. DARRWOGENTU   _ r o _ _ _ _ _ _ _ r

8. TUNLOPLAT   _ _ _ l _ _ _ n _

9. EPITITARINCPO   _ _ _ c _ _ _ t _ _ i _ _

10. ITNIOILRNFAT   _ n _ _ t _ _ _ _ o _

11. ODRLPET   _ r _ _ _ e _

12. NIEDTSOPIO   _ _ _ o _ _ t i _ _

13. WTAEERH   _ _ _ _ h _ r

14. EONNTIGR   n _ _ _ o _ _ _

15. RWANTREAI   r _ _ _ _ _ _ _ r

16. REBGICE   i _ e _ _ _ _

17. TNOAIADRI   _ _ _ _ a _ i _ _

18. EOXNGY   _ x y _ _ _

19. SGOMRNIA   _ _ g _ _ _ _ m

20. YNEDRHOG   _ _ _ r o _ _ _

21. EARTLWTME   _ _ _ _ _ a _ e _

22. COTNCLEOLI   _ o _ _ e _ t _ _ _

23. PAROV   v _ _ _ _

24. NEVOEMTM   _ _ _ _ _ e _ t

25. ORENINTNVEM   e n v _ _ _ _ _ _ _ _

26. OCSANE   _ c _ _ n _

Extra Credit: What is the process of the water cycle?

* Science: The Seasons

First, read the entire passage. After that, go back and fill in the blanks. You can skip the blanks you're unsure about and finish them later.

planet	leaves	North	chicks	green
summer	shines	June	heats	frost

Our _____ has four seasons each year: autumn, winter, spring, and _____.

The Earth spins in a slightly tilted position as it orbits the sun (on an axis tilted 23.5 degrees from a straight-up, vertical position). Because different parts of the planet are angled towards or away from the sun's light throughout the year, this tilt causes our seasons. More or less sunlight and heat influence the length of each day, the average daily temperature, and the amount of rainfall in different seasons.

The tilt has two major effects: the sun's angle to the Earth and the length of the days. The Earth is tilted so that the _____ Pole is more pointed towards the sun for half of the year. The South Pole is pointing at the sun for the other half. When the North Pole is angled toward the sun, the days in the northern hemisphere (north of the equator) receive more sunlight, resulting in longer days and shorter nights. The northern hemisphere _____ up and experiences summer as the days lengthen. As the year progresses, the Earth's tilt shifts to the North Pole points away from the sun, resulting in winter.

As a result, seasons north of the equator are opposed to seasons south of the equator. When Europe and the United States are experiencing winter, Brazil and Australia will be experiencing summer.

We discussed how the length of the day changes, but the angle of the sun also changes. In the summer, the sun _____ more directly on the Earth, providing more energy to the surface and heating it. In the winter, sunlight strikes the Earth at an angle. This produces less energy and heats the Earthless.

The longest day in the Northern Hemisphere is _____ 21st, while the longest night is December 21st. The opposite is true in the Southern Hemisphere, where December 21st is the longest day, and June 21st is the longest night. There are only two days a year when the day and night are the same. These are September 22nd and March 21st.

The amount of time it is light for decreases in autumn, and the _____ begin to change color and fall off the trees. In the United States of America, autumn is referred to as Fall.

Winter brings colder weather, sometimes snow and _____, no leaves on the trees, and the amount of daylight during the day are at its shortest.

The weather usually warms up in the spring, trees begin to sprout leaves, plants begin to bloom, and young animals such as _____ and lambs are born.

The weather is usually warm in the summer, the trees have entire _____ leaves, and the amount of daylight during the day is extended.

* Government History: How Laws Are Made

Congress is the federal government's legislative branch, and it is in charge of making laws for the entire country. Congress is divided into two legislative chambers: the United States Senate and the United States House of Representatives. Anyone elected to either body has the authority to propose new legislation. A bill is a new law proposal.

People living in the United States and its territories are subject to federal laws.

Bills are created and passed by Congress. The president may then sign the bills into law. Federal courts may examine the laws to see if they are in accordance with the Constitution. If a court finds a law to be unconstitutional, it has the authority to overturn it.

The United States government has enacted several laws to help maintain order and protect the country's people. Each new law must be approved by both houses of Congress as well as the President. Before it becomes a new law in the nation, each law must go through a specific process.

The majority of laws in the United States begin as bills. An idea is the starting point for a bill. That thought could come from anyone, including you! The idea must then be written down and explained as the next step. A bill is the name given to the first draft of an idea. The bill must then be sponsored by a member of Congress. The sponsor is someone who strongly supports the bill and wishes to see it become law. A Senator or a member of the House of Representatives can be the sponsor.

The bill is then introduced in either the House or the Senate by the bill's sponsor. Once submitted, the bill is given a number and is officially recorded as a bill.

The bill is assigned to a committee after it is introduced. Committees are smaller groups of congress members who are experts in specific areas. For example, if the bill concerns classroom size in public schools, it would be referred to the Committee on Education. The committee goes over the bill's specifics. They bring in experts from outside Congress to testify and debate the bill's pros and cons.

The committee may decide to make changes to the bill before it is passed. If the committee finally agrees to pass the bill, it will be sent to the House or Senate's main chamber for approval.

If the bill was introduced in the House, it would first be considered by the House. The bill will be discussed and debated by the representatives. House members will then vote on the bill. If the bill is passed, it will be sent to the Senate for consideration.

The Senate will then follow the same procedure. It will discuss and debate the bill before voting. If the Senate approves the bill, it will be sent to the President.

The President's signature is the final step in a bill becoming law. When the President signs the bill, it becomes law.

The President has the option of refusing to sign the bill. This is known as a veto. The Senate and House can choose to override the President's veto by voting again. The bill must now be approved by a two-thirds majority in both the Senate and the House to override the veto.

A bill must be signed into law by the President within 10-days. If he does not sign it within 10-days, one of two things may occur:

1) It will become law if Congress is in session.

2) It will be considered vetoed if Congress is not in session (this is called a pocket veto).

1. If the Senate approves the bill, it will be sent to the _____.
   a. President
   b. House Representee

2. The _____ may decide to make changes to the bill before it is passed.
   a. governor
   b. committee

3. The bill must then be _____ by a member of Congress.
   a. signed
   b. sponsored

4. The President has the option of refusing to sign the bill. This is known as a ___.
   a. voted
   b. veto

5. **The Senate and House can choose to override the President's veto by _____ again.**
    a. creating a new bill
    b. voting

6. **The bill is assigned to a committee after it is _____.**
    a. introduced
    b. vetoed

7. **Bills are created and passed by _____.**
    a. The House
    b. Congress

8. **A bill must be signed into law by the President within ___-days.**
    a. 10
    b. 5

9. **The President's _____ is the final step in a bill becoming law.**
    a. signature
    b. saying yes

10. **If the committee agrees to pass the bill, it will be sent to the House or Senate's main ___ for approval.**
    a. chamber
    b. state

Extra Credit: What are some of the weirdest laws in the world? List at least 5.

* History: The Vikings

First, read the entire passage. After that, go back and fill in the blanks. You can skip the blanks you're unsure about and finish them later.

sail	settle	North	Christianity	raided
Middle	defeated	shallow	cargo	Denmark

During the _____ Ages, the Vikings lived in Northern Europe. They first settled in the Scandinavian lands that are now Denmark, Sweden, and Norway. During the Middle Ages, the Vikings played a significant role in Northern Europe, particularly during the Viking Age, which lasted from 800 CE to 1066 CE.

In Old Norse, the word Viking means "to raid." The Vikings would board their longships and _____ across the seas to raid villages on Europe's northern coast, including islands like Great Britain. In 787 CE, they first appeared in England to raid villages. When the Vikings _____, they were known to attack defenseless monasteries. This earned them a bad reputation as barbarians, but monasteries were wealthy and undefended Viking targets.

The Vikings eventually began to _____ in areas other than Scandinavia. They colonized parts of Great Britain, Germany, and Iceland in the ninth century. They spread into northeastern Europe, including Russia, in the 10th century. They also established Normandy, which means "Northmen," along the coast of northern France.

By the beginning of the 11th century, the Vikings had reached the pinnacle of their power. Leif Eriksson, son of Erik the Red, was one Viking who made it to _____ America. He established a brief settlement in modern-day Canada. This was thousands of years before Columbus.

The English and King Harold Godwinson _____ the Vikings, led by King Harald Hardrada of Norway, in 1066. The defeat in this battle is sometimes interpreted as the end of the Viking Age. The Vikings stopped expanding their territory at this point, and raids became less frequent.

The arrival of Christianity was a major factor at the end of the Viking age. The Vikings became more and more a part of mainland Europe as Scandinavia was converted to _____ and became a part of Christian Europe. Sweden's, Denmark's, and Norway's identities and borders began to emerge as well.

The Vikings were perhaps best known for their ships. The Vikings built longships for exploration and raiding. Longships were long, narrow vessels built for speed. Oars primarily propelled them but later added a sail to help in windy conditions. Longships had a shallow draft, which allowed them to float in _____ water and land on beaches.

The Vikings also built _____ ships known as Knarr for trading. The Knarr was wider and deeper than the longship, allowing it to transport more cargo.

Five recovered Viking ships can be seen at the Viking Ship Museum in Roskilde, _____. It's also possible to see how the Vikings built their ships. The Vikings used a shipbuilding technique known as clinker building. They used long wood planks that overlapped along the edges.

Fun Facts:

- The Viking is the mascot of the Minnesota Vikings of the National Football League.
- Certain Vikings fought with monstrous two-handed axes. They are capable of easily piercing a metal helmet or shield.

* Geography: Castles in Germany

Castles are now iconic symbols of magnificence and mythical tales. Aside from their dazzling appearance and antiquity, they reveal an old vivid, and true fable.

German castles date from the 9th to 10th centuries, when the Great Age of Castles began. Castles embody the need for nations to be protected from invasions by other countries and serve as residences for old royal families. These incredible structures are examples of tactical and solid rocky constructions built by kings and emperors to guard the nation's territories during warfare and impose rule among populaces during peacetime.

German castles evolved during the "Medieval Ages," following the fall of Ancient Rome and the beginning of the Renaissance Period in the 14th century, and are considered an area of art and architecture. The architecture of German castles consists of a combination of towers and fortified walls, with amazingly decorated interior and exterior, located in high peaks of mountains and valleys, near waterways, and allowing total surveillance of the surrounding territory.

Modern Germany has a magnificent castle heritage, with over 2100 castles spread throughout the country. A very bright and amusing history awaits behind the doors of these impressive castles. Around 100 years ago, not so long ago, kings, emperors, and their families visited, lived, and operated there. Historical resolutions were reached there, and many soldiers died there defending their country from invaders.

Let us take some time to explore some of Germany's magnificent castles.

Neuschwanstein Castle: Located in the Bavarian Alps near the town of Füssen in southeast Bavaria, Germany, this is one of Europe's and the world's most impressive castles.

Hohenzollern Castle is situated on the crest of Mount Hohenzollern in the German state of Swabia. It was first built in the 11th century.

Eltz Castle: The beautiful and ancient castle of Eltz is located in the Moselle valley, between Koblenz and Trier, Germany, and is surrounded on three sides by the Eltzbach River. The castle was built as a residence rather than a fortress and served as a residence for the Rodendorf, Kempenich, and Rübenach families.

Heidelberg Castle: Heidelberg Castle (German: *Heidelberger Schloss*) is unquestionably Germany's most famous castle ruin. The magnificent palace commands a commanding position on a hill overlooking historic Heidelberg. Schloss Heidelberg has inspired poets for centuries, so it's no surprise that it's a popular tourist destination and well-known worldwide.

Schwerin Castle: Schwerin Castle is located in the city of Schwerin, Germany. Schwerin Castle is now the seat of the local government and an art museum displaying works from antiquity to the twentieth century. The museum's seventeenth-century Dutch and Flemish paintings are among its most important exhibits.

1. _____ is now the seat of the local government and an art museum.
   a. Schwerin Castle
   b. Swaziland Castle

2. Hohenzollern Castle is situated on the _____ of Mount Hohenzollern.
   a. crest
   b. end

3. The architecture of German castles consists of a combination of towers and _____.
   a. beautiful curtains
   b. fortified walls

4. German castles evolved during the "_____ Ages".
   a. Century
   b. Medieval

5. This castle was built as a residence rather than a fortress.
   a. Eltz Castle
   b. Schwerin Castle

6. Castles are now iconic symbols of magnificence and _____ tales.
   a. real life
   b. mythical

7. _____ has inspired poets for centuries.
   a. Schloss Heidelberg
   b. Steven Spielberg

8. _____ Castle is located in the Bavarian Alps near the town of Füssen.
   a. Norwegian
   b. Neuschwanstein

* Geography: Canada

Canada is the world's second-largest country, covering 10 million square kilometers. Canada's borders are bounded by three oceans: the Pacific Ocean to the west, the Atlantic Ocean to the east, and the Arctic Ocean to the north. The Canada-United States border runs along Canada's southern border.

Queen Victoria, Queen Elizabeth II's great-great-grandmother, chose Ottawa, which is located on the Ottawa River, as the capital in 1857. It is now the fourth largest metropolitan area in Canada. The National Capital Region, which encompasses 4,700 square kilometers around Ottawa, preserves and improves the area's built heritage and natural environment.

Canada is divided into ten provinces and three territories. Each province and territory has a separate capital city. You should be familiar with the capitals of your province or territory, as well as those of Canada.

Below are some of Canada's Territories, Provinces, and Capital Cities. Draw a line through each word you find.

```
R  L  U  G  M  A  N  I  T  O  B  A  N  K  M  E  X  L  S  P
W  K  A  K  B  B  H  A  L  B  E  R  T  A  G  D  K  P  R  R
Q  M  N  Y  N  X  W  I  S  Z  L  X  B  Q  E  K  B  T  X  I
I  Q  A  L  U  I  T  E  G  I  R  T  O  R  O  N  T  O  Y  N
A  B  R  I  T  I  S  H  C  O  L  U  M  B  I  A  E  C  E  C
V  N  N  R  S  Q  H  G  I  W  I  N  N  I  P  E  G  H  L  E
S  O  G  X  Z  G  A  O  N  T  A  R  I  O  F  B  R  A  L  E
T  V  Q  Z  E  D  M  O  N  T  O  N  C  D  F  W  Q  R  O  D
.  A  V  H  B  E  F  R  E  D  E  R  I  C  T  O  N  L  W  W
J  S  V  P  O  Q  U  E  B  E  C  C  I  T  Y  N  W  O  K  A
O  C  Y  J  R  W  S  H  V  C  V  Q  H  W  W  U  L  T  N  R
H  O  E  L  E  E  B  A  A  Z  O  U  Q  G  H  N  V  T  I  D
N  T  W  X  G  A  Q  L  S  T  J  E  F  H  I  A  I  E  F  I
.  I  K  M  I  D  C  I  L  X  L  B  U  V  T  V  C  T  E  S
S  A  C  P  N  C  O  F  T  Z  M  E  U  E  E  U  T  O  N  L
P  Q  Y  F  A  P  L  A  G  P  Y  C  F  M  H  T  O  W  B  A
I  W  S  D  R  Y  W  X  G  W  P  U  E  U  O  G  R  N  M  N
Y  N  E  W  B  R  U  N  S  W  I  C  K  T  R  P  I  C  R  D
R  X  B  T  E  R  V  Y  J  B  H  H  M  K  S  W  A  J  N  Z
G  F  S  A  S  K  A  T  C  H  E  W  A  N  E  Y  U  K  O  N
```

Yukon	Nunavut	Nova Scotia	Prince Edward Island	New Brunswick
Quebec	Ontario	Manitoba	Saskatchewan	Alberta
British Columbia	Victoria	Edmonton	Regina	Winnipeg
Toronto	Quebec City	Fredericton	Charlottetown	Halifax
St. John's	Iqaluit	Yellowknife	Whitehorse	

* Environmental Health: Water Pollution

First, read the entire passage. After that, go back and fill in the blanks. You can skip the blanks you're unsure about and finish them later.

naturally	spills	toxic	crops	causes
streams	Gulf	wastewater	Acid	ill

Water pollution occurs when waste, chemicals, or other particles cause a body of water (e.g., rivers, oceans, lakes) to become _____ to the fish and animals that rely on it for survival. Water pollution can also disrupt and hurt nature's water cycle.

Water pollution can occur _____ due to volcanoes, algae blooms, animal waste, and silt from storms and floods.

Human activity contributes significantly to water pollution. Sewage, pesticides, fertilizers from farms, wastewater and chemicals from factories, silt from construction sites, and trash from people littering are some human _____.

Oil _____ have been some of the most well-known examples of water pollution. The Exxon Valdez oil spill occurred when an oil tanker collided with a reef off the coast of Alaska, causing over 11 million gallons of oil to spill into the ocean. Another major oil spill was the Deepwater Horizon oil spill, which occurred when an oil well exploded, causing over 200 million gallons of oil to spill into the _____ of Mexico.

Water pollution can be caused directly by air pollution. When sulfur dioxide particles reach high altitudes in the atmosphere, they can combine with rain to form acid rain. _____ rain can cause lakes to become acidic, killing fish and other animals.

The main issue caused by water pollution is the impact on aquatic life. Dead fish, birds, dolphins, and various other animals frequently wash up on beaches, killed by pollutants in their environment. Pollution also has an impact on the natural food chain. Small animals consume contaminants like lead and cadmium.

Clean water is one of the most valuable and essential commodities for life on Earth. Clean water is nearly impossible to obtain for over 1 billion people on the planet. They can become _____ from dirty, polluted water, which is especially difficult for young children. Some bacteria and pathogens in water can make people sick to the point of death.

Water pollution comes from a variety of sources. Here are a few of the main reasons:
Sewage: In many parts of the world, sewage is still flushed directly into _____ and rivers. Sewage can introduce dangerous bacteria that can make humans and animals very sick.

Farm animal waste: Runoff from large herds of farm animals such as pigs and cows can enter the water supply due to rain and large storms.

Pesticides: Pesticides and herbicides are frequently sprayed on _____ to kill bugs, while herbicides are sprayed to kill weeds. These potent chemicals can enter the water through rainstorm runoff. They can also contaminate rivers and lakes due to unintentional spills.

Construction, floods, and storms: Silt from construction, earthquakes, and storms can reduce water oxygen levels and suffocate fish.

Factories: Water is frequently used in factories to process chemicals, keep engines cool, and wash things away. Sometimes used _____ is dumped into rivers or the ocean. It may contain pollutants.

Score: _____

Date: _____

* Weather and Climate

The difference between weather and climate is simply a matter of time. Weather refers to the conditions of the atmosphere over a short period of time, whereas climate refers to how the atmosphere "behaves" over a longer period of time.

When we discuss climate change, we are referring to changes in long-term averages of daily weather. Today's children are constantly told by their parents and grandparents about how the snow was always piled up to their waists as they trudged off to school. Most children today have not experienced those kinds of dreadful snow-packed winters. The recent changes in winter snowfall indicate that the climate has changed since their parents were children.

Weather is essentially the atmosphere's behavior, particularly in terms of its effects on life and human activities. The distinction between weather and climate is that weather refers to short-term (minutes to months) changes in the atmosphere, whereas climate refers to long-term changes. Most people associate weather with temperature, humidity, precipitation, cloudiness, brightness, visibility, wind, and atmospheric pressure, as in high and low pressure.

Weather can change from minute to minute, hour to hour, day to day, and season to season in most places. However, the climate is the average of weather over time and space. A simple way to remember the distinction is that climate is what you expect, such as a very hot summer, whereas weather is what you get, such as a hot day with pop-up thunderstorms.

Use the word bank to unscramble the words!

Pressure	Density	Cloudy	Latitude	Elevation	Weather
Absorb	Humid	Precipitation	Windy	Forecast	Climate
Sunshine	Temperature				

1. IUMHD   _ u _ _ _

2. UDLOYC   _ l _ u _ _

3. FSEATOCR   _ _ _ _ _ a _ t

4. UDLTITAE   L _ _ _ _ u _ _

5. IEOCAIIPPTRNT _ _ _ _ _ _ _ t _ _ _ o n

6. TEEERPAURMT   T _ _ _ e _ _ t _ _ _

7. RSEREUPS   _ r e _ _ _ _ _

8. LEICATM   _ _ i _ _ t _

9. SNNIEHUS   S _ _ _ _ i _ _

10. OBBASR   _ b s _ _ _

11. VETIEOANL   _ _ _ _ a t _ _ _

12. EATWRHE   W _ _ _ _ e _

13. NDWIY   _ _ _ _ y

14. TYNEIDS   _ _ _ _ i _ y

Acronym

A common way to make an acronym is to use the first letter of each word in a phrase to make a word that can be spoken. This is a great way to make a longer, more complicated phrase easier to say and shorter.

Carefully choose the acronym for each word or phrase.

1. Also Known As
   a. AKA
   b. KAA

2. Central Standard Time
   a. CST
   b. TCS

3. Doing Business As
   a. DBA
   b. ASDOING

4. Do Not Disturb
   a. NOTDN
   b. DND

5. Electronic Data Systems
   a. SDE
   b. EDS

6. End of Day
   a. EOD
   b. ENDDAY

7. Eastern Standard Time
   a. EST
   b. TSE

8. Estimated Time of Arrival
   a. ET
   b. ETA

9. Human Resources
   a. HRS
   b. HR

10. Masters of Business Administration
    a. MOBA
    b. MBA

11. MST - Mountain Standard Time
    a. MST
    b. MSTS

12. Overtime
    a. OTIME
    b. OT

13. Point Of Service
    a. POS
    b. POOS

14. Pacific Standard Time
    a. PST
    b. PSTE

15. Anti-lock Braking System
    a. LOCKBS
    b. ABS

16. Attention Deficit Disorder
    a. ADD
    b. ATTDD

17. Attention Deficit Hyperactivity Disorder

    a. ADHP

    b. ADHD

18. Acquired Immune Deficiency Syndrome

    a. ACQIMDEF

    b. AIDS

19. Centers for Disease Control and Prevention

    a. CDC

    b. CDCP

20. Dead On Arrival

    a. DONA

    b. DOA

21. Date Of Birth

    a. DOB

    b. DOFB

22. Do It Yourself

    a. DIY

    b. DIYO

23. Frequently Asked Questions

    a. FAQA

    b. FAQ

24. Graphics Interchange Format

    a. GIF

    b. GIFF

25. Human Immunodeficiency Virus

    a. HIV

    b. HIMMV

26. Medical Doctor

    a. MD

    b. MED

27. Over The Counter

    a. OTC

    b. OTHEC

28. Pay Per View

    a. PPV

    b. PAYPPV

29. Sound Navigation And Ranging

    a. SONAR

    b. SONAVR

30. Sports Utility Vehicle

    a. SPOUV

    b. SUV

The History of the Calendar

Tuesday	Saturday	November	February	Monday	March
Friday	weekend	May	Wednesday	Sunday	January
weekday	October	June	September	December	August
April	Thursday	July			

1. rauanjy — J a n u a r y

2. uraeybfr — F e b r u a r y

3. macrh — M a r c h

4. iralp — A p r i l

5. yma — M a y

6. nuej — J u n e

7. luyj — J u l y

8. suagut — A u g u s t

9. ebpmeetrs — S e p t e m b e r

10. btcreoo — O c t o b e r

11. vmbeneor — N o v e m b e r

12. eedcrmbe — D e c e m b e r

13. dmnyoa — M o n d a y

14. saetudy — T u e s d a y

15. deeawysnd — W e d n e s d a y

16. shtayudr — T h u r s d a y

17. rdayfi — F r i d a y

18. yuartdas — S a t u r d a y

19. ydsaun — S u n d a y

20. eenekwd — w e e k e n d

21. kaewedy — w e e k d a y

This, That, These, and Those

This, that, these and those are demonstratives. We use this, that, these, and those to point to people and things. This and that are singular. These and those are plural.

1. _____ orange I'm eating is delicious.
   a. | This |
   b. These
   c. Those
   d. That

2. It is better than _____ apples from last week.
   a. that
   b. | those |
   c. these
   d. this

3. Let's exchange _____ bread for these crackers.
   a. those
   b. this
   c. these
   d. | that |

4. Let's try some of _____ freeze-dried steak.
   a. this
   b. | this here |
   c. them
   d. those there

5. Is _____ water boiling yet?
   a. these here
   b. | that |
   c. that there
   d. this here

6. _____ granola bars are tasty too.
   a. | These |
   b. This here
   c. Them
   d. These here

7. _____ mountains don't look that far away.
   a. This
   b. | Those |
   c. These
   d. That

8. I like _____ pictures better than those.
   a. this
   b. that
   c. those
   d. | these |

9. _____ car at the far end of the lot is mine.
   a. | That |
   b. This
   c. These
   d. Those

10. I like the feel of _____ fabric.
   a. those
   b. this here
   c. that there
   d. | this |

11. In _____ early days, space travel was a dream.
   a. that
   b. them
   c. | those |
   d. this

12. _____ days, we believe humans will go to Mars.
   a. | These |
   b. This
   c. Those
   d. That

Littering

The annual cost of cleaning up litter in the nation's __streets__ , parks, and coastal areas is estimated to be in the millions of dollars. The cleanup of trash has a direct expense, but it also has a __negative__ impact on the surrounding environment, the value of property, and other economic activity. Food packaging, bottles, cans, plastic bags, and paper are the most common sources of litter. Did you know cigarette __butts__ remain the most littered item in the U.S. and across the globe? One of the many strategies that states can use to reduce the amount of litter in their communities is to enact and strictly adhere to laws that carry criminal penalties for the behavior. The penalties for littering vary significantly from state to state, depending on the __amount__ , nature, and location of the litter. The seriousness of the offense is determined by the weight or volume of litter in 10 states, for example. For instance, several states penalize people for disposing of large goods like furniture or major appliances in public places. Legislation addressing trash on public roadways, along the beaches, and in __recreational__ areas has been passed in several states due to these concerns.

In situations that are considered to be relatively small, the courts will typically impose a fine. They may also compel the defendant to perform __community__ service, such as picking up garbage. In Massachusetts, for instance, the minimum __fine__ is $25, whereas, in the state of Maryland, the maximum penalty is $30,000. When a crime is more serious, the offender may be sentenced to up to six years in __jail__ , depending on the state. In addition, the laws in the states of Maryland, Massachusetts, and Louisiana all include provisions that allow the __suspension__ of a driver's license for those who violate the laws. In almost every state, a person's sentence worsens with each subsequent conviction.

It doesn't matter if someone throws trash out on purpose or accidentally; either way, they're contributing to pollution by doing so. Our city's parks, sidewalks, roads, and private property and parks are all impacted by litter. Research has shown that litter leads to the accumulation of even more garbage. A clean __neighborhood__ , on the other hand, lowers the incidence of littering and enhances both the local living standards and the quality of life.

Capitalization Rules Refresher

1. What are the most common pronouns?

   he, she, it, you, her, him, me, I, us, them, they

2. What is a proper noun?

   a name used for an individual person, place, or organization, spelled with initial capital letters

3. Do common nouns name specific persons, places, things, or ideas?

   No: They are not capitalized unless they come at the beginning of a sentence.

4. Always capitalize the first letter in the first word of a sentence?

   Yes

5. Always capitalize the first letter in the first word in a quotation?

   Yes

6. Always capitalize the first letter in the first word of a greeting or closing?

   Yes

7. Always capitalize the first letter in the first and last name of a person?

   Yes

8. Never capitalize the pronoun "I"?   No: I is the only pronoun form that is always capitalized in English.

9. Always capitalize the first letter in the names of: streets, roads, cities, and states?

   Yes

10. Always capitalize the first letter in each part of the name of a specific building or monument: Statue of Liberty, Empire State Building, Pensacola Chamber of Commerce . . .?

    Yes

11. Always capitalize the titles of: video games, stories, movies, and TV shows

    Yes

12. Always capitalize the days of the weeks?

    Yes

13. The names of months should not be capitalized?

    No: Yes, the names of months are always capitalized.

14. Always capitalize major holidays except christmas and thanksgiving?

    No: Christmas and Thanksgiving should be capitalized.

Lumberjack Paul Bunyan

According to legend, it took five massive storks to deliver the infant (already enormous) Paul Bunyan to his parents in **Bangor**, Maine. As he grew older, a single drag of the mighty lumberjack's massive ax **carved** out the Grand Canyon, while the giant footprints of his trusty companion, Babe the **Blue** Ox, filled with water and became Minnesota's 10,000 lakes. There is no way to know for sure, but was Paul Bunyan really a real person? As it turns out, there's more to this iconic figure's past than meets the eye.

Scholars believe that Bunyan was based on a real lumberjack: Fabian Fournier, a French-Canadian who moved south after the Civil War and became the foreman of a logging crew in Michigan after the war. Fournier was **nicknamed** "Saginaw Joe" because he was six feet tall (at a time when the ordinary person was barely five feet) and had huge **hands**. This man was known to have two full sets of teeth and was known to chew off **chunks** of rail in his spare time while also indulging in a bit of drinking and a little brawling. Fournier was killed on a November night in 1875 in the notoriously rowdy lumber town of Bay City, Michigan. People told stories about Saginaw Joe's **complicated** life in logging camps in Michigan, Minnesota, Wisconsin, and other places after his death and the dramatic trial of his alleged killer (who was acquitted).

"Round River," the first Paul Bunyan story, was published in 1906 by **journalist** James MacGillivray for a local newspaper in Oscoda, Michigan. MacGillivray and a poet collaborated on a Bunyan-themed poem for American Lumberman magazine in 1912, giving Paul Bunyan his first **national** exposure. Two years later, the first illustrations of the larger-than-life lumberjack appeared in an ad campaign for Minnesota's Red River Lumber Company. His prominent appearance as Red River's mascot and pamphlets rolling tales of his adventures would help turn Paul Bunyan into a **household** name and an enduring American icon.

Commonly misspelled words that sound alike but are spelled differently

Carefully circle the correct spelling combinations of words.

	A	B	C	D
1.	Sun/Sn	Son/Son	**Sun/Son**	Son/Sn
2.	Hare/Hiar	Harre/Hair	**Hare/Hair**	Harre/Hiar
3.	Cache/Cassh	**Cache/Cash**	Cache/Casch	Cacha/Cash
4.	Cytte/Sight	**Cite/Sight**	Cyte/Sight	Citte/Sight
5.	Worrn/Warn	Wurn/Warn	Wurrn/Warn	**Worn/Warn**
6.	Minerr/Minor	Miner/Minur	**Miner/Minor**	Minerr/Minur
7.	Wratch/Retch	**Wretch/Retch**	Wrretch/Retch	Wrratch/Retch
8.	Floor/Flower	Flloor/Flower	**Flour/Flower**	Fllour/Flower
9.	Whille/Wile	**While/Wile**	Whylle/Wile	Whyle/Wile
10.	Calous/Callus	Caloos/Callus	**Callous/Callus**	Calloos/Callus
11.	Build/Biled	**Build/Billed**	Boild/Billed	Boild/Biled
12.	Marrten/Martin	**Marten/Martin**	Marten/Martyn	Marrten/Martyn
13.	Humerrus/Humorous	**Humerus/Humorous**	Humerus/Humoroos	Humerus/Humoroos
14.	Housse/Hoes	**Hose/Hoes**	House/Hoes	Hosse/Hoes
15.	Mei Be/Maybe	Mai Be/Maybe	**May Be/Maybe**	Mey Be/Maybe
16.	Matal/Metle/Meddle	**Metal/Mettle/Meddle**	Matal/Mettle/Meddle	Metal/Metle/Meddle
17.	**Halve/Have**	Hallva/Have	Hallve/Have	Halva/Have
18.	**Wee/We**	Wea/We	We/We	Wa/We
19.	**Taper/Tapir**	Taperr/Tapyr	Taperr/Tapir	Taper/Tapyr
20.	Timberr/Timbre	Tymber/Timbre	Tymberr/Timbre	**Timber/Timbre**
21.	Minse/Mintts	Mince/Mintts	Minse/Mints	**Mince/Mints**
22.	Eies/Ayes	Eyesc/Ayes	**Eyes/Ayes**	Eyess/Ayes
23.	Guesced/Guest	**Guessed/Guest**	Guesed/Guest	Gueced/Guest
24.	**Yore/Your/You'Re**	Yore/Yoor/You'Re	Yorre/Your/You'Re	Yorre/Yoor/You'Re
25.	Oarr/Or/Ora	Oarr/Or/Ore	**Oar/Or/Ore**	Oar/Or/Ora

#	Option A	Option B	Option C	Option D
26.	Bate/Biat	**Bate/Bait**	Batte/Biat	Batte/Bait
27.	**Tax/Tacks**	Tax/Taks	Tax/Tacksc	Tax/Tackss
28.	Bald/Ballad/Bawled	Bald/Baled/Bawled	**Bald/Balled/Bawled**	Bald/Balad/Bawled
29.	Ewe/Yuo/Yew	Ewe/Yoo/Yew	**Ewe/You/Yew**	Ewe/Yoo/Yw
30.	Eei/I/Aye	Eie/I/Ae	**Eye/I/Aye**	Eie/I/Aye
31.	**Hoes/Hose**	Hoess/Hose	Hoess/House	Hoes/House
32.	Tou/Two/To	Tu/Two/To	To/Two/To	**Too/Two/To**
33.	**Ceres/Series**	Cerres/Series	Ceres/Sereis	Cerres/Sereis
34.	**Hansom/Handsome**	Hansum/Handsome	Hanscom/Handsome	Hanssom/Handsome
35.	Residance/Residents	**Residence/Residents**	Ressidence/Residents	Ressidance/Residents
36.	Surrf/Serf	**Surf/Serf**	Surrph/Serf	Surph/Serf
37.	Siall/Sale	Saill/Sale	**Sail/Sale**	Sial/Sale
38.	Therre's/Thiers	There's/Thiers	**There's/Theirs**	Therre's/Theirs
39.	Roed/Rode	Roed/Rude	**Rued/Rude**	Roed/Rue
40.	Aid/Aie	Ayd/Aide	Ayd/Aie	**Aid/Aide**
41.	Taem/Teem	Taem/Tem	Team/Tem	**Team/Teem**
42.	Ilusion/Allusion	Ilution/Allusion	Illution/Allusion	**Illusion/Allusion**
43.	Hi/Hih	Hy/High	**Hi/High**	Hy/Hih
44.	**Barred/Bard**	Bared/Bard	Barad/Bard	Barrad/Bard
45.	Mewll/Mule	**Mewl/Mule**	Mewll/Mole	Mewl/Mole
46.	Rowss/Rose	**Rows/Rose**	Rowss/Rouse	Rows/Rouse
47.	Chep/Cheap	Cheep/Chaep	**Cheep/Cheap**	Chep/Chaep
48.	Bah/Ba	Beh/Ba	**Bah/Baa**	Beh/Baa
49.	**Gofer/Gopher**	Gopher/Gopher	Gophfer/Gopher	Goffer/Gopher
50.	Don/Doe	Dun/Doe	**Dun/Done**	Don/Done
51.	Ryte/Write/Right	Ritte/Write/Right	Rytte/Write/Right	**Rite/Write/Right**
52.	**Mite/Might**	Mitte/Might	Myte/Might	Mytte/Might
53.	**Latter/Ladder**	Later/Ladder	Latar/Ladder	Lattar/Ladder
54.	Gorred/Goord	**Gored/Gourd**	Gored/Goord	Gorred/Gourd
55.	Ball/Belle	**Bell/Belle**	Bal/Belle	Bel/Belle
56.	Ruscell/Rustle	**Russell/Rustle**	Rusell/Rustle	Rucell/Rustle
57.	Tuat/Taught	Tautt/Taught	Tuatt/Taught	**Taut/Taught**

#	Column 1	Column 2	Column 3	Column 4
58.	**Cozen/Cousin**	Cozen/Coosin	Cozen/Coossin	Cozen/Coussin
59.	**Morn/Mourn**	Morrn/Moorn	Morrn/Mourn	Morn/Moorn
60.	Stare/Stiar	**Stare/Stair**	Sttare/Stiar	Sttare/Stair
61.	Wrrap/Rap	Wrrep/Rap	**Wrap/Rap**	Wrep/Rap
62.	Centts/Ssents	Centts/Scents	**Cents/Scents**	Cents/Ssents
63.	Basste/Based	Baste/Baced	**Baste/Based**	Bascte/Based
64.	Foorr/Fore/For	Foor/Fore/For	Fourr/Fore/For	**Four/Fore/For**
65.	Knikers/Nickers	Knickerrs/Nickers	Knikerrs/Nickers	**Knickers/Nickers**
66.	Marre/Mayor	**Mare/Mayor**	Mare/Meyor	Marre/Meyor
67.	Surrje/Serge	Surje/Serge	Surrge/Serge	**Surge/Serge**
68.	**Steal/Steel**	Steal/Stel	Stael/Steel	Stael/Stel
69.	Haerrt/Hart	**Heart/Hart**	Hearrt/Hart	Haert/Hart
70.	**Holed/Hold**	Huled/Hold	Holled/Hold	Hulled/Hold
71.	Way/Wiegh/Whey	Wai/Wiegh/Whey	Wai/Weigh/Whey	**Way/Weigh/Whey**
72.	Diieng/Dying	Dyieng/Dying	Dieing/Dying	**Dyeing/Dying**
73.	Holay/Holy/Wholly	Holay/Holy/Wholy	Holey/Holy/Wholy	**Holey/Holy/Wholly**
74.	Sworrd/Soared	Swurrd/Soared	Swurd/Soared	**Sword/Soared**
75.	Cane/Cyan	Cane/Cian	Cane/Cayn	**Cane/Cain**
76.	Arreil/Aerial	**Ariel/Aerial**	Arriel/Aerial	Areil/Aerial
77.	**Brut/Brute**	Brrot/Brute	Brot/Brute	Brrut/Brute
78.	Frrays/Phrase	**Frays/Phrase**	Frreys/Phrase	Freys/Phrase
79.	**Throne/Thrown**	Thrrune/Thrown	Thrune/Thrown	Thrrone/Thrown
80.	Ha'd/Hed	**He'd/Heed**	He'd/Hed	He'd/Head
81.	Waerr/Where/Ware	**Wear/Where/Ware**	Wearr/Where/Ware	Waer/Where/Ware
82.	Brraed/Bred	**Bread/Bred**	Braed/Bred	Brread/Bred
83.	We've/Waeve	**We've/Weave**	Wa've/Weave	Wa've/Waeve
84.	Hew/Hoe/Huh	**Hew/Hue/Hugh**	Hew/Hoe/Hugh	Hew/Hoe/Hogh
85.	Nikerrs/Knickers	Nickerrs/Knickers	Nikers/Knickers	**Nickers/Knickers**
86.	Call/Sell	**Cell/Sell**	Cal/Sell	Cel/Sell
87.	Isle/I'l/Aisle	**Isle/I'll/Aisle**	Isle/I'll/Aysle	Isle/I'll/Aysle
88.	Brruice/Brews	**Bruise/Brews**	Brruise/Brews	Bruice/Brews
89.	**Except/Accept**	Exsept/Accept	Exsept/Acept	Except/Acept

Grammar: Homophones vs Homographs vs. Homonyms

1. 'there,' 'their,' or 'they're' are examples of _____.
   a. [Homophones]
   b. Homographs

2. ____ are words that have the same spelling or pronunciation but different meanings.
   a. [Homonyms]
   b. Hemograms

3. Choose the correct homophone for this sentence: Please don't drop and _____ that bottle of hand sanitizer!
   a. brake
   b. [break]

4. Homographs are two or more words that have the same spelling but different ____.
   a. ending sounds
   b. [meanings]

5. Current (A flow of water / Up to date) is both homograph and homophone.
   a. [True]
   b. False

6. To, two and too are _____.
   a. Homagraphs
   b. [Homonyms]

7. The candle filled the _____ with a delicious scent.
   a. heir
   b. [air]

8. Kim drove _____ the tunnel.
   a. threw
   b. [through]

9. John wants to go to _____ house for dinner, but they don't like her, so _____ going to say no.
   a. [their, they're]
   b. there, they're

10. We won a $95,000 _____!
    a. cheque
    b. [check]

11. For example, a pencil is not really made with _____.
    a. led
    b. [lead]

12. Choose the correct homophone for this sentence: Timmy was standing _____ in line.
    a. [fourth]
    b. forth

13. Homophones are two words that sound the same but have a different meanings.
    a. [True]
    b. False

14. The word ring in the following two sentences is considered what? She wore a ruby ring. | We heard the doorbell ring.
    a. hologram
    b. [homograph]

15. A Homograph is a word that has more than one meaning and doesn't have to sound the same.

    a. | True |
    b. False

16. Homophones occur when there are multiple ways to spell the same sound.

    a. | True |
    b. False

17. Select the correct homophone: I have very little (patience/patients) when students do not follow directions.

    a. patients
    b. | patience |

18. The correct homophone (s) are used in the sentence: Personally, I hate the smell of read meet.

    a. True
    b. | False |

19. The correct homophone(s) is used in the sentence: We saw a herd of cattle in the farmer's field.

    a. | True |
    b. False

20. What is NOT an example of a homograph?

    a. | or, oar |
    b. live, live

Grammar: Nouns, Verbs, Adjectives

DIRECTIONS: SORT the words (below) by their corresponding *part-of-speech*.

color	chickens	kittens	banjo	library	goldfish
grieving	adorable	cough	stand	nasty	powerful
dance	build	cry	break	easy	circle
coach	aggressive	careful	eat	adventurous	think
mysterious	face	sticks	drink	guitar	busy
calm	window	worm	coast	draw	polka dot
eager	handsome	explain			

Nouns (13)	Verbs (13)	Adjectives (13)
coast	break	adorable
polka dot	build	busy
sticks	coach	eager
banjo	color	grieving
goldfish	cough	easy
chickens	think	calm
window	cry	handsome
face	dance	careful
library	draw	adventurous
circle	drink	aggressive
guitar	eat	mysterious
kittens	explain	nasty
worm	stand	powerful

*Usage Activity: CHOOSE (12) words from your completed table & WRITE (1) sentence for each form of the words you chose.

[Student worksheet has a 25 line writing exercise here.]

* **Grammar: Compound Nouns**

A compound noun is one that is composed of two or more words. Each word contributes to the meaning of the noun.

Compound nouns can be written three ways:

A single word	Two words	Hyphenated
haircut	rain forest	self-esteem

Instructions: Match the compound noun pairs correctly.

#	Answer	First		Second
1	O	Fund	→	raiser
2	D	News	→	paper
3	C	Sun	→	glasses
4	F	Child	→	hood
5	N	Door	→	way
6	E	heart	→	attack
7	J	tooth	→	paste
8	K	apple	→	sauce
9	M	full	→	moon
10	H, B	hair	→	cut
11	G	air	→	plane
12	I	ear	→	ring
13	A	scare	→	crow
14	P	post	→	office
15	B, H	hair	→	dresser
16	L	note	→	book

* **Grammar: Collective Noun**

A collective noun is a noun that refers to a group of people, animals, or things. They are described as a single entity. Collective nouns are distinct from singular nouns in that singular nouns describe only one person or object.

Many collective nouns are common nouns, but when they are the name of a company or other organization with more than one person, such as Microsoft, they can also be proper nouns.

Find the collective noun in each sentence.

1. Our class visited the natural history museum on a field trip.

   class

2. The bison herd stampeded across the prairie, leaving a massive dust cloud in its wake.

   herd

3. We eagerly awaited the verdict of the jury.

   jury

4. This year's basketball team features three players who stand taller than six feet.

   team

5. At Waterloo, Napoleon's army was finally defeated.

   army

6. The plans for a new park have been approved by the town council.

   council

7. He comes from a large family, as the oldest of eleven children.

   family

8. The rock group has been on tour for several months.

   group

9. When Elvis appeared on stage, the entire audience erupted in applause.

   audience

10. The San Francisco crowd were their usual individualistic selves.

    crowd

11. The crew of sailors boarded the ships.

    crew

12. A mob destroyed the company's new office.

    mob

13. The fleet of ships was waiting at the port.

    fleet

14. It was difficult for the committee to come to a decision.

    committee

* Grammar: Concrete & Abstract Noun

In the English language, both concrete and abstract nouns are essential parts of speech. The primary distinction between concrete and abstract nouns is that concrete nouns refer to people, places, or things that take up physical space, whereas abstract nouns refer to intangible ideas that cannot be physically interacted with.

Words like "luck," "disgust," and "empathy" are examples of abstract nouns. While it is possible to see someone being empathetic, empathy is not a visible or tangible entity. The majority of feelings, emotions, and philosophies can be classified as abstract nouns.

1. FIND THE ABSTRACT NOUN ?

   a. KIND

   b. BOOK

2. FIND THE CONCRETE NOUNS

   a. WINDOW

   b. LOVE

3. FIND THE ABTRACT NOUN: THE KING WAS KNOWN FOR HIS JUSTICE

   a. JUSTICE

   b. KING

4. WHAT ARE THE 5 CONCRETE NOUNS

   a. TASTE, SMELL, WALKING, EYEING, TOUCHING

   b. SMELL,TASTE, SIGHT, HEARING,TOUCH

5. WHICH NOUN BELOW IS AN ABSTRACT NOUN?

   a. TRAIN

   b. LOVE

6. IS THE FOLLOWING NOUN CONCRETE OR ABSTRACT? CUPCAKES

   a. ABSTRACT

   b. CONCRETE

7. WHAT IS A CONCRETE NOUN?

   a. A NOUN THAT YOU CAN EXPERIENCE WITH AT LEAST 1 OF YOUR 5 SENSES.

   b. A NOUN THAT YOU CAN'T EXPERIENCE WITH AT LEAST 1 OF YOUR 5 SENSES.

8. WHICH WORD BELOW IS AN ABSTRACT NOUN?

   a. BRAVERY

   b. FRIEND

9. WHICH WORD BELOW IS NOT A CONCRETE NOUN?

   a. HAMBURGER

   b. ANGER

10. IS THE WORD THOUGHTFULNESS A CONCRETE OR ABSTRACT NOUN?

   a. ABSTRACT

   b. CONCRETE

* Science: Vertebrates

To begin, all animals are classified as either vertebrates or invertebrates. Invertebrates lack a backbone, whereas vertebrates do. Scientists can't stop there, because each group contains thousands of different animals! As a result, scientists divide vertebrates and invertebrates into increasingly smaller groups. Let's talk about vertebrates and some of their classifications.

Vertebrates range in size from a frog to a blue whale. Because there are at least 59,000 different types of vertebrates on the planet, they are further classified into five major groups: mammals, birds, fish, amphibians, and reptiles. Remember that animals are classified into these groups based on what they have in common. Why is an elephant classified as a mammal while a crocodile is classified as a reptile? Let's go over some of the characteristics of each vertebrate group.

Warm-blooded animals are mammals. This means that their bodies maintain their temperature, which is usually higher than the temperature of the surrounding air. They also have hair or fur; they have lungs to breathe air; that they feed milk to their babies; and that most give birth to live young, rather than laying eggs, as a dog does.

- Birds have feathers, two wings (though not all birds, such as the ostrich and penguin, can fly), are warm-blooded, and lay eggs.
- Fish have fins or scales, live in water, and breathe oxygen through gills.
- Like salamanders and frogs, Amphibians have smooth, moist skin (amphibians must keep their skin wet); lay eggs in water; most breathe through their skin and lungs.
- Reptiles have scales (imagine a scaly lizard), are cold-blooded (their body temperature changes as the temperature around them changes), breathe air. Most reptiles, including the crocodile and snake, lay hard-shelled eggs on land.

Vertebrates play several vital roles in an ecosystem. Many predator species are large vertebrates in ecosystems. Lions, eagles, and sharks are examples of predatory vertebrates. Many prey species in ecosystems are also vertebrates. Mice, rabbits, and frogs are examples of these animals. Many vertebrates serve as scavengers in ecosystems. They are significant because they remove dead animals from the environment. Turkey vultures and hyenas, for example, are both vertebrate scavengers. Furthermore, many vertebrates serve as pollinators in ecosystems. Bats and monkeys, for example, may aid in pollen spread by visiting various trees and plants.

Humans value vertebrates for a variety of reasons. Vertebrates are domesticated animals used by humans. These animals are capable of producing milk, food, and clothing. They can also help with work. Agricultural animals are usually vertebrates. Humans also hunt a variety of wild vertebrate animals for food.

1. Vertebrates range in _____ from a frog to a blue whale.
   - a. age
   - b. size

2. Fish have fins or scales, live in water, and breathe ___ through gills.
   - a. oxygen
   - b. water

3. Invertebrates lack a _____, whereas vertebrates _____.
   - a. skin, whereas vertebrates do
   - b. backbone, whereas vertebrates do

4. Warm-blooded animals are _____.
   - a. mammals
   - b. producers

5. Some vertebrates serve as _____, they remove dead animals from the environment.
   - a. scavengers
   - b. invertebrates

6. Lions, eagles, and sharks are examples of _____ vertebrates.
   - a. ecofriendly
   - b. predatory

7. _____ animals are capable of producing milk, food, and clothing.
   - a. Non-producing
   - b. Domesticated

8. Many vertebrates serve as _____ in ecosystems, they may aid in pollen spread by visiting various trees and plants.
   - a. water lilies
   - b. pollinators

* Science:
Invertebrates

Invertebrates can be found almost anywhere. Invertebrates account for at least 95% of all animals on the planet! Do you know what one thing they all have in common? Invertebrates lack a backbone.

Your body is supported by a backbone, which protects your organs and connects your other bones. As a result, you are a vertebrate. On the other hand, invertebrates lack the support of bones, so their bodies are often simpler, softer, and smaller. They are also cold-blooded, which means their body temperature fluctuates in response to changes in the air or water around them.

Invertebrates can be found flying, swimming, crawling, or floating and provide essential services to the environment and humans. Nobody knows how many different types of invertebrates there are, but there are millions!

Just because an invertebrate lacks a spinal column does not mean it does not need to eat. Invertebrates, like all other forms of animal life, must obtain nutrients from their surroundings. Invertebrates have evolved two types of digestion to accomplish this. The use of intracellular digestion is common in the most simple organisms. The food is absorbed into the cell and broken down in the cytoplasm at this point. Extracellular digestion, in which cells break down food through the secretion of enzymes and other techniques, is used by more advanced invertebrates. All vertebrates use extracellular digestion.

Still, all animals, invertebrates or not, need a way to get rid of waste. Most invertebrates, especially the simplest ones, use the process of diffusion to eliminate waste. This is merely the opposite of intracellular digestion. However, more advanced invertebrates have more advanced waste disposal mechanisms. Similar to our kidneys, specialized glands in these animals filter and excrete waste. But there is a happy medium. Even though some invertebrates do not have complete digestive tracts like vertebrates, they do not simply flush out waste through diffusion. Instead, the mouth doubles as an exit.

Scientists have classified invertebrates into numerous groups based on what the animals have in common. Arthropods have segmented bodies, which means that they are divided into sections. Consider an ant!

Arthropods are the most numerous group of invertebrates. They can live on land, as spiders and insects do, or in water, as crayfish and crabs do. Because insects are the most numerous group of arthropods, many of them fly, including mosquitoes, bees, locusts, and ladybugs.

They also have jointed legs or limbs to help them walk, similar to how you have knees for your legs and elbows for your arms. The majority of arthropods have an exoskeleton, tough outer skin, or shell that protects their body. Have you ever wondered why when you squish a bug, it makes that crunching sound? That's right; it's the exoskeleton!

Mollusks are the second most numerous group of invertebrates. They have soft bodies and can be found on land or in water. Shells protect the soft bodies of many mollusks, including snails, oysters, clams, and scallops. However, not all, such as octopus, squid, and cuttlefish, have a shell.

1. Invertebrates lack a _____.
   a. backbone
   b. tailbone

2. Invertebrates are also ____.
   a. cold-blooded
   b. warm-blooded

3. _____ can live on land, as spiders and insects do, or in water, as crayfish and crabs do.
   a. Vertebrates
   b. Arthropods

4. All animals, invertebrates or not, need a way to get rid of ____.
   a. their skin
   b. waste

5. _____ have soft bodies and can be found on land or in water.
   a. Arthropods
   b. Mollusks

6. Just because an invertebrate lacks a _____ column does not mean it does not need to eat.
   a. spinal
   b. tissues

7. Your body is supported by a backbone, which protects your ____ and connects your other bones.
   a. organs
   b. muscles

8. Invertebrates lack the support of bones, so their bodies are often simpler, ___, and smaller.
   a. softer and bigger
   b. softer and smaller

* Science: Organelles

Do you and your dog have a similar appearance? We are all aware that people and dogs appear to be very different on the outside. However, there are some similarities on the inside. Cells make up all animals, including humans and dogs.

All animal cells appear to be the same. They have a cell membrane that contains cytoplasm, which is a gooey fluid. Organelles float in the cytoplasm. Organelles function as tiny machines that meet the needs of the cell. The term organelle refers to a "miniature organ." This lesson will teach you about the various organelles found in animal cells and what they do.

The nucleus of the cell is the cell's brain. It is in charge of many of the cell's functions. The nucleus is where DNA, the genetic instructions for building your body, is stored. DNA contains vital information! Your nucleus has its membrane to protect this essential information, similar to the membrane that surrounds the entire cell.

Your cells require energy. Energy is produced by mitochondria, which are oval-shaped organelles. Mitochondria convert the nutrients that enter the cell into ATP. Your cells use ATP for energy. Because they are the cell's powerhouses, you might think of these organelles as the mighty mitochondria.

The nutrients must be digested before they can be converted into energy by the mitochondria. Digestion is carried out by a group of organelles known as lysosomes. Digestive enzymes are found in lysosomes. Enzymes can sometimes be released into the cell. Because the enzymes kill the cell, lysosomes are known as "suicide bags."

Use Google or your preferred source to help match each term with a definition.

1	L	nucleus	→	where DNA is stored
2	B	lysosomes	→	degradation of proteins and cellular waste
3	J	Golgi Apparatus	→	modification of proteins; "post-office" of the cell
4	I	Mitochondria	→	powerhouse of the cell
5	D	SER	→	lipid synthesis
6	K	RER	→	protein synthesis + modifications
7	A	Microtubules	→	responsible for chromosome segregation
8	C	ribosomes	→	protein synthesis
9	H	peroxysomes	→	degradation of H2O2
10	G	cell wall	→	prevents excessive uptake of water, protects the cell (in plants)
11	E	chloroplast	→	site of photosynthesis
12	F	central vacuole	→	stores water in plant cells

WATER CYCLE ANSWERS

1. NMSALIITBOU   sublimation

2. IARTASRPONTIN   transpiration

3. OMLLECUE   molecule

4. NEIRAVOTAOP   evaporation

5. ALEIGCR   glacier

6. TONOINSNCEDA   condensation

7. DARRWOGENTU   groundwater

8. TUNLOPLAT   pollutant

9. EPITITARINCPO   precipitation

10. ITNIOILRNFAT   infiltration

11. ODRLPET   droplet

12. NIEDTSOPIO   deposition

13. WTAEERH   weather

14. EONNTIGR   nitrogen

15. RWANTREAI   rainwater

16. REBGICE   iceberg

17. TNOAIADRI   radiation

18. EOXNGY   oxygen

19. SGOMRNIA   organism

20. YNEDRHOG   hydrogen

21. EARTLWTME   meltwater

22. COTNCLEOLI   collection

23. PAROV   vapor

24. NEVOEMTM   movement

25. ORENINTNVEM   environment

26. OCSANE   oceans

* Science: The Seasons

Our __planet__ has four seasons each year: autumn, winter, spring, and __summer__ .

The Earth spins in a slightly tilted position as it orbits the sun (on an axis tilted 23.5 degrees from a straight-up, vertical position). Because different parts of the planet are angled towards or away from the sun's light throughout the year, this tilt causes our seasons. More or less sunlight and heat influence the length of each day, the average daily temperature, and the amount of rainfall in different seasons.

The tilt has two major effects: the sun's angle to the Earth and the length of the days. The Earth is tilted so that the __North__ Pole is more pointed towards the sun for half of the year. The South Pole is pointing at the sun for the other half. When the North Pole is angled toward the sun, the days in the northern hemisphere (north of the equator) receive more sunlight, resulting in longer days and shorter nights. The northern hemisphere __heats__ up and experiences summer as the days lengthen. As the year progresses, the Earth's tilt shifts to the North Pole points away from the sun, resulting in winter.

As a result, seasons north of the equator are opposed to seasons south of the equator. When Europe and the United States are experiencing winter, Brazil and Australia will be experiencing summer.

We discussed how the length of the day changes, but the angle of the sun also changes. In the summer, the sun __shines__ more directly on the Earth, providing more energy to the surface and heating it. In the winter, sunlight strikes the Earth at an angle. This produces less energy and heats the Earthless.

The longest day in the Northern Hemisphere is __June__ 21st, while the longest night is December 21st. The opposite is true in the Southern Hemisphere, where December 21st is the longest day, and June 21st is the longest night. There are only two days a year when the day and night are the same. These are September 22nd and March 21st.

The amount of time it is light for decreases in autumn, and the __leaves__ begin to change color and fall off the trees. In the United States of America, autumn is referred to as Fall.

Winter brings colder weather, sometimes snow and __frost__ , no leaves on the trees, and the amount of daylight during the day are at its shortest.

The weather usually warms up in the spring, trees begin to sprout leaves, plants begin to bloom, and young animals such as __chicks__ and lambs are born.

The weather is usually warm in the summer, the trees have entire __green__ leaves, and the amount of daylight during the day is extended.

* Government History: How Laws Are Made

1. If the Senate approves the bill, it will be sent to the _____.
   a. President
   b. House Representee

2. The _____ may decide to make changes to the bill before it is passed.
   a. governor
   b. committee

3. The bill must then be _____ by a member of Congress.
   a. signed
   b. sponsored

4. The President has the option of refusing to sign the bill. This is known as a ___.
   a. voted
   b. veto

5. The Senate and House can choose to override the President's veto by _____ again.
   a. creating a new bill
   b. voting

6. The bill is assigned to a committee after it is _____.
   a. introduced
   b. vetoed

7. Bills are created and passed by _____.
   a. The House
   b. Congress

8. A bill must be signed into law by the President within ___-days.
   a. 10
   b. 5

9. The President's _____ is the final step in a bill becoming law.
   a. signature
   b. saying yes

10. If the committee agrees to pass the bill, it will be sent to the House or Senate's main ___ for approval.
    a. chamber
    b. state

Extra Credit: What are some of the weirdest laws in the world? List at least 5. (Independent student's answers)

[Student worksheet has a 19 line writing exercise here.]

* History: The Vikings

During the __Middle__ Ages, the Vikings lived in Northern Europe. They first settled in the Scandinavian lands that are now Denmark, Sweden, and Norway. During the Middle Ages, the Vikings played a significant role in Northern Europe, particularly during the Viking Age, which lasted from 800 CE to 1066 CE.

In Old Norse, the word Viking means "to raid." The Vikings would board their longships and __sail__ across the seas to raid villages on Europe's northern coast, including islands like Great Britain. In 787 CE, they first appeared in England to raid villages. When the Vikings __raided__, they were known to attack defenseless monasteries. This earned them a bad reputation as barbarians, but monasteries were wealthy and undefended Viking targets.

The Vikings eventually began to __settle__ in areas other than Scandinavia. They colonized parts of Great Britain, Germany, and Iceland in the ninth century. They spread into northeastern Europe, including Russia, in the 10th century. They also established Normandy, which means "Northmen," along the coast of northern France.

By the beginning of the 11th century, the Vikings had reached the pinnacle of their power. Leif Eriksson, son of Erik the Red, was one Vikings who made it to __North__ America. He established a brief settlement in modern-day Canada. This was thousands of years before Columbus.

The English and King Harold Godwinson __defeated__ the Vikings, led by King Harald Hardrada of Norway, in 1066. The defeat in this battle is sometimes interpreted as the end of the Viking Age. The Vikings stopped expanding their territory at this point, and raids became less frequent.

The arrival of Christianity was a major factor at the end of the Viking age. The Vikings became more and more a part of mainland Europe as Scandinavia was converted to __Christianity__ and became a part of Christian Europe. Sweden's, Denmark's, and Norway's identities and borders began to emerge as well.

The Vikings were perhaps best known for their ships. The Vikings built longships for exploration and raiding. Longships were long, narrow vessels built for speed. Oars primarily propelled them but later added a sail to help in windy conditions. Longships had a shallow draft, which allowed them to float in __shallow__ water and land on beaches.

The Vikings also built __cargo__ ships known as Knarr for trading. The Knarr was wider and deeper than the longship, allowing it to transport more cargo.

Five recovered Viking ships can be seen at the Viking Ship Museum in Roskilde, __Denmark__. It's also possible to see how the Vikings built their ships. The Vikings used a shipbuilding technique known as clinker building. They used long wood planks that overlapped along the edges.

* **Geography: Castles in Germany**

1. _____ is now the seat of the local government and an art museum.
   a. Schwerin Castle
   b. Swaziland Castle

2. Hohenzollern Castle is situated on the _____ of Mount Hohenzollern.
   a. crest
   b. end

3. The architecture of German castles consists of a combination of towers and _____.
   a. beautiful curtains
   b. fortified walls

4. German castles evolved during the "_____ Ages".
   a. Century
   b. Medieval

5. This castle was built as a residence rather than a fortress.
   a. Eltz Castle
   b. Schwerin Castle

6. Castles are now iconic symbols of magnificence and _____ tales.
   a. real life
   b. mythical

7. _____ has inspired poets for centuries.
   a. Schloss Heidelberg
   b. Steven Spielberg

8. _____ Castle is located in the Bavarian Alps near the town of Füssen.
   a. Norwegian
   b. Neuschwanstein

* Geography: Canada

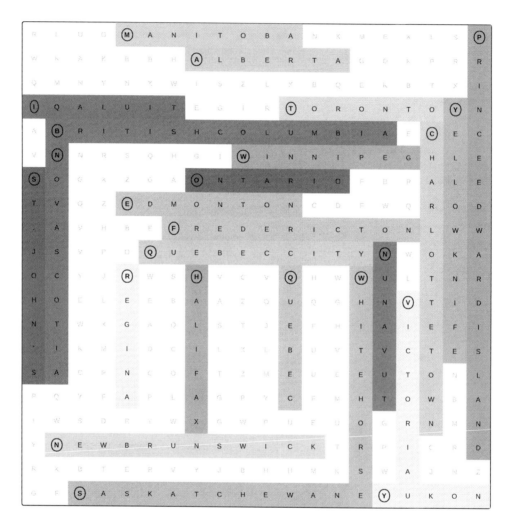

Yukon → | Nunavut ↓ | Nova Scotia ↓ | Prince Edward Island ↓ | New Brunswick → | Quebec ↓ | Ontario → | Manitoba →

Saskatchewan → | Alberta → | British Columbia → | Victoria ↓ | Edmonton → | Regina ↓ | Winnipeg → | Toronto →

Quebec City → | Fredericton → | Charlottetown ↓ | Halifax ↓ | St. John's ↓ | Iqaluit → | Yellowknife ↓ | Whitehorse ↓

24 words in Wordsearch: 11 vertical, 13 horizontal, 0 diagonal. (0 reversed.)

* Environmental Health: Water Pollution

First, read the entire passage. After that, go back and fill in the blanks. You can skip the blanks you're unsure about and finish them later.

naturally	spills	toxic	crops	causes
streams	Gulf	wastewater	Acid	ill

Water pollution occurs when waste, chemicals, or other particles cause a body of water (e.g., rivers, oceans, lakes) to become __toxic__ to the fish and animals that rely on it for survival. Water pollution can also disrupt and hurt nature's water cycle.

Water pollution can occur __naturally__ due to volcanoes, algae blooms, animal waste, and silt from storms and floods.

Human activity contributes significantly to water pollution. Sewage, pesticides, fertilizers from farms, wastewater and chemicals from factories, silt from construction sites, and trash from people littering are some human __causes__.

Oil __spills__ have been some of the most well-known examples of water pollution. The Exxon Valdez oil spill occurred when an oil tanker collided with a reef off the coast of Alaska, causing over 11 million gallons of oil to spill into the ocean. Another major oil spill was the Deepwater Horizon oil spill, which occurred when an oil well exploded, causing over 200 million gallons of oil to spill into the __Gulf__ of Mexico.

Water pollution can be caused directly by air pollution. When sulfur dioxide particles reach high altitudes in the atmosphere, they can combine with rain to form acid rain. __Acid__ rain can cause lakes to become acidic, killing fish and other animals.

The main issue caused by water pollution is the impact on aquatic life. Dead fish, birds, dolphins, and various other animals frequently wash up on beaches, killed by pollutants in their environment. Pollution also has an impact on the natural food chain. Small animals consume contaminants like lead and cadmium.

Clean water is one of the most valuable and essential commodities for life on Earth. Clean water is nearly impossible to obtain for over 1 billion people on the planet. They can become __ill__ from dirty, polluted water, which is especially difficult for young children. Some bacteria and pathogens in water can make people sick to the point of death.

Water pollution comes from a variety of sources. Here are a few of the main reasons:

Sewage: In many parts of the world, sewage is still flushed directly into __streams__ and rivers. Sewage can introduce dangerous bacteria that can make humans and animals very sick.

Farm animal waste: Runoff from large herds of farm animals such as pigs and cows can enter the water supply due to rain and large storms.

Pesticides: Pesticides and herbicides are frequently sprayed on __crops__ to kill bugs, while herbicides are sprayed to kill weeds. These potent chemicals can enter the water through rainstorm runoff. They can also contaminate rivers and lakes due to unintentional spills.

Construction, floods, and storms: Silt from construction, earthquakes, and storms can reduce water oxygen levels and suffocate fish. Factories - Water is frequently used in factories to process chemicals, keep engines cool, and wash things away. Sometimes used __wastewater__ is dumped into rivers or the ocean. It may contain pollutants.

*: Weather and Climate

The difference between weather and climate is simply a matter of time. Weather refers to the conditions of the atmosphere over a short period of time, whereas climate refers to how the atmosphere "behaves" over a longer period of time.

When we discuss climate change, we are referring to changes in long-term averages of daily weather. Today's children are constantly told by their parents and grandparents about how the snow was always piled up to their waists as they trudged off to school. Most children today have not experienced those kinds of dreadful snow-packed winters. The recent changes in winter snowfall indicate that the climate has changed since their parents were children.

Weather is essentially the atmosphere's behavior, particularly in terms of its effects on life and human activities. The distinction between weather and climate is that weather refers to short-term (minutes to months) changes in the atmosphere, whereas climate refers to long-term changes. Most people associate weather with temperature, humidity, precipitation, cloudiness, brightness, visibility, wind, and atmospheric pressure, as in high and low pressure.

Weather can change from minute to minute, hour to hour, day to day, and season to season in most places. However, the climate is the average of weather over time and space. A simple way to remember the distinction is that climate is what you expect, such as a very hot summer, whereas weather is what you get, such as a hot day with pop-up thunderstorms.

Use the word bank to unscramble the words!

Pressure	Density	Cloudy	Latitude	Elevation	Weather
Absorb	Humid	Precipitation	Windy	Forecast	Climate
Sunshine	Temperature				

1. IUMHD — Humid

2. UDLOYC — Cloudy

3. FSEATOCR — Forecast

4. UDLTITAE — Latitude

5. IEOCAIIPPTRNT — Precipitation

6. TEEERPAURMT — Temperature

7. RSEREUPS — Pressure

8. LEICATM — Climate

9. SNNIEHUS — Sunshine

10. OBBASR — Absorb

11. VETIEOANL — Elevation

12. EATWRHE — Weather

13. NDWIY — Windy

14. TYNEIDS — Density

A= Above Standards S=	93-97 A	80-82 B	68-69 D+		
Meets Standards N=	90-92 A	78-79 C+	62-67 D	Track overall daily grade(s)	
Needs Improvement	88-89 B+	73-77 C	60-62 D		
98-100 A+	83-87 B	70-72 C	59 & Below F		

Week	Monday	Tuesday	Wednesday	Thursday	Friday
1					
2					
3					
4					
5					
6					
7					
8					
9					
10					
11					
12					
13					
14					
15					
16					
17					
18					

Notes

Week	Monday	Tuesday	Wednesday	Thursday	Friday
1					
2					
3					
4					
5					
6					
7					
8					
9					
10					
11					
12					
13					
14					
15					
16					
17					
18					

Notes

A= Above Standards S=	93-97 A	80-82 B	68-69 D+	Track overall daily grade(s)	
Meets Standards N=	90-92 A	78-79 C+	62-67 D		
Needs Improvement	88-89 B+	73-77 C	60-62 D		
98-100 A+	83-87 B	70-72 C	59 & Below F		

Week	Monday	Tuesday	Wednesday	Thursday	Friday
1					
2					
3					
4					
5					
6					
7					
8					
9					
10					
11					
12					
13					
14					
15					
16					
17					
18					

Notes

End of the Year Evaluation

Name: _____

Grade/Level: _____ Date: _____

Subjects Studied: _____
_____
_____

Goals Accomplished: _____
_____
_____
_____

Most Improved Areas: _____
_____
_____
_____

Areas of Improvement: _____
_____
_____

Main Curriculum Evaluation	Satisfied	A= Above Standards S= Meets Standards N= Needs Improvement	Final Grades
_____	Yes No	98-100 A+ 93-97 A	_____
_____	Yes No	90-92 A 88-89 B+	_____
_____	Yes No	83-87 B 80-82 B	_____
_____	Yes No	78-79 C+ 73-77 C 70-72 C	_____
_____	Yes No	68-69 D+ 62-67 D	_____
_____	Yes No	60-62 D 59 & Below F	_____

Most Enjoyed: _____
_____

Least Enjoyed: _____
_____

Cut out book

Academic Transcript

STUDENT INFORMATION		SCHOOL INFORMATION	
Name:		**School Name:**	
Address:		**Address:**	
Date of Birth:	**Sex:**	**Phone Number:**	
Date of Graduation:		**Email Address:**	
Credits Earned:	**GPA:**	*I do hereby affirm that this official academic record is accurate and complete.*	
		Administrator's Signature:	

COURSE	1ST SEM	2ND SEM	FINAL GRADE	CREDIT	COURSE	1ST SEM	2ND SEM	FINAL GRADE	CREDIT
9th GRADE		**YEAR:**			**10th GRADE**		**YEAR:**		
9TH GRADE CREDITS:		**9TH GRADE GPA:**			**10TH GRADE CREDITS:**		**10TH GRADE GPA:**		
11th GRADE:		**YEAR:**			**12th GRADE:**		**YEAR:**		
11TH GRADE CREDITS:		**11TH GRADE GPA:**			**12TH GRADE CREDITS:**		**12TH GRADE GPA:**		

Special Awards/ Activities: